Understa
Fractions, Percent, and Decimals

Understanding Fractions series is available in print or eBook form:

Understanding Fractions

Understanding Fractions, Percent, and Decimals

Written by

Robert Femiano

THE CRITICAL THINKING CO.™

www.CriticalThinking.com

Phone: 800-458-4849 • Fax: 541-756-1758

1991 Sherman Ave., Suite 200 • North Bend • OR 97459

ISBN 978-1-60144-985-6

Printed in the United States of America by Hatteras, Inc., Plymouth, MI (Dec. 2023)

Table of Contents

Using This Book

This all-in-one set of lessons enables both the student and teacher/parent to cooperately work together through fun, yet challenging activities. A high-level mastery of fractions and percent is inevitable with this step-by-step, hands-on approach! And by rounding it off with an introduction to decimals, students will understand the interrelatedness between fractions, percent, and decimals and be at ease in moving between them as needed in solving real-life problems.

To ensure a smooth start, it is most important that the student attempts the initial three pages without adult help. If they struggle with more than a few problems, the teacher should consider having them review the first book in this series, *Understanding Fractions*.

As new topics are introduced, jointly read over the pages while using the provided cut-out fraction bars and/or hundreds grid – see below. This will boost students understanding and motivation to apply themselves during the follow-up practice. Spot-checking those completed worksheets by asking students to explain (justify) their reasoning on a few problems is mathematically valuable as it deepens their understanding and enhances their ability to mentally manipulate fractions.

Multiplication Table, Decimal 100's Grid, and Fraction Bars

There is a multiplication table cut-out on page 65. Be sure to review how to use it and importantly become a 'warm demander' encouraging they memorize these facts, as it is the single most vital step in developing confidence in their math abilities going forward. The decimal 100's grid cut-out is also on page 65. This is useful when working through percent and decimals activities.

The fraction bars cut-outs on page 67 are used as support and free exploration for students to "see" how fractions work. These can provide a helpful aid when topics are introduced (follow along with the examples in the lesson) as well as during practice exercises.

- To increase durability, glue or paste the page to heavier stock, such as a file folder or thin cardboard, prior to cutting out
- Fastening an envelope to the inside back cover will allow storage of the cut-outs.

A free PDF (www.CriticalThinking.com/tablefractions) of these cut-outs is also available to download and print.

Extra for Experts

Most activities in this book end with a starred problem (★) which provides a higher-level learning option for those up to a challenge! These more difficult problems are not required to solve the riddles in the "check yourself" portion.

About the Author

Robert Femiano won the highest honor in education, the Presidential Award for Excellence in Mathematics and Science Teaching in 2002. For more than 30 years he was an elementary teacher in Seattle public schools, and adjunct faculty at Seattle Pacific University, conducting math methods courses. Publications include *Algebraic Problem Solving in the Primary Grades* article in National Council of Teachers of Math journal and the award-winning *Balance Math™ & More* series by The Critical Thinking Co.™ His interest in using logic puzzles for teaching math resulted in the best-selling series/Apps, *Balance Benders™* by The Critical Thinking Co.™

Fractions Review Part 1

Before moving on to a thorough study of fractions, let's review some of the basics. Use these next three pages to self-assess your comfort level in having mastered these concepts covered in Book 1, *Understanding Fractions.*

In the blank next to the problem, write the letter for the correct answer. Then complete the "check yourself" below.

Problem	Answer choices
_____ 1. What fraction of \$1 is 5¢?	o $\frac{1}{6}$
_____ 2. What part of a day is 6 hours?	t $\frac{2}{3}$
_____ 3. Which fraction has a numerator of 3?	e $\frac{1}{10}$
_____ 4. What fraction is eight out of a dozen?	m $\frac{6}{24}$
_____ 5. What part of an hour is 20 minutes?	s $\frac{3}{4}$
_____ 6. Which fraction has a denominator of 6?	p $\frac{1}{4}$
_____ 7. What fraction of the digits, 0-9, are even?	t $\frac{5}{10}$
_____ 8. What portion of \$4.00 is 4 dimes?	o $\frac{5}{100}$
	a $\frac{1}{3}$

Check yourself: Write the letter for each problem in the numbered spaces below to answer this riddle.

What has toes but no legs?

__ __ __ __ __ __ __ __
7 1 2 5 4 6 8 3

Review Part 2

In the blank next to the problem, write the letter for each correct answer, then complete the "check yourself" below.

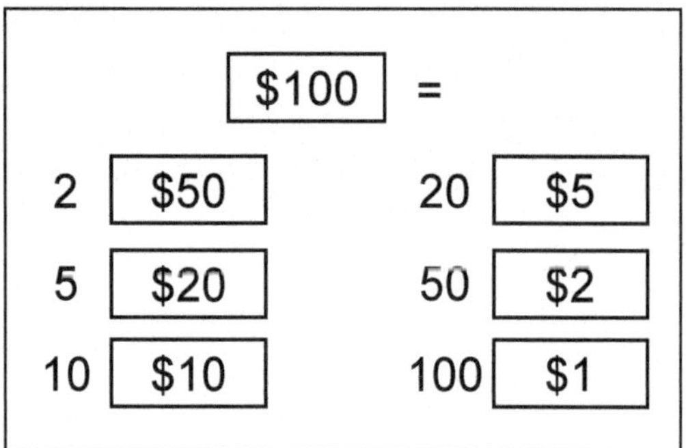

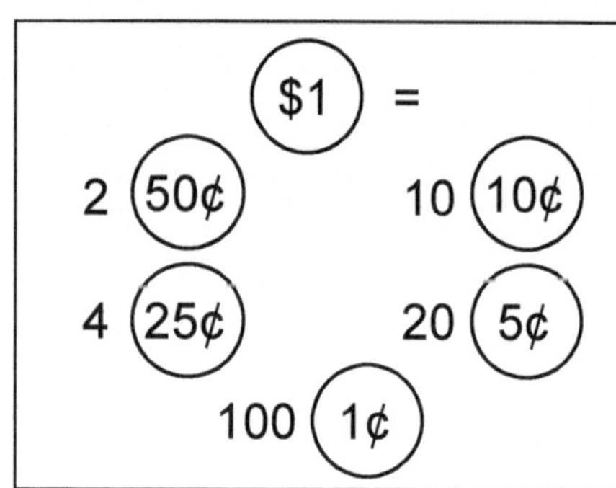

____ 1. What fraction of [$100] is 2 [$10]?

____ 2. What part of ($1) is 3 (25¢)?

____ 3. What fraction of [$100] is 3 [$50]?

____ 4. What portion of [$5] is ($1) (50¢)?

____ 5. What part of [$10] is (50¢)?

____ 6. What fraction of [$2] is (5¢)?

____ 7. 20 (10¢) is what fraction of [$20]?

1 Year =
365 days = 52 weeks = 12 months = 4 seasons

____ 8. Fraction of a year that is 1 week.

____ 9. Fraction of $1\frac{1}{2}$ years that is 3 months.

____ 10. Fraction of a year that is 4 seasons.

____ 11. Portion of a year that is 13 months.

____ 12. Fraction of a year that is 4 weeks.

r $\frac{1}{6}$
e $\frac{1}{13}$
m $\frac{365}{365}$
s $\frac{3}{10}$
r $\frac{1}{10}$
d $\frac{1}{52}$
y $\frac{1}{20}$
a $\frac{13}{12}$
n $\frac{1}{4}$
u $\frac{1}{40}$
r $\frac{1}{5}$
u $\frac{3}{4}$
l $\frac{12}{13}$
o $\frac{3}{2}$

Check yourself: Write the letter for each problem in the numbered spaces below to answer this riddle.

What part of your body can make music?

__ __ __ __   __ __ __ __ __ __ __ __
5 3 2 1   12 11 7 8 9 6 10 4

Review Part 3

In the blank next to the problem, write the letter for each correct answer. Then complete the "check yourself" below.

Problem	Answer
____ 1. Which is least: $\frac{1}{5}, \frac{1}{4}, \frac{1}{6}$?	o $\frac{2}{3}$
____ 2. Which is the greatest: $\frac{3}{6}, \frac{3}{7}, \frac{3}{8}$?	u $\frac{3}{4}$
____ 3. Which is more: $\frac{3}{2}$ or $\frac{3}{4}$?	b $\frac{1}{4}$
____ 4. Equivalent fraction for $\frac{1}{5}$	o 10
____ 5. $\frac{1}{8} + \frac{1}{8} + \frac{1}{8} + \frac{1}{8} + \frac{1}{4}$	r $\frac{1}{6}$
____ 6. $\frac{2}{3} = ?$	y $\frac{3}{15}$
____ 7. $(\frac{1}{2}$ of $18) + (\frac{1}{3}$ of $18)$	n $\frac{1}{2}$
____ 8. $(\frac{1}{3}$ of $30) - (\frac{1}{4}$ of $20)$	s $\frac{3}{8}$
____ 9. $\frac{2}{3} = \frac{?}{15}$	t 12
____ 10. $\frac{3}{4}$ of $16 = ?$	t 15
____ 11. $\frac{4}{1} + \frac{12}{3} = ?$	f 8
____ 12. $\frac{1}{2} + \frac{1}{6} = ?$	p 5
____ 13. [figure] Fraction shaded?	e $\frac{3}{6}$
	s $\frac{6}{9}$
____ 14. ★ $\frac{2}{3}$ of $\frac{3}{4}$ of $\frac{5}{5}$	o $\frac{3}{2}$

Check yourself: Write the letter for each problem in the numbered spaces below to answer this riddle.

What is it that the more you take, the more you leave behind?

__ __ __ __   __ __ __ __ __ __ __ __ __

4 3 5 1   11 12 9 7 13 10 2 8 6

Equivalent Fractions

Remember, multiplying or dividing fractions by 1 does not change their value, only their appearance. Also, 2 out of 2 parts or $\frac{2}{2}$ means one whole. Similarly, $\frac{3}{3}$ . . . $\frac{100}{100}$ . . . all equal 1.

Changing a fraction into an equivalent fraction, whether larger or reduced to lowest terms, is quicker and more fun when you've memorized the multiplication table. Until then, use the cut-out table on page 59 to help you.

How to Use the Multiplication Table*

To solve $\frac{3}{4} = \frac{\square}{28}$, what form of 1 is needed to multiply $\frac{3}{4}$ by? Well, what times 4 = 28? Look down the 4's column until you see 28. Then look across that row to find the outside number is 7. That tells us 7 x 4 = 28 and to use $\frac{7}{7}$ as the multiplier. So, $\frac{7}{7} \times \frac{3}{4} = \frac{7 \times 3}{4 \times 4} = \frac{\square}{28}$. So what is 7 x 3? Move one finger down the 7's column and one finger across the 3's row. They meet at 21. So, 7 x 3 = 21 and therefore $\frac{3}{4} = \frac{21}{28}$.

x	1	2	3	4	5	6	7	8
1	1	2	3	4	5	6	7	8
2	2	4	6	8	10	12	14	16
3	3	6	9	12	15	18	21	
4	4	8	12	16	20	24	28	
5	5	10	15	20				
6	6	12	18	24				
7	7	14	21	28				

* Students should explore how the multiplication table is repeated addition or skip counting if they are not clear, e.g., 3 x 7 is the same as 7 + 7+ 7, and the same as seven 3's.

Using the Multiplication Table

Show your multiplier in the form of 1. In the blank next to the problem, write the letter for the correct answer. Then complete the "check yourself" below.

__n__ 1. $\frac{6}{6} \times \frac{1}{6} = \frac{6}{36}$

____ 2. $\_ \times \frac{4}{5} = \frac{\_}{35}$

____ 3. $\_ \times \frac{3}{4} = \frac{\_}{36}$

____ 4. $\_ \times \frac{1}{9} = \frac{\_}{45}$

____ 5. $\_ \times \frac{5}{7} = \frac{\_}{42}$

____ 6. $\_ \times \frac{9}{10} = \frac{\_}{100}$

____ 7. $\_ \times \frac{3}{8} = \frac{\_}{40}$

____ 8. $\_ \times \frac{5}{4} = \frac{\_}{36}$

____ 9. $\_ \times \frac{8}{9} = \frac{\_}{63}$

____ 10. $\_ \times \frac{4}{6} = \frac{\_}{54}$

____ 11. $\_ \times \frac{9}{10} = \frac{72}{?}$

____ 12. $\_ \times \frac{6}{8} = \frac{48}{?}$

____ 13. $\_ \times \frac{?}{8} = \frac{28}{32}$

____ 14. $\_ \times \frac{?}{9} = \frac{70}{63}$

____ 15. $\_ \times \frac{6}{?} = \frac{42}{56}$

____ 16. $\_ \times \frac{3}{1} = \frac{\_}{3}$

____ 17. $\_ \times 2\frac{1}{2} = \frac{\_}{8}$

____ 18. ★ $\_ \times 1\frac{7}{8} = \frac{75}{?}$

p 35	i 56	s 15	n 10	r 20	i 27	a 90
g 30	b 40	c 36	a 80	e 45	w 64	f 32
d 5	n 6	i 7	t 8	s 9	a 28	y 16

Check yourself: Write the letter for each problem in the numbered spaces below to answer this riddle.

What goes up and down and around but never moves?

__ (2)   __ (12) __ (3) __ (14) __ (4) __ (9) __ (1) __ (5)   __ (16) __ (15) __ (6) __ (13) __ (17) __ (10) __ (11) __ (7) __ (8)

Reducing Fractions to Simplest Form

It is much easier to think about, and to do calculations, using "smaller" fractions such as $\frac{1}{2}$ rather than "larger" (but equal) numbers such as $\frac{25}{50}$ or $\frac{128}{256}$. For this reason, mathematicians prefer to reduce all fractions to their lowest terms or simplest form.

Remember, a fraction can be reduced by dividing (always by 1), multiple times if needed. The larger the numbers, the less the steps needed to reach lowest terms. For example:

a. $\frac{12}{24} \div \frac{2}{2} = \frac{6}{12} \div \frac{2}{2} = \frac{3}{6} \div \frac{3}{3} = \frac{1}{2}$

b. $\frac{12}{24} \div \frac{6}{6} = \frac{2}{4} \div \frac{2}{2} = \frac{1}{2}$

c. $\frac{12}{24} \div \frac{12}{12} = \frac{1}{2}$

You'll know a fraction is reduced to simplest form when both the numerator and denominator can no longer be evenly divided by any form of 1. For example, $\frac{2}{5}$ cannot be divided by $\frac{2}{2}$ since $5 \div 2$ is not a whole number, so it is in lowest terms. The same is true for $\frac{3}{5}$ and $\frac{4}{5}$.

Any time the numerator is 1, such as $\frac{1}{7}$ or $\frac{1}{8}$, or anytime the difference between the numerator and denominator is 1, as in $\frac{5}{6}$ or $\frac{9}{10}$, the fraction is in simplest form.

Let's reduce one more: $\frac{16}{24}$. Here again the multiplication table can help. Is there any column with both 16 and 24 in it? Yes, both 4 and 8, so let's use the larger number to save steps. $\frac{16}{24} \div \frac{8}{8} = \frac{2}{3}$. This is lowest terms, since the numerator and denominator differ by only 1.

Reducing Fractions to Simplest Form

Use the multiplication table to reduce these fractions to their lowest terms. Show your work. Write the answer in the blank. A shortcut is to look down the columns in the multiplication table to see if both the numerator and denominator are in the same column. For example, 24 and 30 are both in the 6's column, so $\frac{24}{30}$ can be divided by $\frac{6}{6} = \frac{4}{5}$.

$\frac{1}{3}$ 1. $\frac{6}{18} \div \frac{6}{6} = \frac{1}{3}$

____ 2. $\frac{15}{25}$

____ 3. $\frac{30}{42}$

____ 4. $\frac{9}{21}$

____ 5. $\frac{12}{27}$

____ 6. $\frac{18}{30}$

____ 7. $\frac{25}{40}$

____ 8. $\frac{8}{18}$

____ 9. $\frac{12}{36}$

____ 10. $\frac{20}{45}$

____ 11. $\frac{14}{35}$

____ 12. $\frac{54}{72}$

____ 13. $\frac{24}{36}$

____ 14. $\frac{16}{24}$

____ 15. $\frac{36}{48}$

____ 16. $\frac{28}{32}$

____ 17. $\frac{21}{28}$

____ 18. $\frac{24}{72}$

____ 19. $\frac{28}{40}$

____ 20. $\frac{42}{54}$

____ 21. $\frac{72}{81}$

____ 22. $\frac{48}{66}$

____ 23. $\frac{50}{75}$

____ 24. ★ $\frac{100}{60}$

Reducing Fractions to Simplest Form

Find the 9 fractions that are not in their lowest form and reduce them. Write the letter that is next to those 9 fractions in the blanks above the correctly reduced fractions in "check yourself" below.

m $\frac{1}{3}$	p $\frac{3}{7}$	a $\frac{15}{45}$	l $\frac{3}{11}$
t $\frac{10}{12}$	r $\frac{2}{5}$	c $\frac{3}{10}$	h $\frac{20}{30}$
b $\frac{17}{20}$	w $\frac{2}{50}$	d $\frac{12}{13}$	f $\frac{1}{100}$
v $\frac{5}{8}$	y $\frac{15}{16}$	m $\frac{7}{9}$	n $\frac{3}{20}$
l $\frac{8}{19}$	e $\frac{25}{28}$	o $\frac{19}{38}$	g $\frac{20}{27}$
i $\frac{49}{100}$	j $\frac{4}{33}$	s $\frac{13}{20}$	a $\frac{45}{50}$
d $\frac{19}{24}$	o $\frac{4}{31}$	t $\frac{16}{25}$	d $\frac{6}{99}$
c $\frac{18}{90}$	x $\frac{2}{69}$	g $\frac{21}{35}$	u $\frac{11}{21}$

Check yourself: Write the letter for each problem in the numbered spaces below to answer the riddle

What animal always knows what time it is?

___   ___ ___ ___ ___ ___ ___ ___ ___

$\frac{1}{3}$ $\frac{1}{25}$ $\frac{9}{10}$ $\frac{5}{6}$ $\frac{1}{5}$ $\frac{2}{3}$ $\frac{2}{33}$ $\frac{1}{2}$ $\frac{3}{5}$

Comparing Fractions

Which is more; $\frac{2}{3}$ or $\frac{3}{5}$ and by how much?

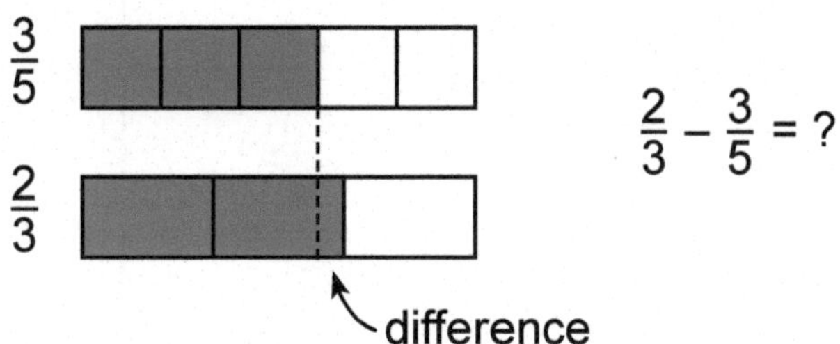

$\frac{2}{3}$ is greater than $\frac{3}{5}$, but how much greater? If they both had a common denominator, they would line up so that the difference could be counted between them. An easy way to make a denominator they share is by multiplying the two denominators. In this case 3 x 5 = 15. So, let's change them to fifteenths.

$$\frac{3}{3} \times \frac{3}{5} = \frac{9}{15}$$

$$\frac{5}{5} \times \frac{2}{3} = \frac{10}{15}$$

difference = $\frac{1}{15}$

Let's try another one. Compare $\frac{2}{5}$ to $\frac{3}{8}$. First make equivalent fractions with the same denominator. Since 5 x 8 = 40, use that. So $\frac{2}{5} = \frac{?}{40}$ and $\frac{3}{8} = \frac{?}{40}$.

$$\frac{8}{8} \times \frac{2}{5} = \frac{16}{40} \text{ and } \frac{5}{5} \times \frac{3}{8} = \frac{15}{40}. \text{ So, } \frac{2}{5} > \frac{3}{8} \text{ by } \frac{1}{40}$$

Sometimes you can spot a smaller common denominator and save a little work.

Comparing $\frac{3}{4}$ and $\frac{4}{6}$ can use 12, for example, instead of 24.

$$\frac{3}{4} = \frac{9}{12} \text{ and } \frac{4}{6} = \frac{8}{12}. \quad \frac{9}{12} - \frac{8}{12} = \frac{1}{12}$$

$$\frac{3}{4} = \frac{18}{24} \text{ and } \frac{4}{6} = \frac{16}{24}. \quad \frac{18}{24} - \frac{16}{24} = \frac{2}{24} = \frac{1}{12}.$$

Comparing Fractions

Complete the chart. Then identify <, =, > in ◯ for the fractions below.

	Equivalent fractions with common denominators	Difference
1. $\frac{1}{2}$ (>) $\frac{4}{9}$	$\frac{1}{2} = \frac{9}{18}$, $\frac{4}{9} = \frac{8}{18}$	$\frac{9}{18} - \frac{8}{18} = \frac{1}{18}$
2. $\frac{4}{7}$ ◯ $\frac{1}{2}$		
3. $\frac{3}{4}$ ◯ $\frac{2}{3}$		
4. $\frac{3}{5}$ ◯ $\frac{10}{15}$ Hint: 15ths		
5. $\frac{5}{9}$ ◯ $\frac{2}{3}$		
6. $\frac{3}{4}$ ◯ $\frac{9}{12}$		
7. $\frac{2}{6}$ ◯ $\frac{2}{5}$		
8. $\frac{3}{7}$ ◯ $\frac{1}{3}$		
9. $\frac{1}{6}$ ◯ $\frac{2}{9}$ Hint: 18ths		
10. $\frac{5}{8}$ ◯ $\frac{3}{5}$		
11. $\frac{7}{10}$ ◯ $\frac{2}{3}$		
12. $\frac{1}{2}$ ◯ $\frac{14}{28}$		
13. ★ $\frac{1}{12}$ ◯ $\frac{8}{100}$		

Comparing Fractions

Complete the chart. Then identify <, =, > in ◯ for the fractions below. It may be easier to convert mixed numbers to improper fractions first.

	Equivalent fractions with common denominators	Difference
1. $\frac{3}{4} \bigcirc 1\frac{1}{3}$		
2. $\frac{5}{7} \bigcirc \frac{4}{6}$		
3. $2\frac{1}{3} \bigcirc \frac{21}{9}$		
4. $\frac{5}{11} \bigcirc \frac{1}{3}$		
5. $\frac{5}{6} \bigcirc \frac{6}{7}$		
6. $\frac{5}{12} \bigcirc \frac{3}{8}$		
7. $\frac{3}{2} \bigcirc \frac{8}{5}$		
8. $\frac{12}{8} \bigcirc \frac{10}{6}$		
9. $\frac{15}{6} \bigcirc 2\frac{2}{5}$		
10. $1\frac{3}{4} \bigcirc \frac{21}{12}$		
11. $\frac{7}{8} \bigcirc \frac{7}{9}$		
12. $1\frac{9}{10} \bigcirc \frac{76}{40}$		
13. ★ $\left(\frac{8}{9} - \frac{7}{8}\right) \bigcirc \frac{2}{100}$		

Improper Fractions and Mixed Numbers

Remember, the fraction bar not only means "out of" as in 2 out of 3 or $\frac{2}{3}$, it also represents division as in 2 cookies, 3 friends where everyone receives $\frac{2}{3}$ of a cookie.

Improper fractions, such as $\frac{3}{2}$ and $\frac{15}{4}$, also represent division. As always the denominator tells how many parts are in the "whole." $\frac{3}{2}$ means 3 half-cookies. Of course, two halves $(\frac{2}{2})$ are needed to make one whole cookie.

So $3 \div 2 = 1$ whole + $\frac{1}{2}$. $\frac{2}{2} + \frac{1}{2} = \frac{3}{2} = 1\frac{1}{2}$.

Similarly $\frac{15}{4}$ means fifteen $\frac{1}{4}$ths. A "whole" takes $\frac{4}{4}$ so $15 \div 4 = 3$ whole cookies + $\frac{3}{4}$.

$\frac{4}{4} + \frac{4}{4} + \frac{4}{4} + \frac{3}{4} = \frac{15}{4} = 3\frac{3}{4}$.

Improper fractions are larger than 1 whole, so they always convert to a mixed number.

$\frac{10}{2} = 10 \div 2 = 5$ (whole cookies).

Change these improper fractions to mixed numbers. Reduce to lowest terms.

1. $\frac{7}{2} =$
2. $\frac{9}{3} =$
3. $\frac{17}{5} =$
4. $\frac{20}{6} =$
5. $\frac{42}{6} =$
6. $\frac{34}{4} =$
7. $\frac{37}{7} =$
8. $\frac{42}{8} =$
9. $\frac{54}{8} =$
10. $\frac{33}{6} =$
11. $\frac{39}{5} =$
12. $\frac{28}{3} =$
13. $\frac{77}{9} =$
14. $\frac{50}{7} =$
15. $\frac{60}{9} =$
16. $\frac{102}{10} =$
17. $\frac{121}{20} =$
18. ★ $\frac{225}{15} =$

Reciprocals

When a fraction is flipped upside down, the denominator becomes the numerator and the numerator becomes the denominator. This is called the reciprocal (re-sip-ro-cull) or inverse. To find the reciprocal of $\frac{3}{4}$, invert the fraction to $\frac{4}{3}$.

Multiplying a fraction by its reciprocal always makes the product of 1.

For example: $\frac{2}{3} \times \frac{3}{2} = \frac{6}{6} = 1$; $\frac{9}{10} \times \frac{10}{9} = \frac{90}{90} = 1$. Remember, a whole number is assumed to be a fraction with a denominator of 1 ($5 = \frac{5}{1}$). So its inverse is $\frac{1}{5}$ in this case.

Mixed numbers need to be changed to improper fractions to find their reciprocals. For example, $3\frac{1}{2} = \frac{7}{2}$ so $\frac{2}{7}$ is the inverse.

Shortcut: To change a mixed number to an improper fraction, multiply the whole number by the denominator, then add the numerator. Put this new number over the original denominator. Examples: $2\frac{1}{3} = (3 \times 2) + 1 = \frac{7}{3}$. $4\frac{3}{5} = (5 \times 4) + 3 = \frac{23}{5}$.

Write the reciprocal for these mixed numbers in the blank.

$\frac{2}{5}$ 1. $2\frac{1}{2} = \frac{5}{2}$ ____ 2. $3\frac{3}{4} =$ ____ 3. $6\frac{1}{5} =$

____ 4. $7\frac{1}{8} =$ ____ 5. $3\frac{5}{9} =$ ____ 6. $8\frac{1}{8} =$

____ 7. $9\frac{1}{5} =$ ____ 8. $5\frac{3}{8} =$ ____ 9. $7\frac{3}{4}$

____ 10. $6\frac{5}{6} =$ ____ 11. $7\frac{4}{8} =$ ____ 12. $9\frac{1}{7} =$

____ 13. $9\frac{1}{5} =$ ____ 14. $4\frac{3}{8} =$ ____ 15. $10\frac{4}{5}$

____ 16. $50\frac{1}{3} =$ ____ 17. $9\frac{99}{100} =$ ____ 18. ★ $99\frac{999}{10,000}$

Addition of Fractions

What is the sum of $\frac{2}{3}$ plus $\frac{2}{3}$? It's easy because they have the same (or common) denominator; $\frac{2}{3} + \frac{2}{3} = \frac{4}{3}$ or $1\frac{1}{3}$. What about $\frac{1}{2}$ plus $\frac{2}{5}$?

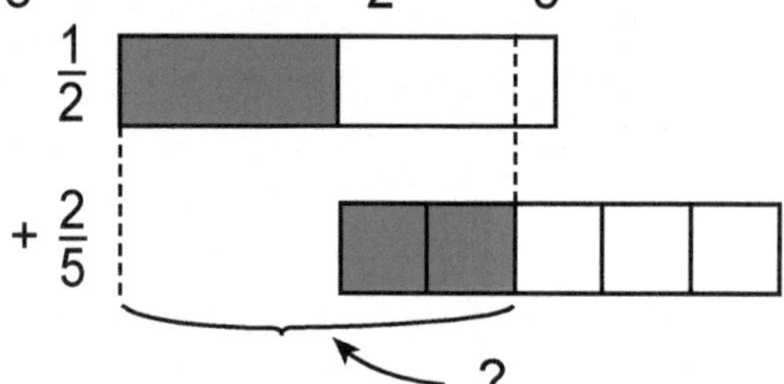

We need common denominators.

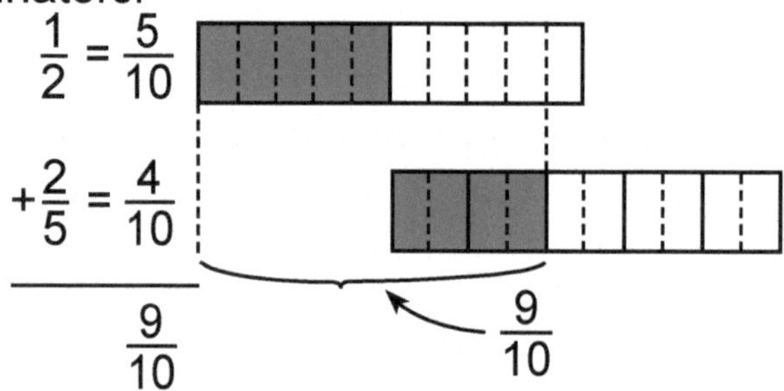

When it comes to adding mixed numbers as in $2\frac{3}{4} + 3\frac{1}{3}$, begin by adding the fractions, to see if there is enough to make a whole. First, change them to common denominator of 12. $\frac{3}{4} = \frac{9}{12}$ and $\frac{1}{3} = \frac{4}{12}$ so together they add to $\frac{13}{12}$ or 1 whole plus $\frac{1}{12}$. Add the 1 to the other two whole numbers for a total answer of $6 + \frac{1}{12}$ or $6\frac{1}{12}$.

Let's do another: what is the sum of $3\frac{1}{5}$ and $2\frac{7}{8}$?

$$3\frac{1}{5} = 3\frac{8}{40}$$

$$+\,2\frac{7}{8} = 2\frac{35}{40}$$

$$5\frac{43}{40} = 5 + 1\frac{3}{40} = 6\frac{3}{40}$$

There can also be 3 (or more) addends*, as in $\frac{2}{3} + \frac{3}{4} + \frac{11}{12}$, as long as they share a common denominator. Here, 12 works fine. $\frac{2}{3} = \frac{8}{12}$; $\frac{3}{4} = \frac{9}{12}$. So $\frac{8}{12} + \frac{9}{12} + \frac{11}{12} = \frac{28}{12} = 2\frac{1}{3}$.

*An addend is any number or fraction that is being added in an addition problem.

Addition of Fractions*

Add the following fractions and write the answer in the blank. Show equivalent fractions. Then complete the "check yourself" below.

____ 1. $\frac{1}{2} + \frac{1}{4}$

____ 2. $\frac{2}{3} + \frac{1}{4}$

____ 3. $\frac{3}{4} + \frac{3}{5}$

____ 4. $1\frac{2}{5} + \frac{1}{2}$

____ 5. $3\frac{5}{6} + 3\frac{2}{12}$

____ 6. $5\frac{3}{8} + 2\frac{3}{4}$

____ 7. $3\frac{7}{10} + 1\frac{3}{5}$

____ 8. $\frac{1}{8} + \frac{1}{9}$

____ 9. $3\frac{4}{7} + 3\frac{4}{6}$

____ 10. $\frac{1}{4} + \frac{1}{2} + \frac{6}{8}$

____ 11. $4\frac{1}{3} + 3\frac{5}{7}$

____ 12. $5\frac{1}{4} + 2\frac{5}{6}$

____ 13. $\frac{1}{3} = \frac{\square}{18}$, $\frac{7}{9}$, $+ \frac{4}{6}$

____ 14. $\frac{3}{4}$, $\frac{5}{6}$, $+ \square$ = $1\frac{17}{24}$

____ 15. $\frac{1}{2} + \frac{1}{3} + \frac{1}{10} + \square = 1$

____ 16. ★ $\frac{1}{25} + \frac{1}{50} + \frac{1}{100} + \frac{1}{5} + \frac{1}{10} + \frac{1}{2} + \frac{1}{4}$

s $\frac{1}{8}$	y 7	o $\frac{17}{72}$	l $\frac{1}{15}$	p $\frac{3}{4}$	h $\frac{11}{12}$	r $7\frac{5}{21}$	a $8\frac{1}{21}$
e $1\frac{7}{20}$	e $1\frac{7}{9}$	y $1\frac{1}{2}$	e $1\frac{9}{10}$	b $1\frac{3}{25}$	a $8\frac{1}{8}$	u $5\frac{3}{10}$	e $8\frac{1}{12}$

Check yourself: Write the letter for each problem in the numbered spaces below to answer the riddle.

What one question can never be answered "YES?"

_ _ _, _ _ _ _ _ _ _ _ _ _ _ _?
2 3 5 6 9 4 10 8 7 11 14 15 13 12 1

*See page 53 set A for extra practice with this skill.

Subtraction of Fractions

Subtraction is simply finding the difference between two amounts, which is why the answer to any subtraction problem is called the difference. You already know how to compare and find the difference between 2 fractions, but let's review the steps again, using the fraction bars.

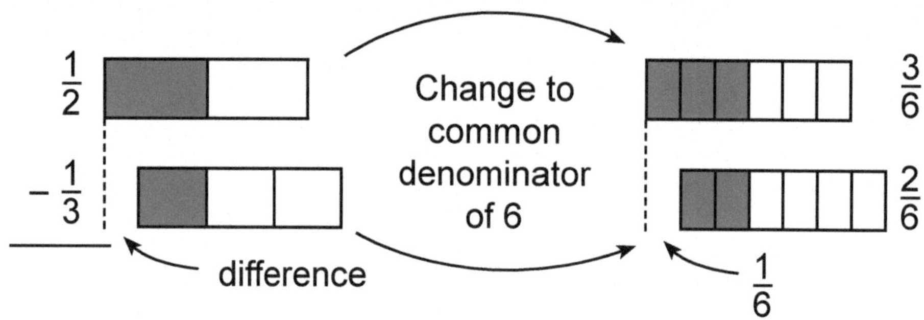

So $\frac{1}{2}$ is $\frac{1}{6}$ greater than $\frac{1}{3}$ and $\frac{1}{3}$ is $\frac{1}{6}$ less than $\frac{1}{2}$.

Show the equivalent fractions. Write the answer in the blanks.

____ 1. $\frac{2}{3} - \frac{1}{5}$ $\quad \frac{2}{3} = \frac{\_\_}{15}; \ \frac{1}{5} = \frac{\_\_}{15}$

____ 2. $\frac{3}{4} - \frac{1}{3}$

____ 3. $\frac{3}{5} - \frac{1}{4}$

____ 4. $\frac{2}{3} - \frac{1}{7}$

____ 5. $\frac{5}{6} - \frac{3}{5}$

____ 6. $\frac{1}{6} - \frac{1}{8}$

____ 7. $\frac{3}{4} - \frac{1}{9}$

____ 8. $\frac{4}{7} - \frac{1}{4}$

____ 9. $\frac{4}{6} - \frac{2}{9}$

____ 10. $\frac{3}{8} - \frac{2}{7}$

____ 11. $\frac{5}{6} - \frac{3}{7}$

____ 12. $\frac{1}{9} - \frac{1}{11}$

____ 13. ★ $\frac{1}{99} - \frac{1}{100}$

Subtracting Mixed Numbers

When subtracting mixed numbers, just as in regular subtraction, make sure they have the same denominators then start on the right side in case you need to “borrow” or “trade in” as you’ll see below.

Example A: $4\frac{1}{2} - 1\frac{1}{3}$. Let’s start by writing the problem vertically and changing the fractions to a common denominator. The subtraction is easy after that.

$$\begin{array}{rr} 4\frac{1}{2} = & 4\frac{3}{6} \\ -\,1\frac{1}{3} = & -\,1\frac{2}{6} \\ \hline & 3\frac{1}{6} \end{array}$$

Sometimes the fraction you need to subtract from is not there. For example, how do you give away $\frac{1}{2}$ of a granola bar when you have 5 whole bars? By breaking one into 2 parts, you have 4 whole and $\frac{2}{2}$ and can now give away a half bar. It looks like this:

Example B:

$$\begin{array}{r} 5 \\ -\,\frac{1}{2} \\ \hline \end{array} \xrightarrow{\text{RENAMED}} \begin{array}{r} 4\frac{2}{2} \\ -\,\frac{1}{2} \\ \hline 4\frac{1}{2} \end{array} \xrightarrow{\text{SHORTCUT}} \begin{array}{r} \overset{4\frac{2}{2}}{\cancel{5}} \\ -\,\frac{1}{2} \\ \hline 4\,\frac{1}{2} \end{array}$$

Other times the fraction you need to subtract from is too small as in $7\frac{1}{4} - \frac{3}{4}$. You’ll need to “cash in” a whole again, this time as $\frac{4}{4}$. Added to the $\frac{1}{4}$, you now have enough fourths $\left(\frac{5}{4}\right)$ to subtract the $\frac{3}{4}$. Here’s how this looks:

Example C:

$$\begin{array}{r} 7\,\frac{1}{4} \\ -\,\frac{3}{4} \\ \hline \end{array} \xrightarrow{\text{RENAMED}} \begin{array}{r} 6\,\frac{4}{4} + \frac{1}{4} = 6\,\frac{5}{4} \\ -\,\frac{3}{4} \\ \hline 6\frac{2}{4} = 6\frac{1}{2} \end{array} \xrightarrow{\text{SHORTCUT}} \begin{array}{r} \overset{6}{\cancel{7}}\frac{\overset{5}{\cancel{1}}}{4} \\ -\,\frac{3}{4} \\ \hline 6\frac{2}{4} = 6\frac{1}{2} \end{array}$$

Subtracting Mixed Numbers*

Example D:

$$\begin{array}{rcccc} 6\frac{3}{5} = & 6\frac{18}{30} & = 5\frac{30}{30} + \frac{18}{30} & = & 5\frac{48}{30} \\ -1\frac{5}{6} = & 1\frac{25}{30} & = & & -1\frac{25}{30} \\ \hline & & & & 4\frac{23}{30} \end{array}$$

Subtract the problems below.

1. $\begin{array}{r} 8 \\ -\frac{1}{8} \\ \hline \end{array}$

2. $\begin{array}{r} 12\frac{1}{4} \\ -7\frac{3}{4} \\ \hline \end{array}$

3. $\begin{array}{r} 6\frac{1}{3} \\ -1\frac{1}{2} \\ \hline \end{array}$

4. $\begin{array}{r} 15\frac{1}{5} \\ -3\frac{1}{3} \\ \hline \end{array}$

5. $\begin{array}{r} 9\frac{1}{4} \\ -2\frac{2}{5} \\ \hline \end{array}$

6. $\begin{array}{r} 14\frac{1}{5} \\ -3\frac{1}{7} \\ \hline \end{array}$

7. $\begin{array}{r} 6\frac{5}{9} \\ -1\frac{1}{4} \\ \hline \end{array}$

8. $\begin{array}{r} 3\frac{1}{6} \\ -\frac{4}{7} \\ \hline \end{array}$

9. $\begin{array}{r} 1\frac{1}{6} \\ -\frac{7}{8} \\ \hline \end{array}$

10. ★ $\begin{array}{r} 1\frac{1}{11} \\ -\frac{11}{12} \\ \hline \end{array}$

*See page 53 SET B for extra practice with this skill.

Addition and Subtraction Practice

1. What is the difference between $\frac{3}{4}$ and $\frac{1}{16}$?

2. What is the sum of $\frac{1}{2} + \frac{1}{3} + \frac{1}{4}$?

3. What do you add to $\frac{2}{5}$ to make $\frac{3}{4}$?

4. How much do you subtract from $8\frac{1}{3}$ to have $7\frac{1}{8}$?

5. $\frac{7}{3} + \frac{9}{5}$

6. $\frac{1}{6} - \frac{1}{7}$

7. What number is $2\frac{3}{8}$ less than $4\frac{1}{4}$?

8. What number is $3\frac{2}{9}$ more than $\frac{4}{5}$?

9. $8 - \frac{29}{9} = ?$

10. A car stops for gas 3 times while driving on vacation, using $8\frac{1}{2}$ gallons, $9\frac{2}{5}$ gallons, and $10\frac{1}{10}$ gallons. How many gallons is this?

11. Compare (a.) to (b.) a. $\frac{5}{6} + \frac{3}{4}$ b. $2\frac{2}{3} - 1\frac{1}{4}$ a ◯ b

12. Which is smaller and by how much? (a) $\frac{12}{9}$ or (b) $\frac{21}{15}$

13. How much larger is $1\frac{8}{7}$ than $1\frac{7}{8}$?

14. ★ Show that $\left(6 + \frac{1}{4}\right) \times \left(5 - \frac{1}{5}\right) = 6 \times 5$.

Multiplying Fractions

Multiplying fractions is done the same way as making equivalent fractions. Simply multiply across the numerators and multiply across the denominators, keeping the fraction form. You can even multiply three or more fractions. For example: $\frac{1}{2} \times \frac{1}{3} \times \frac{1}{4} = \frac{1 \times 1 \times 1}{2 \times 3 \times 4} = \frac{1}{24}$.

In math, the word "of" means to multiply, as in half of a dozen, which is $\frac{1}{2} \times \frac{12}{1} = \frac{12}{2} = 6$. If someone says "in $\frac{1}{4}$ of an hour," you know that is $\frac{1}{4} \times \frac{60}{1} = \frac{60}{4} = 15$ minutes.

Multiplication of fractions means you are taking a part of a part. For example, what is $\frac{1}{2}$ of $\frac{1}{3}$? What does that look like?

$\frac{1}{3}$ $\frac{1}{2}$ of $\frac{1}{3}$ $= \frac{1}{6}$ $\frac{1}{2} \times \frac{1}{3} = \frac{1 \times 1}{2 \times 3} = \frac{1}{6}$

What about $\frac{1}{4}$ of $\frac{1}{3}$?

$\frac{1}{3}$ $\frac{1}{4}$ of $\frac{1}{3}$ $= \frac{1}{12}$ $\frac{1}{4} \times \frac{1}{3} = \frac{1 \times 1}{4 \times 3} = \frac{1}{12}$

How about $\frac{2}{3}$ of $\frac{3}{4}$?

$\frac{3}{4}$

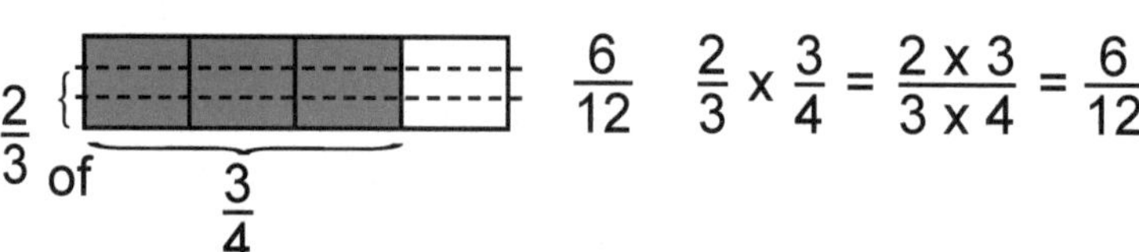

You could have looked at $\frac{2}{3}$ of $\frac{3}{4}$ this way too.

$\frac{3}{4}$ 2 out of the 4 = $\frac{1}{2}$

2 out of 3 = $\frac{2}{3}$

What is $\frac{1}{2}$ of $\frac{3}{4}$? Draw and show the math.

Check your work on the next page.

In multiplication, changing the order of the factors (multipliers) does not change the answer. This is known as the commutative property of multiplication.

Even when there are multiple factors, you may switch any of them around if it helps your thinking or computation.

For example 3 x 4 = 12 and 4 x 3 = 12. The same is true with fractions. Let's use the previous problem, $\frac{1}{2}$ of $\frac{3}{4}$, to see it taking half of $\frac{3}{4}$ is the same as taking three-fourths of $\frac{1}{2}$.

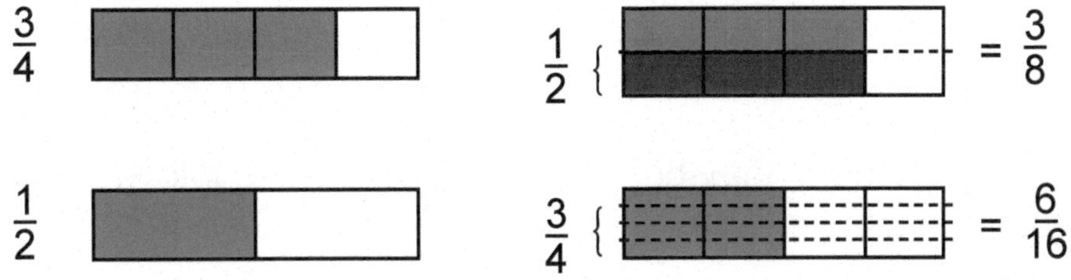

$\frac{3}{4}$ $\frac{1}{2}$ { $= \frac{3}{8}$

$\frac{1}{2}$ $\frac{3}{4}$ { $= \frac{6}{16} = \frac{3}{8}$

In the blank next to the problem, write the letter for the correct answer. Then complete the "check yourself" below.

___ 1. $\frac{1}{2} \times \frac{1}{4}$

___ 2. $\frac{3}{4}$ of $\frac{2}{4}$

___ 3. $\frac{3}{5} \times \frac{5}{7}$

___ 4. $\frac{2}{3}$ of $\frac{5}{6}$

___ 5. $\frac{2}{4} \times \frac{3}{8}$

___ 6. $\frac{4}{5}$ of $\frac{10}{12}$

___ 7. $\frac{8}{9} \times \frac{9}{8}$

___ 8. $\frac{6}{7} \times \frac{1}{4}$

___ 9. $\frac{1}{2} \times \frac{2}{3} \times \frac{1}{4}$

___ 10. $\frac{1}{6}$ of $\frac{2}{3}$

___ 11. $\frac{4}{5} \times \frac{3}{4} \times \square = 1$

(Hint: reciprocal)

___ 12. ★ $\frac{6}{5}$ of $\frac{4}{21} \times \frac{15}{6}$

g $\frac{5}{9}$	d $\frac{1}{9}$	a $\frac{2}{3}$	o 1	i $\frac{3}{8}$	n $\frac{3}{7}$	r $\frac{3}{16}$
b $\frac{4}{7}$	a $\frac{1}{12}$	n $\frac{1}{8}$	p $\frac{3}{14}$	m $\frac{3}{4}$	a $\frac{5}{3}$	

Check yourself: Write the letter for each problem in the numbered spaces below to answer this riddle.

What has keys but cannot open any locks?

___ ___ ___ ___ ___ ___   ___ ___ ___ ___ ___
6 4 5 9 1 10   8 2 11 3 7

Multiplying Mixed Numbers

Mixed numbers can also be multiplied but it is quickest to change them to improper fractions first. For example, to find $\frac{1}{2}$ of $1\frac{1}{2}$ cookies (2 friends sharing) we can take half of 1 whole and half of the $\frac{1}{2}$ to end up with $\frac{3}{4}$ cookie each, but instead of 2 steps, it's faster to simply multiply. Substituting "times" for "of" gives $\frac{1}{2} \times 1\frac{1}{2}$ and converting the mixed number to an improper fraction makes it: $\frac{1}{2} \times \frac{3}{2} = \frac{1 \times 3}{2 \times 2} = \frac{3}{4}$.

In the case of 2 mixed numbers, they both need to be changed into improper fractions before multiplying. For example,

$$2\frac{1}{2} \times 3\frac{1}{4} = \frac{5}{2} \times \frac{13}{4} \qquad \frac{5 \times 13}{2 \times 4} = \frac{65}{8} = 8\frac{1}{8}$$

Reduce answers to lowest terms. Show your work.

____ 1. $\frac{3}{4}$ of $2\frac{2}{4}$

____ 2. $1\frac{1}{3} \times 3$

____ 3. $1\frac{4}{5} \times 3\frac{1}{2}$

____ 4. $6\frac{3}{4} \times \frac{1}{9}$

____ 5. $1\frac{1}{2}$ of $2\frac{1}{2}$

____ 6. $3\frac{2}{3} \times \frac{6}{11}$

____ 7. $3\frac{1}{7}$ times $1\frac{1}{11}$

____ 8. $\frac{1}{4}$ of $2\frac{1}{6}$

____ 9. $1\frac{1}{3} \times 1\frac{1}{3} \times 1\frac{1}{3}$

____ 10. $\frac{1}{2}$ of $\frac{1}{3}$ of 4

____ 11. $10\frac{1}{10} \times \square = 1$

____ 12. ★ $1\frac{3}{4} \times \square \times \frac{1}{3} = 1$

Multiplying Fractions Shortcut*

Take the problem $\frac{3}{4} \times \frac{4}{5}$. Notice that the numerator and denominator are both multiplied by 4. This means that you will also divide by 4 when reducing the new fraction to its simplest form. Let's see: $\frac{3 \times 4}{4 \times 5} = \frac{12}{20} \div \frac{4}{4} = \frac{3}{5}$

A shortcut is to "cancel" out the 4's before doing the multiplying and dividing.

A number is canceled with a single strike-through. Since 4 ÷ 4 = 1, a small 1 is put next to both canceled numbers.

$$\frac{3}{_1\cancel{4}} \times \frac{\cancel{4}^1}{5} = \frac{3 \times 1}{1 \times 5} = \frac{3}{5}$$

You can cross-cancel a numerator anytime it will evenly divide into a denominator, or the other way around. Explain these examples step-by-step.

a. $\frac{5}{6} \times \frac{7}{10} = \frac{^1\cancel{5}}{6} \times \frac{7}{\cancel{10}_2} = \frac{1 \times 7}{6 \times 2} = \frac{7}{12}$

b. $\frac{6}{8} \times \frac{4}{6} = \frac{^1\cancel{6}}{_2\cancel{8}} \times \frac{\cancel{4}^1}{\cancel{6}_1} = \frac{1 \times 1}{2 \times 1} = \frac{1}{2}$

c. $1\frac{3}{5} \times 7\frac{1}{2} = \frac{^4\cancel{8}}{_1\cancel{5}} \times \frac{\cancel{15}^3}{\cancel{2}_1} = \frac{4 \times 3}{1 \times 1} = 12$

d. $1\frac{2}{4} \times \frac{4}{5} \times \frac{2}{3} = \frac{^2\cancel{6}}{_1\cancel{4}} \times \frac{\cancel{4}^1}{5} \times \frac{2}{\cancel{3}_1} = \frac{2 \times 1 \times 2}{1 \times 5 \times 1} = \frac{4}{5}$

Multiply the following fractions using cross-cancelling when possible.

1. $\frac{4}{7} \times \frac{1}{4}$
2. $\frac{5}{8} \times \frac{2}{5}$
3. $\frac{4}{6} \times \frac{6}{16}$
4. $\frac{3}{4} \times \frac{20}{30}$
5. $\frac{2}{3} \times \frac{12}{14}$
6. $\frac{2}{6} \times \frac{24}{30}$
7. $1\frac{1}{4} \times \frac{12}{20}$
8. $3\frac{1}{5} \times \frac{3}{8}$
9. $4\frac{1}{6} \times 3\frac{3}{5}$
10. $8\frac{3}{4} \times 1\frac{3}{5}$
11. ★ $1\frac{1}{3} \times \frac{6}{8} \times \frac{4}{5} \times 1\frac{1}{4}$

*See page 54 SET C for extra practice.

Dividing Fractions

How many halves are in $2\frac{1}{4}$? You could subtract $\frac{1}{2}$ repeatedly:

$2\frac{1}{4} - \underline{\frac{1}{2}} = 1\frac{3}{4} - \underline{\frac{1}{2}} = 1\frac{1}{4} - \underline{\frac{1}{2}} = \frac{3}{4} - \underline{\frac{1}{2}} = \frac{1}{4}$. So, 4 halves with $\frac{1}{4}$ leftover. Recognize $\frac{1}{4}$ is actually half of $\frac{1}{2}$ so, you know there are $4\frac{1}{2}$ halves in $2\frac{1}{4}$. Another way to think about it: how many halves are in 2 cookies (4) and the $\frac{1}{4}$ cookies left is halfway to being a full half. So there are 4 halves and $\frac{1}{2}$ half or $4\frac{1}{2}$ halves in 2 $\frac{1}{4}$ cookies. A quicker way is to use division, again changing mixed numbers to improper fractions. In this case, it is written $2\frac{1}{4} \div \frac{1}{2} = \square$ or $\frac{9}{4} \div \frac{1}{2} = \square$.

Remember fractions are actually division problems, with the fraction bar as the division symbol (divisor on bottom), so you can write the above problem as $\frac{\frac{9}{4}}{\frac{1}{2}}$. If you multiply this complex-looking fraction by 1, using the reciprocal of this divisor in the form of $\frac{\frac{2}{1}}{\frac{2}{1}}$, you have $\frac{\frac{9}{4}}{\frac{1}{2}} \times \frac{\frac{2}{1}}{\frac{2}{1}}$. The denominators cancel to 1, so $\frac{\frac{9}{4} \times \frac{2}{1}}{1}$ or simply $\frac{9}{4} \times \frac{2}{1} = \frac{9}{\cancel{4}_2} \times \frac{\cancel{2}^1}{1} = \frac{9}{2} = 4\frac{1}{2}$.

The key to dividing fractions is to use the inverse of the denominator over itself, as a form of 1. That way the denominator always turns into 1, and then you can ignore it. Explain the steps in:

$$3\frac{1}{2} \div \frac{1}{3} \text{ (how many } \tfrac{1}{3}\text{'s in } 3\tfrac{1}{2}\text{?).}$$

$$\frac{3\frac{1}{2}}{\frac{1}{3}} = \frac{\frac{7}{2}}{\frac{1}{3}} \times \frac{\frac{3}{1}}{\frac{3}{1}} = \frac{\frac{7}{2} \times \frac{3}{1}}{1} = \frac{7 \times 3}{2 \times 1} = \frac{21}{2} = 10\frac{1}{2} \text{ thirds are in } 3\frac{1}{2}.$$

Show $12 \div 1\frac{1}{2} = 8$. Check your work on next page.

Fraction Division Shortcuts*

So the first step in solving $\frac{\frac{12}{1}}{\frac{3}{2}}$ from the previous page, is to make the denominator 1, by multiplying it by its reciprocal, in the form of 1. The inverse of $\frac{3}{2}$ is $\frac{2}{3}$, so use $\frac{\frac{2}{3}}{\frac{2}{3}}$.

$\frac{\frac{12}{1}}{\frac{3}{2}} \times \frac{\frac{2}{3}}{\frac{2}{3}} = \frac{\frac{12}{1} \times \frac{2}{3}}{1} = \frac{\overset{4}{\cancel{12}}}{1} \times \frac{2}{\underset{1}{\cancel{3}}} = 8$. Is that what you found?

Want to see a shortcut for this problem, $\frac{12}{1} \div \frac{3}{2}$? Notice, that if the divisor is inverted and the division sign is changed to a multiplication sign, you have $\frac{12}{1} \times \frac{2}{3}$ for the same answer of 8.

Let's try another: How many eights are in $\frac{1}{2}$? $\frac{1}{2} \div \frac{1}{8} = \square$

The reciprocal to the divisor is $\frac{8}{1}$, which becomes the new multiplier. Since $\frac{1}{2} \times \frac{8}{1} = 4$, you now know there are four $\frac{1}{8}$'s in $\frac{1}{2}$ or $\frac{1}{2} \div \frac{1}{8} = 4$.

> Rule: To divide fractions, invert the divisor, then multiply.
> Caution: Inverting the dividend (instead of divisor) will give an inverted quotient (answer). So be careful to invert the second fraction.

Divide the following problems.* Show your work. The divisor is the second number. Look for cross-canceling shortcuts.

1. $\frac{3}{5} \div \frac{1}{5} = \frac{3}{5} \times \frac{5}{1}$
2. $4 \div \frac{2}{3}$
3. $2\frac{1}{2} \div 3$
4. $\frac{3}{4} \div \frac{5}{6}$
5. $\frac{8}{10} \div 2\frac{2}{3}$
6. $2\frac{1}{5} \div 1\frac{1}{6}$
7. $\frac{7}{40} \div \frac{21}{25}$
8. $4\frac{1}{5} \div 1\frac{4}{10}$
9. $1\frac{1}{4} \div 1\frac{7}{8}$
10. How many $\frac{1}{100}$ are in $\frac{1}{10}$?
11. ★ $(2\frac{1}{2} \div 1\frac{1}{2}) \div \frac{1}{2}$

*See page 54 SET D for extra practice.

Checking Your Work

Whether you're adding, subtracting, multiplying, or dividing, errors will happen from time to time. You're only human, and not a computer! To double-check that an answer is correct, it is best to re-work it from a different angle so you don't inadvertently make the same mistake (if you made one the first time).

Addition and subtraction are inverse operations, each "undoing" the other. Similarly multiplication and division are opposite operations. You can use these inverse operations to check the accuracy of your answer. For example, check whether 2 + 3 = 7 is correct by using subtraction. Does 7 – 3 = 2? No, so 7 is incorrect. 2 + 3 = 5, right? Check: Does 5 – 3 = 2? Yes, so 5 is the correct answer—mistake caught!

Look at these examples and correct the mistakes.

Problem		Check	
$\frac{1}{2} + \frac{1}{3} = \square$	$\square = \frac{5}{6}$	$\frac{5}{6} - \frac{1}{2} \stackrel{?}{=} \frac{1}{3}$	Yes. $\frac{5}{6} - \frac{3}{6} = \frac{1}{3}$
$\frac{1}{2} - \frac{1}{3} = \square$	$\square = \frac{1}{4}$	$\frac{1}{4} + \frac{1}{3} \stackrel{?}{=} \frac{1}{2}$	No. $\frac{3}{12} + \frac{4}{12} = \frac{7}{12} \neq \frac{1}{2}$
$\frac{1}{2} \times \frac{1}{3} = \square$	$\square = \frac{1}{6}$	$\frac{1}{6} \div \frac{1}{3} \stackrel{?}{=} \frac{1}{2}$	Yes. $\frac{1}{6} \times 3 = \frac{3}{6} = \frac{1}{2}$
$\frac{1}{2} \div \frac{1}{3} = \square$	$\square = 1\frac{1}{3}$	$1\frac{1}{3} \times \frac{1}{3} \stackrel{?}{=} \frac{1}{3}$	No. $\frac{4}{3} \times \frac{1}{3} = \frac{4}{9} \neq \frac{1}{2}$

When checking addition or multiplication, use the answer along with either number in the inverse operation. Does it equal the third number?

When checking subtraction, add the answer to the smaller number. Does it equal the third number?

When checking division, multiply the answer with the divisor only. Does it equal the third number?

Solve the following problems, then check. Show your work.

Problem	Check
1. $1\frac{1}{2} + 1\frac{3}{8} = \square$	$\square - 1\frac{3}{8} \stackrel{?}{=} 1\frac{1}{2}$
2. $6\frac{1}{3} - \frac{3}{4} = \square$	$\square + \frac{3}{4} \stackrel{?}{=} 6\frac{1}{3}$
3. $3\frac{3}{4} \times 1\frac{1}{5} = \square$	$\square \div 1\frac{1}{5} \stackrel{?}{=} 3\frac{3}{4}$
4. $1\frac{1}{6} \div \frac{3}{4} = \square$	$\square \times \frac{3}{4} \stackrel{?}{=} 1\frac{1}{6}$
5. $6\frac{2}{3} + 3\frac{9}{10} = \square$	$\square - 3\frac{9}{10} \stackrel{?}{=} 6\frac{2}{3}$
6. $2\frac{3}{5} - \frac{2}{7} = \square$	$\square + \frac{2}{7} \stackrel{?}{=} 2\frac{3}{5}$
7. $2\frac{1}{4} \times 1\frac{5}{9} = \square$	$\square \div 1\frac{5}{9} \stackrel{?}{=} 2\frac{1}{4}$
8. $3\frac{4}{8} \div 14 = \square$	$\square \times 14 \stackrel{?}{=} 3\frac{4}{8}$
9. $1\frac{1}{12} + \frac{7}{8} = \square$	$\square - \frac{7}{8} \stackrel{?}{=} 1\frac{1}{12}$
10. $2\frac{5}{6} - \frac{1}{7} = \square$	$\square + \frac{1}{7} \stackrel{?}{=} 2\frac{5}{6}$
11. $2\frac{1}{3} \times 2\frac{1}{3} = \square$	$\square \div 2\frac{1}{3} \stackrel{?}{=} 2\frac{1}{3}$
12. $\dfrac{3\frac{1}{7}}{7\frac{1}{3}} = \square$	$\square \times 7\frac{1}{3} \stackrel{?}{=} 3\frac{1}{7}$

13. ★ $\dfrac{1\frac{2}{5} \times 1\frac{2}{3}}{10 \div 1\frac{1}{2}} \times \square = 1$

Word Problems

Using math in our everyday life means translating thought and words into number sentences. For example, how old will someone be in 10 years means 10 added to some number. It may help to make a word equation using parenthesis first.

(ten) (added to) (some number)

Then you can substitute math symbols and use (□) for any unknown.

In this case: 10 + □

Another example: A boy is two years younger than his sister. This means he is (2) (less than) (a number) which means subtract.

□ – 2.

Study these common signal words and their translations. Then translate the phrases below.

SIGNAL WORD	TRANSLATION
is, equal, is equal to, the same as . . .	=
of, the product, times, multiplied by . . .	x
plus, more, more than, sum, added to . . .	+
difference, less, less than, decreased . . .	–
divided by, out of, divide . . .	÷

1. one more than a number
2. a number 5 less than it.
3. three-fourths of a dozen
4. a number divided in half
5. difference between a half and a third.
6. one-third of a quantity is equal to $\frac{3}{4}$.

Several types of word problems involving fractions routinely pop-up that look scary but really aren't when you go step-by-step. Practice translating three examples:

a. $\frac{4}{7}$ of $2\frac{1}{2}$ is what number?

$\left(\frac{4}{7}\right)$ (of) $\left(2\frac{1}{2}\right)$ (is) (what number)?

↓ ↓ ↓ ↓ ↓

$\frac{4}{7} \times 2\frac{1}{2} = \square$

b. What fraction of $2\frac{1}{3}$ is $1\frac{1}{4}$?

(what fraction) (of) $\left(2\frac{1}{3}\right)$ (is) $\left(1\frac{1}{4}\right)$?

↓ ↓ ↓ ↓ ↓

$\square \times 2\frac{1}{3} = 1\frac{1}{4}$

c. $\frac{3}{4}$ of what number equals $1\frac{1}{2}$?

$\left(\frac{3}{4}\right)$ (of) (what number) (equals) $\left(1\frac{1}{2}\right)$

↓ ↓ ↓ ↓ ↓

$\frac{3}{4} \times \square = 1\frac{1}{2}$

Example (a) is easy to solve now that you know how to multiply mixed numbers. (b) is a bit more difficult to decide what to do. It often helps to change the numbers in a problem to "easy" numbers to think the problem through. Keep the numbers in the same order and relative size; here, we drop the fraction and use only the whole numbers.

$$\square \times 2 = 1.$$

To solve, we divide 1 by 2 so to solve the problem (b), use division as well.

$$1\frac{1}{4} \div 2\frac{1}{3} = \frac{5}{4} \div \frac{7}{3} = \frac{5}{4} \times \frac{3}{7} = \frac{15}{28} \quad \text{Check: } \frac{15}{28} \times 2\frac{1}{3} = 1\frac{1}{4}$$

In Example (c) it is easiest to again simplify the numbers first, to figure out how to solve it, as in $2 \times \square = 10$. Your brain divided 10 into 2 parts to find the answer 5, so do the same for Example (c).

$$1\frac{1}{2} \div \frac{3}{4} = \frac{3}{2} \times \frac{4}{3} = 2 \quad \text{Check: } \frac{3}{4} \text{ of } 2 = \frac{6}{4} = 1\frac{1}{2}.$$

Translate and solve this problem. Check answer on next page.

$\frac{2}{3}$ of me is $\frac{1}{4}$. What fraction am I?

$$\left(\frac{2}{3}\right) \text{ (of) (me) (is) } \left(\frac{1}{4}\right)$$
$$\downarrow \quad \downarrow \quad \downarrow \quad \downarrow \quad \downarrow$$
$$\frac{2}{3} \times \square = \frac{1}{4}$$

Change this to a simple problem to help think about how to solve it. Keeping the numbers in their proper order and relative size, you might say "three times what equals 1?" or $3 \times \square = 1$. The answer is $\frac{1}{3}$, but your brain thought $1 \div 3 = \frac{1}{3}$. So use division.

(You may also recognize this problem is similar to Example (b) on previous page, which also required division.)

$$\square = \frac{1}{4} \div \frac{2}{3} \rightarrow \square = \frac{1}{4} \times \frac{3}{2} = \frac{3}{8}$$

Check: Is $\frac{2}{3}$ of $\frac{3}{8} = \frac{1}{4}$? Yes, $\frac{2}{3} \times \frac{3}{8} = \frac{1}{4}$ so "me" is $\frac{3}{8}$.

Translate the problems into equations and solve. Place the letter for the correct answer in the blank. Then complete the "check yourself" below.

____ 1. What fraction of $\frac{3}{4}$ is $\frac{1}{2}$?

____ 2. $1\frac{1}{3}$ of what fraction is $\frac{2}{3}$?

____ 3. $1\frac{1}{2}$ of $1\frac{1}{2}$ equals what?

____ 4. $1\frac{1}{4}$ of what number is $1\frac{2}{3}$?

____ 5. $\square \times \frac{3}{8} = 1\frac{5}{16}$

____ 6. $1\frac{7}{8} \times \square = \frac{5}{16}$

____ 7. What part of $8\frac{3}{4}$ is $\frac{7}{12}$?

____ 8. ★ Find a number such that $\frac{1}{3}$ of $\frac{3}{11}$ of it is $\frac{1}{4}$ of $\frac{3}{11}$.

t $3\frac{1}{2}$	u $1\frac{1}{3}$	a $\frac{3}{4}$	l $\frac{1}{15}$
n $2\frac{1}{3}$	r $\frac{2}{3}$	b $\frac{1}{2}$	e $2\frac{1}{4}$
m $1\frac{2}{3}$	o $\frac{1}{6}$	p = not here	

Check yourself: Write the letter for each problem in the numbered spaces below to answer this riddle.

What is easy to find your way into but hard to find the way out?

___ ___ ___ ___ ___ ___ ___
5 1 6 4 2 7 3

Word Problems

1. Mercer solves 20 fraction problems in 40 minutes. At this rate, how many will he solve in 50 minutes?

   a. How many minutes does it take to do 1 problem?

      $40 \div 20 = \square$ _______ minutes to do 1 problem.

   b. How many can be done in 50 minutes?

      $50 \div \square$ minutes = _______ problems.

2. Kelly completes $2\frac{1}{2}$ pages of math in 2 hours. How much could she do in 3 hours?

   a. How many pages can she do in 1 hour?

      $2\frac{1}{2} \div 2 = \square$ _______ pages in 1 hour

   b. How many pages can she do in 3 hours?

      $\square \times 3 =$ _______ pages

3. Bridget completes $1\frac{1}{3}$ problem every $2\frac{1}{2}$ minutes. How quickly can she do a dozen problems?

   a. How long does it take to do 1 problem?

      $2\frac{1}{2} \div 1\frac{1}{3} = \square$ _______ minutes for each problem.

   b. To do a dozen? _______ minutes. Show your work.

4. Dominic walks $12\frac{1}{2}$ blocks to school in $\frac{2}{5}$ hour.

   a. How far can Dominic walk in 1 hour? _______ blocks

      i. How many $\frac{2}{5}$ are in 1 hour? _______

      ii. Multiply by $12\frac{1}{2}$ = _______ per hour

   b. How long would it take to walk 100 blocks? _______ hours

Word Problems

Show your work.

1. A gumball machine is $\frac{3}{5}$ full with 4 dozen gumballs.

   How many gumballs would be in a full machine? _______ gumballs
   (Hint: How many in $\frac{1}{5}$ of machine)

2. Bobby is $\frac{3}{4}$ done with his math homework in $1\frac{1}{20}$ hours.

   By the time he is finished, how long will it have taken? _______ hours

3. Margo runs $3\frac{3}{4}$ laps on the track in $\frac{3}{10}$ hour.

   a. How long will it take to run $12\frac{1}{2}$ laps? _______ hours

   b. How many laps can be run in $2\frac{1}{10}$ hours? _______ laps

4. A car uses $10\frac{1}{2}$ gallons of gasoline to go 210 miles.

   a. How far can it go on $12\frac{1}{2}$ gallons? _______ miles

   b. How many gallons are needed to go $10\frac{1}{2}$ miles? _______ gallons

5. A factory can assemble $2\frac{2}{3}$ trucks every $\frac{1}{4}$ hour

   a. How many trucks can it build in $3\frac{3}{4}$ hours? _______ trucks

   b. How long would it take to assemble 100 trucks? _______ hours

6. ★ The temperature increases 3 degrees every $\frac{2}{5}$ hour. If it is noon, at what time will it be 20 degrees warmer? _______ p.m.

Review #1

Solve and reduce the answers to lowest terms. Write the letter of the correct answer in the blank. Then complete the "check yourself" below.

____ 1. $\frac{5}{6} + \frac{1}{4}$

____ 2. $1\frac{2}{5} + 2\frac{1}{3}$

____ 3. $\frac{5}{7} - \frac{2}{5}$

____ 4. $2\frac{1}{3} - \frac{3}{8}$

____ 5. $1\frac{2}{3} + 2\frac{3}{4} + 1\frac{5}{6}$

____ 6. $2\frac{3}{5} - 1\frac{7}{8}$

____ 7. $\frac{9}{15} \times \frac{5}{3}$

____ 8. $1\frac{5}{7} \times 3\frac{3}{4}$

____ 9. $\frac{2}{3} \div \frac{3}{5}$

____ 10. $1\frac{3}{16} \div 4\frac{3}{4}$

____ 11. $1\frac{3}{5} \times 1\frac{4}{6} \times 2\frac{1}{2}$

____ 12. $3\frac{3}{7} \div 1\frac{7}{14}$

____ 13. What fraction of $4\frac{2}{3}$ is $3\frac{1}{2}$?

____ 14. What fraction of 50 is $4\frac{1}{2}$?

____ 15. $1\frac{2}{3}$ of what number is $\frac{7}{15}$?

____ 16. ★ It takes a snail $4\frac{1}{2}$ hours to crawl 30 feet. How far can it move in $1\frac{1}{8}$ hour? _______ feet

k $2\frac{2}{7}$	r $\frac{7}{25}$	a $6\frac{2}{3}$	b $\frac{9}{100}$	n $\frac{1}{4}$	f $6\frac{1}{4}$	s 1	d $1\frac{1}{9}$
i $\frac{3}{4}$	t $1\frac{1}{12}$	e $1\frac{23}{24}$	m $7\frac{1}{2}$	a $\frac{11}{35}$	e $\frac{29}{40}$	r $3\frac{11}{15}$	n $6\frac{3}{7}$

Check yourself: Write the letter for each problem in the numbered space below to answer this riddle.

What 2 things can you not eat at lunch time?

___ ___ ___ ___ ___ ___ ___ ___ ___ , ___ ___ ___ ___ ___ ___
14 15 6 3 12 5 11 7 1 , 9 13 8 10 4 2

% Percent %

Closely related to fractions is percent. Notice how the percent symbol (%) even looks like a fraction!

50% OFF SALE!

SAVE 20% TODAY!

The word percent is actually two words: per and cent. When their meanings are put together you'll see the mathematics.

Let's start with "per." Recall the fraction bar stands for "out of" as in 1 out of 2 or $\frac{1}{2}$. Another word for "out of" is per, so it too is represented by the fraction bar. "Per" is often used in ways such as: maximum 2 tickets per person, 40 miles per hour speed limit, 3 outs per innings, or even the very old saying of an apple per day keeps the doctor away. Below, 1 out of every 2 circles are shaded.

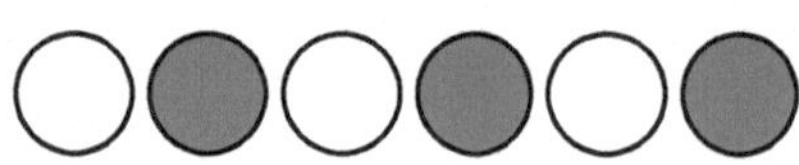
1 shaded per every 2 circles

The word "cent" means one hundred, as in the word century, which means 100 years. 100 centimeters are in a meter and yes, a few varieties of centipedes do have 100 legs!" The penny coin is called a cent because it is $\frac{1}{100}$ of a dollar. A centimeter is $\frac{1}{100}$ as long as a meter.

So the word percent literally means "out of 100" or $\frac{\square}{100}$. Any fraction with a denominator of 100 can also be written using the percent symbol: %. $\frac{5}{100}$ = 5%. Percents are mathematically created by changing fractions into equivalent fractions of hundredths.

$$\frac{1}{2} = \frac{50}{100} = 50 \text{ per } 100 = 50\%$$

$$\frac{2}{2} = \frac{100}{100} = 100 \text{ per } 100 = 100\%$$

Challenge Yourself: Use the hundreds grid on p. 65, to prove:

(a) 10% of the total grid = $\frac{1}{10}$

(b) 75% of the total grid = $\frac{3}{4}$

(c) 1/20 of the grid = 5%

(d) $\frac{4}{5}$ of the grid = 80%

To convert a fraction to a percent, find its equivalence in hundredths.

$$\frac{1}{4} = \frac{\square}{100} \qquad \frac{25}{25} \times \frac{1}{4} = \frac{25}{100} = 25\%$$

$$\frac{3}{5} = \frac{\square}{100} \qquad \frac{20}{20} \times \frac{3}{5} = \frac{60}{100} = 60\%$$

To convert a percent to a fraction, put it in fraction form with a denominator of 100, then reduce to simplest terms.

$$10\% = \frac{10}{100} \div \frac{10}{10} = \frac{1}{10}$$

$$75\% = \frac{75}{100} \div \frac{25}{25} = \frac{3}{4}$$

Complete the tables below.

	FRACTION	EQUIVALENT (Per hundredths)	PERCENT
1.	$\frac{1}{5}$		
2.	$\frac{3}{4}$		
3.	$\frac{7}{10}$		
4.	$\frac{1}{20}$		
5.	$\frac{49}{50}$		
6.	$\frac{2}{4}$		
7.	$\frac{4}{5}$		
8.	$\frac{10}{10}$		
9.	$\frac{3}{5}$		
10.	$\frac{11}{25}$		

	PERCENT	FRACTION (Per hundredths)	REDUCED?
11.	50%		
12.	30%		
13.	8%		
14.	15%		
15.	90%		
16.	2%		
17.	42%		
18.	25%		
19.	3%		
20.	4%		

Some fractions, such as $\frac{1}{3}$, can only be made into an equivalent fraction in hundredths by using a mixed number as the multiplier.

$$\frac{1}{3} \times \frac{33\frac{1}{3}}{33\frac{1}{3}} = \frac{33\frac{1}{3}}{100} = 33\frac{1}{3}\%$$

$$\frac{1}{6} \times \frac{16\frac{2}{3}}{16\frac{2}{3}} = \frac{16\frac{2}{3}}{100} = 16\frac{2}{3}\%$$

Use the cut-out hundreds grid (page 65) to see if three – $33\frac{1}{3}$'s make 100 and whether six – $16\frac{2}{3}$'s total 100.

Study the following "cheat sheet" and refer to it as you work through the remainder of this book.

CHEAT SHEET

FRACTION	PERCENT
$\frac{1}{100}$	1%
$\frac{1}{50}$	2%
$\frac{1}{25}$	4%
$\frac{1}{20}$	5%
$\frac{1}{12}$	$8\frac{1}{3}\%$
$\frac{1}{11}$	$9\frac{1}{11}\%$
$\frac{1}{10}$	10%
$\frac{1}{9}$	$11\frac{1}{9}\%$
$\frac{1}{8}$	$12\frac{1}{2}\%$
$\frac{1}{7}$	$14\frac{2}{7}\%$

FRACTION	PERCENT
$\frac{1}{6}$	$16\frac{2}{3}\%$
$\frac{1}{5}$	20%
$\frac{1}{4}$	25%
$\frac{1}{3}$	$33\frac{1}{3}\%$
$\frac{1}{2}$	50%
$\frac{2}{3}$	$66\frac{2}{3}\%$
$\frac{3}{4}$	75%
$\frac{3}{8}$	$37\frac{1}{2}\%$
$\frac{5}{8}$	$62\frac{1}{2}\%$
$\frac{7}{8}$	$87\frac{1}{2}\%$
$\frac{5}{6}$	$83\frac{1}{3}\%$

What Percent?

Write the letter of the correct answer in the blank. Refer to "cheat sheet" on page 36 as needed. Then complete the "check yourself" below.

____ 1. What percent of a year is two seasons?

____ 2. What percent of a dollar is 7 nickels?

____ 3. What percent of a year is 13 weeks?

____ 4. What percent of an hour is 12 minutes?

____ 5. What percent of a day is 3 hours?

____ 6. What percent of 2 days is 4 hours?

____ 7. What percent of a dozen is 8?

____ 8. What percent of months begin with 'M'?

____ 9. What percent of $1\frac{1}{2}$ hours is 10 minutes?

____ 10. What percent of a week is the weekend?

____ 11. What percent of \$20 is \$3?

____ 12. What percent of 1 minute is 50 seconds?

____ 13. What percent of a century is 36 months?

____ 14. ★ What percent of \$5 is $\$1\frac{1}{2}$?

o 15%
u 20%
o $16\frac{2}{3}\%$
m $28\frac{4}{7}\%$
f 3%
e $83\frac{1}{3}\%$
s 35%
p $8\frac{1}{3}\%$
i 25%
l 30%
r $11\frac{1}{9}\%$
r $12\frac{1}{2}\%$
s $66\frac{2}{3}\%$
b 75%
y 50%

Check yourself: Write the letter for each problem in the numbered space below to answer this riddle.

What is it that if you break them you cannot keep them?

__ __ __ __   __ __ __ __ __ __ __ __
1 11 4 9   6 5 8 10 3 7 12 2

Percent Word Problems

A farmer donates 20% of her 60 chicken eggs to a food bank. How many is this?

20% of 60

↓ ↓ ↓

$$\frac{20}{100} \times \frac{60}{1} \quad \text{Reduce } \frac{20}{100} \text{ to } \frac{1}{5}$$

$$\frac{1}{5} \times \frac{60}{1} = \frac{60}{5} = 12 \text{ eggs}$$

In the following problems, start by converting the percent to a fraction in lowest terms. Use "cheat sheet" on page 36 when helpful.

1. 25% of the 2 dozen loaves of bread are whole wheat. How many is this? ________
2. How much is a 15% tip on $40? ________
3. A trucker has driven 85% of a 1,000 mile trip. How much is left? ________
4. A store owner pays 4% of its $1,200 sales to charity. How much is this? ________
5. The bike shop will take $33\frac{1}{3}$% off the price of $180. What is the new price? ________
6. ★ His $3.50 tip was $16\frac{2}{3}$% of the bill, so what was the bill? ________
7. 40% of 60 = ________
8. 12% of $10 = ________
9. 90% of 50 = ________
10. $66\frac{2}{3}$% of 300 = ________
11. $12\frac{1}{2}$% of 64 = ________
12. 5% of $20.20 = ________
13. 27% of 1 = ________
14. 50% of 1,000 = ________
15. 75% x 400 = ________
16. $83\frac{1}{3}$% of a dozen = ________
17. $87\frac{1}{2}$% of 32 = ________
18. ★ 5% of 10% of 10,000 = ________

Percentage is the result of finding a percent.

Example: 5% of what number is 1?

$$\frac{1}{20} \times \square = 1$$

$$\square = 1 \div \frac{1}{20} = \frac{1}{1} \times \frac{20}{1} = 20$$

Check: Is 5% x 20 = 1? Yes, $\frac{5}{100} \times \frac{20}{1} = 1$, so 20 is correct.

Solve and check each problem.

1. 20% of the total cost is $3. Total cost = ________

2. $33\frac{1}{3}$% of the theatre audience were 125 children. How many people were in the audience? ________

3. 4% of the cooking time for rice in 2 minutes. How long is the total cooking time? ________

4. 50 is 10% of what number? ________

5. What number, multiplied by 75%, makes 60? ________

6. $8\frac{1}{3}$% of the doughnuts a baker is making requires 12 minutes, so how long will it take to make 100%? ________

7. $66\frac{2}{3}$ of the math problems are done. 7 are left, so how many were there in all? ________

8. 15% of me is $1\frac{1}{2}$. What number am I? ________

9. 50% of 50% of me is $6\frac{1}{4}$. What number am I? ________

10. 75% of the track race is 1,800 meters. How long is the whole race? ________

11. ★ $44\frac{4}{9}\% \times \square = 16\frac{2}{3}\%$? ________

What Percent of ? is ?

What percent of 40 is 10? You know how to find the answer if the question was, What <u>fraction</u> of 40 is 10? $\frac{10}{40}$ means you divided so use division in the percent problems.

What percent of 40 is 10?

↓ ↓ ↓ ↓ ↓

☐ % x 40 = 10

☐ % = 10 ÷ 40 = $\frac{10}{40} = \frac{1}{4}$

$25\% = \frac{1}{4}$

Check: Is 25% of 40 = 10? $\frac{25}{\cancel{100}_5} \times \frac{\cancel{40}^2}{1} = \frac{1}{4} \times \frac{40}{1} = 10.$

Solve each problem and check your work.

1. What percent of a 12-slice pizza is 3 slices? ________

2. If 6 pieces out of a 16-piece jigsaw puzzle are left, what percent is this? ________

3. What percent of 10 is $\frac{1}{2}$? ________

4. $\frac{3}{4}$ is what percent of 3? ________

5. What percent of a \$20 board game is \$$2\frac{1}{2}$ off? ________

6. What percent of the 50 states are the 8 states that begin with "M?" ________

7. What percent of $2\frac{1}{2}$ is $\frac{4}{5}$? ________

8. $1\frac{3}{4}$ is what percent of $10\frac{1}{2}$? ________

9. What percent of 240 is 80? ________

10. ★ What percent of 97 is $84\frac{7}{8}$? ________
    (Hint: 97 x 7 = 679)

Percent Increase/Decrease

When an amount changes, whether it increases or decreases, the change can be described in percentage.

If a baby weighs 8 pounds at birth and a week later weighs 9 pounds, the baby gained 1 pound. What percent of 8 pounds is 1 pound? $\square$ % x 8 = 1; $\square = 1 \div 8 = \frac{1}{8}$; $\frac{1}{8} = 12\frac{1}{2}\%$.

Looked at another way, the weight went up 1 pound out of 8 pounds, or increased by $\frac{1}{8}$, and $\frac{1}{8} = 12\frac{1}{2}\%$.

Check: Is $12\frac{1}{2}\%$ of 8 = 1? $12\frac{1}{2}\% = \frac{25}{2} \div 100 = \frac{25}{2} \times \frac{1}{100} = \frac{25}{200}$.

Is $\frac{25}{200}$ of 8 = 1? Yes, $\frac{25}{200} \times 8 = \frac{200}{200}$.

Solve and check each problem. Show your work.

1. A bag of apples is on sale from \$5 to \$4. What percentage has the price been reduced? (Dropped 1 out of 5.) ________

2. A 3 year old turns 4. What percentage increase of years is this? ________

3. The outside temperature drops from 60° to 50°. What percentage change is this? ________

4. A cup of hot tea went from boiling at 100° to $28\frac{1}{2}$° when ice was added. What percentage drop in temperature was this? ________

5. The price of an item went from \$4.50 to \$9.00. What percentage increase is this? ________

6. 3 slices remain from two 12-slice pizzas. What percentage was eaten? ________

7. A student grew from 4 feet 2 inches to 4 feet 5 inches. What percentage taller did the student grow? ________

8. ★ A can of tomatoes has been down-sized from 16 ounces to $14\frac{2}{5}$ ounces. What percentage change in weight is this? ________

More Than 100%

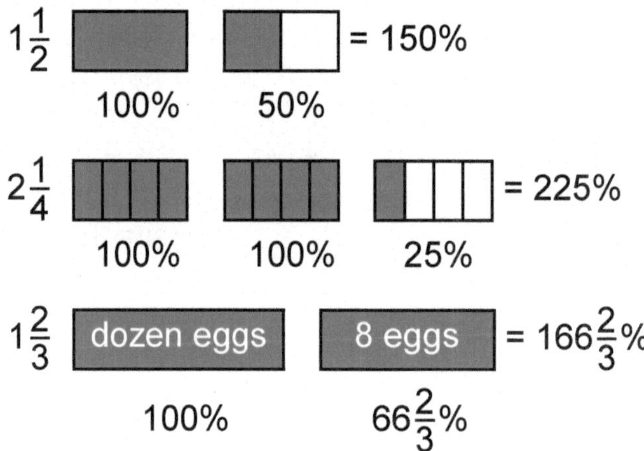

Suppose you are assembling bikes, and you have 7 wheels. Two wheels is 100% of what a bike needs, right? So 7 wheels would be much more than 100%, but how much more?

$7 \div 2 = 3\frac{1}{2}$ bikes. That's 300% and 50% of the fourth bike or 350% of the wheels needed for 1 bike.

Solve each problem. Show your work.

1. A recipe used 4 eggs. You have a half dozen. What percentage do you have if a recipe = 100%?

2. Each carnival ride uses 5 tickets. You have 16 tickets, so what percentage do you have if 5 tickets = 100%.

3. If a dozen oranges per bag = 100%, what percentage is 40 oranges?

4. A recipe uses $1\frac{1}{4}$ sticks of butter. You have 150% of what you need. How many sticks of butter do you have?

5. ★ A recipe uses $2\frac{1}{4}$ teaspoons of vanilla. You have $6\frac{3}{4}$ teaspoons. What percent do you have compared to what you need?

Just For fun: They say when someone is trying their hardest, they're giving 110% effort.

More Than 100%

Example: 120% of 10 = ? $\frac{120}{\cancel{100}_{10}} \times \frac{\cancel{10}^{1}}{1} = \frac{120}{10} = 12$

Check: 100% of 10 = 10; 20% of 10 = 2; so 120% = 10 + 2 = 12

You may find it easier to convert the percent to a fraction before starting.

Example: 250% of what number makes 10? 250% = $\frac{250}{100} = 2\frac{1}{2}$.

$2\frac{1}{2} \times \square = 10$

$10 \div 2\frac{1}{2} = \frac{10}{1} \times \frac{2}{5} = 4$. Check: Is $2\frac{1}{2} \times 4 = 10$? Yes.

Solve each problem. Show your work.

1. 110% of 50 = $1\frac{1}{10} \times 50$
2. 200% of 35
3. 175% of 20
4. 450% of 1
5. 140% of 5
6. $166\frac{2}{3}$% of 900
7. 250% of $\frac{3}{5}$
8. 325% of 300
9. A library loans 600 books daily. It had $133\frac{1}{3}$% increase in borrowed books. What is the new total?
10. A teacher assigns 20 math problems. A student does those plus 3 extra credit problems. What percentage of the assignment did the student do?
11. 225% of me is 90. What number am I?
12. What percent of 20 is 110?
13. What percent of $\frac{1}{4}$ is $\frac{1}{10}$?
14. ★ $1\frac{2}{3}$ is what percent of $\frac{1}{4}$?

Review #2

1. Which are greater than 80%?

   a. $\frac{5}{5}$ b. $\frac{4}{5}$ c. $\frac{9}{10}$ d. $\frac{15}{18}$

2. Which are less than 10%?

   a. $\frac{1}{11}$ b. $\frac{1}{9}$ c. $\frac{7}{100}$ d. $\frac{4}{50}$

3. What percent of cookies are eaten from 3 dozen, if 9 remain?

   a. $33\frac{1}{3}\%$ b. $66\frac{2}{3}\%$ c. 25% d. 75% e. none of these

4. What percent of fingers and toes are not thumbs?

   a. 90% b. 80% c. 75% d. 10% e. none of these

5. What fraction(s) equal 88%?

   a. $8\frac{8}{10}$ b. $\frac{880}{1,000}$ c. $\frac{22}{25}$ d. $\frac{44}{50}$ e. none of these

6. What fraction(s) equal 275%?

   a. $\frac{11}{4}$ b. $2\frac{3}{5}$ c. $\frac{27\frac{1}{2}}{10}$ d. $2\frac{75}{100}$ e. none of these

7. $14\frac{2}{7}\%$ of $3\frac{1}{2}$ is what percent of 1?

   a. 25% b. $33\frac{1}{3}\%$ c. 7% d. 40% e. none of these

8. What is 300% of $\frac{5}{3}$?

   a. $\frac{5}{9}$ b. 15 c. 3 d. 5 e. none of these

9. What is $12\frac{1}{2}\%$ of 4?

   a. $12\frac{1}{2} \times 4$ b. 50% of 1 c. $\frac{4}{12\frac{1}{2}}$ d. $\frac{12\frac{1}{2}}{4}$ e. none of these

10. What is 110% more than 100? a. 200 b. 210 c. 110 d. 120

11. 63 months is what percentage in years? a. 525% b. $\frac{12}{63}\%$ c. 475% d. 630%

12. A book is marked down from \$16 to \$10. What percent "on sale" is it?

    a. 35% b. $37\frac{1}{2}\%$ c. 40% d. 60% e. $62\frac{1}{2}\%$

Fractions as Decimals

$1 (10¢) (10¢) (10¢) (10¢) (10¢)

This amount of money can be described as $1\frac{1}{2}$ dollars, but it is sometimes more convenient and easier to understand when the fraction part is written using a decimal point as in $1.50. This is read as "one dollar and fifty-cents" but also as "one and fifty hundredths" ($1\frac{50}{100}$) dollars, since $\frac{1}{2} = \frac{50}{100}$. The decimal point is read as "and," it separates the whole from the fraction.

$2\frac{1}{4} = 2\frac{25}{100} = 2.25$ (two and twenty-five hundredths).

To understand the math connection between fractions and decimals, below is a short review of <u>base 10</u> or the <u>decimal system</u>. The place value system is based on ones, tens, and multiples of tens (10 x 10, 100 x 10, 1000 x 10 ...)

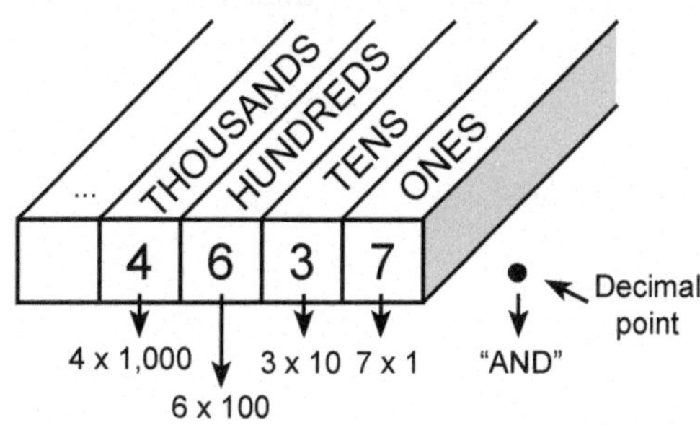

Whole numbers, such as 4,637 are usually written without the decimal point since there is no fractional part to separate out. The decimal point is implied to be there, as in 4,637.0, but is unnecessary to write.

<u>Expanded notation</u> is a good way to understand the decimal system.

For example:

(a) 365
(3 x 100) + (6 x 10) + (5 x 1)

(b) 1,492
(1 x 1,000) + (4 x 100) + (9 x 10) + (2 x 1)

Just For Fun: Decimal comes from the Latin root word "Decem" meaning 10 or 10th. A decade is 10 years and a decimeter is 1/10 of a meter. In the old Roman calendar, December was the 10th month!

To the left of the decimal, place value changes by multiples of 10, starting with the ones. To the right of the decimal point, place value changes by dividing by 10's, again starting with the ones place.

$1 \div 10 = \frac{1}{10}$; $\frac{1}{10} \div 10 = \frac{1}{100}$; $\frac{1}{100} \div 10 = \frac{1}{1{,}000}$ ...

0.123 =

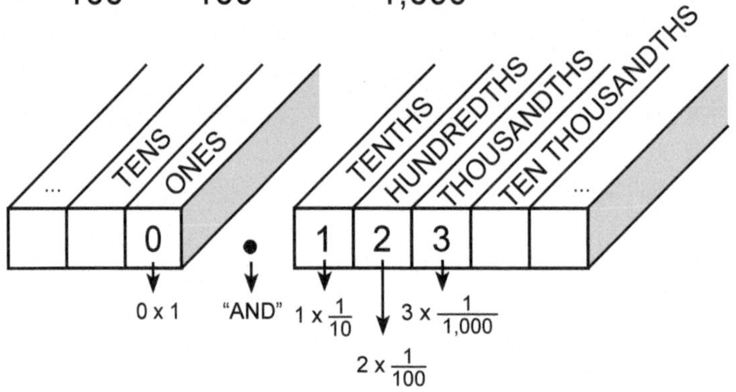

TENS ONES TENTHS HUNDREDTHS THOUSANDTHS TEN THOUSANDTHS

...		0	•	1	2	3		...
		0×1	"AND"	$1 \times \frac{1}{10}$	$2 \times \frac{1}{100}$	$3 \times \frac{1}{1{,}000}$		

There are no ones – only a fraction of one, divided into thousandths. Specifically 123 out of the 1,000, or $\frac{123}{1{,}000}$ or one hundred twenty-three thousandths. It is customary to write the zero but not necessary to say. Notice the relationship between the number of digits in the decimal unit and the number of zeros in the fraction place value.

$$0.\underbrace{9}_{\text{1 digit}} = \frac{9}{\underbrace{10}_{\text{1 zero}}} \qquad 0.\underbrace{25}_{\text{2 digits}} = \frac{25}{\underbrace{100}_{\text{2 zeros}}} \qquad 4.\underbrace{388}_{\text{3 digits}} = 4\frac{388}{\underbrace{1{,}000}_{\text{3 zeros}}}$$

Using expanded notation with decimals:

0.275

$$(0 \times 1) + (2 \times \frac{1}{10}) + (7 \times \frac{1}{100}) + (5 \times \frac{1}{1{,}000})$$

\$12.69

$$(1 \times \$10) + (2 \times \$1) + (6 \times \$\frac{1}{10}) + (9 \times \$\frac{1}{100})$$

For practice read these aloud, then write the letter of the correct answer in the blank.

a. 0.30 b. 1.42 c. 26.04 d. 3.025 e. 1.0001

_____ 1. one and one-ten-thousandth

_____ 2. three and twenty-five thousandths

_____ 3. thirty hundredths

_____ 4. twenty-six and four hundredths

_____ 5. one and forty-two hundredths

Just For Fun: In Olympic sports, races are timed in thousandths of a second. Imagine dividing one second into one thousand parts. Now that's fast!

Decimal Practice

Write the letter for the correct answer in blank. Then complete the "check yourself" below. An answer may be used more than once.

____ 1. Which number has 5 hundredths but no tens?

____ 2. Which number shows $(2 \times 1) + (4 \times 10) + (1 \times \frac{1}{10})$?

____ 3. $(0 \times 100) + (4 \times 10) + (2 \times 1) + (2 \times \frac{1}{100}) = ?$

____ 4. $(4 \times \$\frac{1}{10}) + (4 \times \$1) + (2 \times \$\frac{1}{100}) = ?$

____ 5. Which number is $\frac{1}{10}$ of $\frac{42}{100}$?

____ 6. The digit in the tenths place is half the tens digit.

____ 7. $4\frac{1}{5} = ?$

____ 8. $\frac{402}{100} = ?$

____ 9. four and one-half?

____ 10. 420%?

____ 11. $(4 \times 10) + (2 \times \frac{1}{1,000})$?

____ 12. 25% of $16\frac{1}{5}$?

t 0.042	i 4.02	e 42.02	s 4.50	r 4.05	h 4.200	u 4.21
o 40.002	l 0.0042	a 40.25	n 40.20	w 42.1	d 4.42	m 0.420

Check yourself: Write the letter for each problem in the numbered space below to answer this riddle.

What is it that everyone has and no one loses it?

___ ___ ___ ___ ___   ___ ___ ___ ___ ___ ___
5 10 3 8 1   9 7 6 4 11 2

Comparing Decimals

How do you know which is more: 0.1 or 0.3? You could think of them as fractions ($\frac{1}{10}$ versus $\frac{3}{10}$) which makes it easy, right? You can also compare place value digits from left to right. Whichever has a larger digit, in the same place value column, is the largest number.

Example: Compare 12.60 and 12.49. They both have 1 ten and 2 ones but the tenths digits are not the same. 6 > 4, so 12.60 > 12.49. (Check: 60 > 49)

Compare 3.18 and 3.182. Make sure they have the same number of digits each so 3.18 = 3.180. Comparing digits, left to right, from the thousandths place value 3.180 < 3.182, since 0 < 2. (Check: 180 < 182).

Underline the greatest number in each set below. Use that in the "check yourself" below.

1. (n) 3.72 (o) 3.27 (l) 2.795 (c) 3.717

2. (i) 0.03 (e) 0.13 (m) 0.015 (t) 0.116

3. (b) 67.3 (o) 67.31 (a) 76.032 (p) 67.311

4. (e) 2.01 (f) 2.001 (g) 2.005 (u) 0.29

5. (n) 126.95 (i) 126.899 (o) 126.99 (c) 126.991

6. (t) $1\frac{6}{1,000}$ (e) $\frac{1,005}{1,000}$ (p) 0.061 (f) 1.0061

Check yourself: Write the letter for each problem in the numbered space below to answer this riddle.

What runs around a yard but doesn't move?

___ ___ ___ ___ ___ ___
3 6 4 1 5 2

Just For Fun: Toes and fingers are called digits. The decimal system uses 10 digits too (0 – 9), and that may be why!

Converting Fractions to Decimals

If a fraction has an equivalent fraction in tenths or hundredths or thousandths, it is easy to change it into decimal form. Example: (a) $\frac{1}{2} = \frac{\square}{10}$; $\frac{5}{10} = 0.5$. Also, $\frac{1}{2} = \frac{50}{100}$ or 0.50; $\frac{1}{2} = \frac{500}{1{,}000} = 0.500$ (b) $\frac{2}{5} = \frac{\square}{10}$; $\frac{4}{10} = 0.4$. Also, $\frac{2}{5} = \frac{40}{100} = 0.40$ and $\frac{2}{5} = \frac{400}{1{,}000} =$ 0.400 (c) $\frac{1}{4} \neq \frac{\square}{10}$ but $\frac{1}{4} = \frac{25}{100} = 0.25$; $\frac{1}{4} = \frac{250}{1{,}000} = 0.250\ldots$

Recall that $\frac{1}{8} = 12\frac{1}{2}\%$, so $\frac{1}{8}$ has no equivalent fraction in tenths or hundredths but it does in thousandths. $\frac{1}{8} = \frac{125}{1{,}000}$ or 0.125. See the similarity between $12\frac{1}{2}\%$ and $\frac{125}{1{,}000}$ where $\frac{1}{2} = 0.5$?

Write $\frac{1}{20}$ as a decimal. Hint: $\frac{1}{20} = \frac{\square}{100}$

Did you find it was five hundredths? Notice what happens in converting $\frac{2}{20}$ to a decimal, $\frac{2}{20} = \frac{10}{100} = 0.10 = 0.1$. If you reduce it first, $\frac{2}{20}$ to $\frac{1}{10}$, you can see the decimal immediately: $\frac{1}{10} = 0.1$.

A few are more tricky, such as $\frac{1}{3}$ and $\frac{2}{3}$. There are no equivalent fractions in tenths, hundredths, or any 10's place value. $3 + 3 + 3 \neq 10$; $33 + 33 + 33 \neq 100$, $333 + 333 + 333 \neq 1{,}000$, etc. There is always 1 left over for the three groups, which why it is expressed as $33\frac{1}{3}\%$, for example. $\frac{1}{3} = \frac{3\frac{1}{3}}{10} = \frac{33\frac{1}{3}}{100} = \frac{333\frac{1}{3}}{1{,}000}\ldots$

In decimal numbers, fractions cannot be used, so $0.33\frac{1}{3}$ is not correct. But the 3's never end, so then what to do?

In math, a repeating number is shown by using a bar over the digit(s) that repeat. Thus $\frac{1}{3} = 0.3\overline{3}$ or $0.33\overline{3}$ or simply $0.\overline{3}$.

Similarly, $\frac{2}{3} = \frac{6\frac{2}{3}}{10} = \frac{66\frac{2}{3}}{100}$ $0.\overline{6}$ or $0.6\overline{6}$ = $\frac{666\frac{2}{3}}{1{,}000}$. So $\frac{2}{3} = 0.66\overline{6}$ or $0.6\overline{6}$ or simple $0.\overline{6}$.

Decimal/Fraction Equivalents

Some fractions are used so often it is worth while memorizing them. These are indicated by ★.

★ $\frac{1}{2} = 0.5$

★ $\frac{1}{3} = 0.3\overline{3}$ rounded to 0.33 ★ $\frac{2}{3} = 0.6\overline{6}$ rounded to 0.67

★ $\frac{1}{4} = 0.25$ ★ $\frac{2}{4} = \frac{1}{2} = 0.5$ ★ $\frac{3}{4} = 0.75$

★ $\frac{1}{5} = 0.2$ ★ $\frac{2}{5} = 0.4$ ★ $\frac{3}{5} = 0.6$ ★ $\frac{4}{5} = 0.8$

$\frac{1}{6} = 0.1\overline{6}$ rounded to 0.17 $\frac{5}{6} = 0.8\overline{3}$ rounded to 0.83

$\frac{1}{8} = 0.125$ $\frac{3}{8} = 0.375$ $\frac{5}{8} = 0.625$ $\frac{7}{8} = 0.875$

$\frac{1}{12} = 0.08\overline{3}$ $\frac{1}{20} = 0.05$ $\frac{1}{25} = 0.04$ $\frac{1}{50} = 0.02$

Decimal/Fraction Practice

1. To change decimals into fractions, write its fraction form and then reduce to lowest terms. For example,

a. $0.56 = \frac{56}{100} = \frac{14}{25}$ b. $4.225 = 4\frac{225}{1{,}000}\ (\div \frac{25}{25}) = 4\frac{9}{40}$

Write these decimal numbers as fractions in their lowest terms.

a. 0.25 = b. 0.44 = c. 1.6 d. 0.75 =
e. 0.500 = f. 5.35 = g. 0.16 = h. 0.002 =
i. 3.05 = j. 0.080 = k. 0.85 = l. 0.625 =
m. 0.0002 = n. 1.375 = o. $0.3\overline{3}$ = p. ★ 1.0875 =

2. Convert these fractions and mixed numbers into decimals. Look for ways to change fractions into equivalent in tenths, hundredths, or reducing them first. Then use the chart.

a. $\frac{4}{8} =$ b. $\frac{8}{12} =$ c. $\frac{9}{12} =$ d. $1\frac{52}{100} =$
e. $\frac{12}{200} =$ f. $1\frac{10}{1{,}000} =$ g. $\frac{32}{10{,}000} =$ h. $\frac{12}{144} =$
i. $4\frac{6}{20} =$ j. $3\frac{35}{42} =$ k. $\frac{3}{25} =$ l. $\frac{70}{500} =$
m. $9\frac{45}{12} =$ n. $\frac{40}{48} =$ o. $\frac{400}{10{,}000} =$ p. ★ $\frac{1}{3} + \frac{1}{4} + \frac{1}{6} + 0.25 =$

Final Review

1. Write the improper fraction and decimal for $2\frac{5}{100}$.

2. Convert $1\frac{7}{20}$ to a percent and a decimal.

3. A $33\frac{1}{3}$% drop in price from $24.99 is what new price?

4. What is the sum of the digits in the thousands and thousandths place in the number 20,423.9103

5. $1\frac{2}{8} \times \square = 1$

6. What percent of 6 is $1\frac{1}{2}$?

7. How many $\frac{3}{4}$'s are in 60?

8. What percentage increase is it from $\frac{1}{2}$ to $2\frac{1}{4}$?

9. $1\frac{1}{2} + 2\frac{2}{3} + \square = 10\frac{1}{8}$

10. $1\frac{1}{2} \times 2\frac{2}{3} \times \square = 10\frac{1}{8}$

11. 2% of 50 = $\square + \frac{1}{6} + \frac{1}{9}$

12. What percentage decrease is it from 90 to 54?

13. What is 25% of $\frac{1}{4}$ of $\frac{1}{3}$ of $\frac{1}{2}$?

14. 25 is what percent of 1,000?

15. ★ By what percent must you decrease $4\frac{1}{2}$ to have $\frac{1}{2}$? ("Cheat Sheet" on page 36 may be useful)

Brain Teasers

1. What percent is shaded?

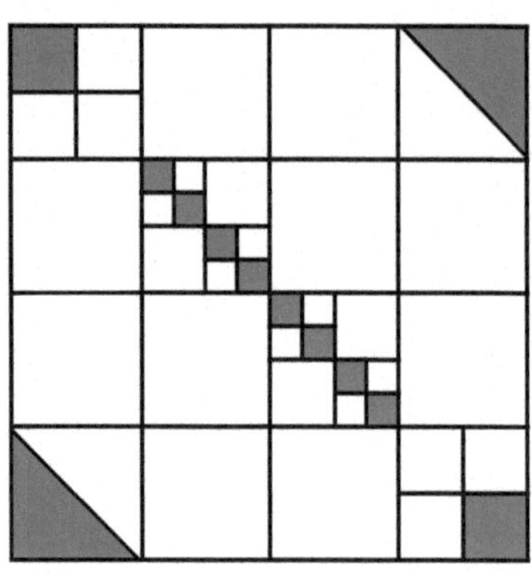

2. If □ ◿ = 6.9, then what is □ □ ◿?

3. If ● = 0.01 and ●●● ●●● is 40% of the total ●'s then what decimal would represent the total?

4. A father offers his daughter either (a) $6\frac{1}{4}$% of 20% of \$800 or (b) $\frac{1}{2}$% of \$2,000. What should she do?

5. What percentage of a day is $\frac{24}{25}$ of an hour?

6-7 Use the clues in each box to fill in the missing blanks.

6.

a = $\frac{1}{3}$ b = ? c = $\frac{3}{8}$ d = ?

a + c	d – a
?	$\frac{1}{4}$
b + c	**b – d**
$1\frac{1}{4}$	?

7.

a = ? b = $\frac{2}{7}$ c = ? d = ?

a x c	a ÷ d
$\frac{5}{48}$	$1\frac{7}{18}$
b x c	**b ÷ d**
$\frac{1}{28}$	?

8. What percent is $\frac{1}{2}$ out of 0.00625? (Hint: $0.0625 = \frac{1}{16}$)

9. If $\frac{1}{3}$ = ⊠ ⊠ ⊠ then ✳ ✳ △ =

10. Complete the magic square on the right. Rows, columns and main diagonals sum to the same number.

3		1	$2\frac{1}{2}$
$\frac{1}{3}$	$2\frac{1}{6}$	2	
		$1\frac{1}{6}$	
	$2\frac{2}{3}$	$2\frac{5}{6}$	

Extra Practice

FOR USE AFTER PAGE 15. SET A

Add, then reduce to lowest terms if possible.

1. $\frac{17}{32} + \frac{19}{32} =$
2. $\frac{1}{2} + \frac{1}{3} + \frac{1}{4} =$
3. $\frac{3}{5} + \frac{5}{6} =$
4. $\frac{9}{10} + 1\frac{2}{5} =$
5. $1\frac{3}{4} + 2\frac{4}{5} =$
6. $3\frac{1}{3} + 4\frac{4}{5} =$
7. $4\frac{1}{6} + 2\frac{7}{8} =$
8. $\frac{8}{9} + \frac{1}{4} =$
9. $4\frac{2}{7} + \frac{3}{4} =$
10. $\frac{1}{4} + \frac{1}{5} + \frac{1}{3} =$
11. $\frac{5}{6} + \frac{7}{9} + \frac{2}{3} =$
12. $\frac{4}{5} + \frac{5}{6} + \frac{9}{10} + \frac{14}{15} =$
13. $1\frac{5}{8} + 2\frac{3}{7} =$
14. $10\frac{3}{5} + 1\frac{5}{9} =$
15. $6\frac{6}{7} + 4\frac{3}{4} =$

FOR USE AFTER PAGE 18. SET B

Subtract. Reduce to simplest form.

1. $2\frac{3}{4} - 1\frac{1}{4} =$
2. $9\frac{1}{3} - \frac{1}{4} =$
3. $4\frac{1}{2} - \frac{3}{5} =$
4. $7\frac{2}{3} - \frac{4}{8} =$
5. $4\frac{3}{7} - 3\frac{2}{3} =$
6. $2\frac{3}{4} - \frac{8}{9} =$
7. $3\frac{5}{12} - 1\frac{1}{16} =$
8. $6\frac{1}{2} - 1\frac{7}{12} =$
9. $\frac{7}{8} - \frac{1}{4} - \frac{1}{12} =$
10. $3\frac{1}{6} - 2\frac{1}{5} =$
11. $14\frac{1}{2} - 10\frac{1}{15} =$
12. $\frac{2}{3} - \frac{11}{20} =$
13. $8\frac{1}{8} - 2\frac{1}{3} =$
14. $\frac{90}{100} - \frac{1}{20} - \frac{1}{4} =$
15. $\frac{5}{6} - \frac{1}{5} - \frac{1}{4} =$

FOR USE AFTER PAGE 23. SET C

Multiply and reduce to lowest form. Look for chances to cross-cancel.

1. $\frac{3}{4}$ of $\frac{4}{5}$ =
2. $\frac{5}{7} \times \frac{7}{8} \times \frac{1}{5}$ =
3. $\frac{1}{6}$ of $\frac{9}{10}$ =
4. $1\frac{1}{3} \times 2\frac{3}{4}$ =
5. $6\frac{2}{5} \times \frac{20}{24}$ =
6. $3\frac{1}{2} \times 4\frac{4}{5}$ =
7. $1\frac{1}{12} \times 1\frac{1}{5}$ =
8. $6\frac{6}{7} \times 1\frac{6}{8}$ =
9. $4\frac{4}{9} \times 2\frac{1}{4}$ =
10. $4\frac{1}{2} \times 4\frac{1}{2}$ =
11. $\frac{1}{2}$ of $\frac{1}{3}$ of $\frac{3}{4}$ =
12. $1\frac{1}{3} \times 1\frac{2}{3} \times \frac{3}{5} \times \frac{6}{8}$ =
13. $3\frac{3}{5} \times 2\frac{1}{9}$ =
14. $10\frac{5}{10} \times \frac{4}{5}$ =
15. $1\frac{1}{2}$ of $2\frac{1}{3}$ of $2\frac{4}{14}$ =

FOR USE AFTER PAGE 25 SET D

Divide and reduce to simplest form. Cross-cancel when possible.

1. $\frac{2}{3} \div \frac{3}{4}$ =
2. $\frac{4}{5} \div \frac{1}{10}$ =
3. $2\frac{1}{4} \div \frac{2}{3}$ =
4. $6\frac{3}{4} \div 3$ =
5. $4 \div 1\frac{1}{4}$ =
6. $3\frac{1}{6} \div 1\frac{1}{6}$ =
7. $6\frac{2}{7} \div 1\frac{1}{10}$ =
8. $1\frac{5}{16} \div \frac{3}{8}$ =
9. $6\frac{3}{4} \div 4\frac{1}{2}$ =
10. $\frac{7}{12} \div 8\frac{3}{4}$ =
11. $10 \div 6\frac{2}{3}$ =
12. $100 \div 8\frac{1}{3}$ =
13. $3\frac{1}{3} \div 16\frac{4}{6}$ =
14. $5\frac{4}{12} \div \frac{8}{9}$ =
15. $100 \div 62\frac{1}{2}$=

Answers

Page 1

1 o ($\frac{5}{100}$) 2 m ($\frac{6}{24}$) 3 s ($\frac{3}{4}$) 4 t ($\frac{8}{12} = \frac{2}{3}$) 5 a ($\frac{20}{60} = \frac{1}{3}$) 6 o ($\frac{1}{6}$)

7 t ($\frac{5}{10}$) (zero is even) 8 e ($\frac{40}{400} = \frac{1}{10}$) Check Yourself tomatoes

Page 2

1 r ($\frac{20}{100} = \frac{1}{5}$) 2 u ($\frac{75}{100} = \frac{3}{4}$) 3 o ($\frac{150}{500} = \frac{3}{2}$) 4 s ($\frac{150}{500} = \frac{3}{10}$) 5 y ($\frac{50}{1{,}000} = \frac{1}{20}$)

6 u ($\frac{5}{200} = \frac{1}{40}$) 7 r ($\frac{200}{2{,}000} = \frac{1}{20}$) 8 d ($\frac{1 \text{ week}}{52}$) 9 r ($\frac{3}{18} = \frac{1}{6}$) 10 m ($\frac{4}{4} = \frac{365}{365}$)

11 a ($\frac{12}{13}$) 12 e ($\frac{4}{52} = \frac{1}{13}$) Check Yourself your eardrums

Page 3

1 r ($\frac{1}{6}$) 2 e ($\frac{3}{6}$) 3 o ($\frac{3}{2}$) 4 y ($\frac{3}{15}$) 5 u ($\frac{6}{8} = \frac{3}{4}$) 6 s ($\frac{6}{9}$) 7 t (9 + 6 = 15)

8 p (10 – 5 = 5) 9 o ($\frac{2}{3} \times \frac{5}{5} = \frac{10}{15}$) 10 t (12) 11 f (4 + 4 = 8) 12 o ($\frac{3}{6} + \frac{1}{6} = \frac{4}{6} = \frac{2}{3}$)

13 s ($\frac{1}{4} + \frac{2}{16} = \frac{6}{16} = \frac{3}{8}$) 14 n ($\frac{2}{3} \times \frac{3}{4} = \frac{1}{2}$ (x 1) = $\frac{1}{2}$) Check Yourself your footsteps

Page 5

2 a ($\frac{7}{7}$, 28) 3 i ($\frac{9}{9}$, 27) 4 d ($\frac{6}{6}$, 5) 5 g ($\frac{6}{6}$, 30) 6 a ($\frac{10}{10}$, 90) 7 s ($\frac{5}{5}$, 15)

8 e ($\frac{9}{9}$, 45) 9 i ($\frac{7}{7}$, 56) 10 c ($\frac{10}{10}$, 36) 11 a ($\frac{8}{8}$, 80) 12 w ($\frac{8}{8}$, 64) 13 i ($\frac{4}{4}$, 7)

14 n ($\frac{7}{7}$, 10) 15 t ($\frac{7}{7}$, 8) 16 s ($\frac{3}{3}$, 9) 17 r ($\frac{4}{4}$, $\frac{5}{2} = \frac{20}{8}$) 18 b ($\frac{5}{5}$, $\frac{15}{8} = \frac{75}{40}$)

Check Yourself a winding staircase

Page 7

2 $\frac{3}{5}$ ($\div \frac{5}{5} = \frac{3}{5}$) 3 $\frac{5}{7}$ ($\div \frac{6}{6} = \frac{5}{7}$) 4 $\frac{3}{7}$ ($\div \frac{3}{3} = \frac{3}{7}$) 5 $\frac{4}{9}$ ($\div \frac{3}{3} = \frac{4}{9}$) 6 $\frac{3}{5}$ ($\div \frac{6}{6} = \frac{3}{5}$)

7 $\frac{5}{8}$ ($\div \frac{5}{5} = \frac{5}{8}$) 8 $\frac{4}{9}$ ($\div \frac{2}{2} = \frac{4}{9}$) 9 $\frac{1}{3}$ ($\div \frac{12}{12} = \frac{1}{3}$) 10 $\frac{4}{9}$ ($\div \frac{5}{5} = \frac{4}{9}$) 11 $\frac{2}{5}$ ($\div \frac{7}{7} = \frac{2}{5}$)

12 $\frac{3}{4}$ ($\div \frac{18}{18} = \frac{3}{4}$) 13 $\frac{2}{3}$ ($\div \frac{12}{12} = \frac{2}{3}$) 14 $\frac{2}{3}$ ($\div \frac{8}{8} = \frac{2}{3}$) 15 $\frac{3}{4}$ ($\div \frac{12}{12} = \frac{3}{4}$) 16 $\frac{7}{8}$ ($\div \frac{4}{4} = \frac{7}{8}$)

17 $\frac{3}{4}$ ($\div \frac{7}{7} = \frac{3}{4}$) 18 $\frac{1}{3}$ ($\div \frac{24}{24} = \frac{1}{3}$) 19 $\frac{7}{10}$ ($\div \frac{4}{4} = \frac{7}{10}$) 20 $\frac{7}{9}$ ($\div \frac{6}{6} = \frac{7}{9}$) 21 $\frac{8}{9}$ ($\div \frac{9}{9} = \frac{8}{9}$)

22 $\frac{8}{11}$ ($\div \frac{6}{6} = \frac{8}{11}$) 23 $\frac{2}{3}$ ($\div \frac{25}{25} = \frac{2}{3}$) 24 $\frac{5}{3}$ ($\div \frac{20}{20} = \frac{5}{3}$)

Page 8

a $\frac{1}{3}$ ($\frac{15}{45} = \frac{1}{3}$) w $\frac{1}{25}$ ($\frac{2}{50} = \frac{1}{25}$) a $\frac{9}{10}$ ($\frac{45}{50} = \frac{9}{10}$) t $\frac{5}{6}$ ($\frac{10}{12} = \frac{5}{6}$) c $\frac{1}{5}$ ($\frac{18}{90} = \frac{1}{5}$)

h $\frac{2}{3}$ ($\frac{20}{30} = \frac{2}{3}$) d $\frac{2}{33}$ ($\frac{6}{99} = \frac{2}{33}$) o $\frac{1}{2}$ ($\frac{19}{38} = \frac{1}{2}$) g $\frac{3}{5}$ ($\frac{21}{35} = \frac{3}{5}$) Check Yourself a watchdog

Page 10

2 $\frac{4}{7} > \frac{1}{2}$; $\frac{4}{7} = \frac{8}{14}$, $\frac{1}{2} = \frac{7}{14}$; $\frac{8}{14} - \frac{7}{14} = \frac{1}{14}$ 3 $\frac{3}{4} > \frac{2}{3}$; $\frac{3}{4} = \frac{9}{12}$, $\frac{2}{3} = \frac{8}{12}$; $\frac{9}{12} - \frac{8}{12} = \frac{1}{12}$

4 $\frac{3}{5} < \frac{10}{15}$; $\frac{3}{5} = \frac{9}{15}$; $\frac{10}{15} - \frac{9}{15} = \frac{1}{15}$ 5 $\frac{5}{9} < \frac{2}{3}$; $\frac{2}{3} = \frac{6}{9}$; $\frac{6}{9} - \frac{5}{9} = \frac{1}{9}$ 6 $\frac{3}{4} = \frac{9}{12}$; $\frac{3}{4} = \frac{9}{12}$; $\frac{3}{4} - \frac{9}{12} = 0$ 7 $\frac{2}{6} < \frac{2}{5}$; $\frac{2}{6} = \frac{10}{30}$, $\frac{2}{5} = \frac{12}{30}$; $\frac{12}{30} - \frac{10}{30} = \frac{1}{15}$ 8 $\frac{3}{7} > \frac{1}{3}$; $\frac{3}{7} = \frac{9}{21}$, $\frac{1}{3} = \frac{7}{21}$; $\frac{9}{21} - \frac{7}{21} = \frac{2}{21}$

9 $\frac{1}{6} < \frac{2}{9}$; $\frac{1}{6} = \frac{3}{18}$, $\frac{2}{9} = \frac{4}{18}$; $\frac{4}{18} - \frac{3}{18} = \frac{1}{18}$ 10 $\frac{5}{8} > \frac{3}{5}$; $\frac{5}{8} = \frac{25}{40}$, $\frac{3}{5} = \frac{24}{40}$; $\frac{25}{40} - \frac{24}{40} = \frac{1}{40}$

11 $\frac{7}{10} > \frac{2}{3}$; $\frac{7}{10} = \frac{21}{30}$, $\frac{2}{3} = \frac{20}{30}$; $\frac{21}{30} - \frac{20}{30} = \frac{1}{30}$ 12 $\frac{1}{2} = \frac{14}{28}$; $\frac{1}{2} = \frac{14}{28}$; $\frac{1}{2} - \frac{14}{28} = 0$

13 $\frac{1}{12} > \frac{8}{100}$; $\frac{1}{12} = \frac{100}{1{,}200}$, $\frac{8}{100} = \frac{96}{1{,}200}$; $\frac{100}{1{,}200} - \frac{96}{1{,}200} = \frac{4}{1{,}200} = \frac{1}{300}$

Page 11

1 $\frac{3}{4} < 1\frac{1}{3}$; $\frac{3}{4} = \frac{9}{12}$, $1\frac{1}{3} = \frac{4}{3} = \frac{16}{12}$; $\frac{16}{12} - \frac{9}{12} = \frac{7}{12}$ 2 $\frac{5}{7} > \frac{4}{6}$; $\frac{5}{7} = \frac{30}{42}$, $\frac{4}{6} = \frac{28}{42}$; $\frac{30}{42} - \frac{28}{42} = \frac{1}{21}$

3 $2\frac{1}{3} = \frac{21}{9}$; $2\frac{1}{3} = \frac{7}{3} = \frac{21}{9}$; $\frac{7}{3} - \frac{21}{9} = 0$ 4 $\frac{5}{11} > \frac{1}{3}$; $\frac{5}{11} = \frac{15}{33}$, $\frac{1}{3} = \frac{11}{33}$; $\frac{15}{33} - \frac{11}{33} = \frac{4}{33}$

5 $\frac{5}{6} < \frac{6}{7}$; $\frac{5}{6} = \frac{35}{42}$, $\frac{6}{7} = \frac{36}{42}$; $\frac{36}{42} - \frac{35}{42} = \frac{1}{42}$ 6 $\frac{5}{12} > \frac{3}{8}$; $\frac{5}{12} = \frac{10}{24}$, $\frac{3}{8} = \frac{9}{24}$; $\frac{10}{24} - \frac{9}{24} = \frac{1}{24}$

7 $\frac{3}{2} < \frac{8}{5}$; $\frac{3}{2} = \frac{15}{10}$, $\frac{8}{5} = \frac{16}{10}$; $\frac{16}{10} - \frac{15}{10} = \frac{1}{10}$ 8 $\frac{12}{8} < \frac{10}{6}$; $\frac{12}{8} = \frac{36}{24}$, $\frac{10}{6} = \frac{40}{24}$; $\frac{40}{24} - \frac{36}{24} = \frac{1}{6}$

9 $\frac{15}{6} > 2\frac{2}{5}$; $\frac{15}{6} = \frac{75}{30}$, $2\frac{2}{5} = \frac{12}{5} = \frac{72}{30}$; $\frac{75}{30} - \frac{72}{30} = \frac{1}{10}$ 10 $1\frac{3}{4} = \frac{21}{12}$; $1\frac{3}{4} = \frac{7}{4} = \frac{21}{12}$; $\frac{7}{4} - \frac{21}{12} = 0$

11 $\frac{7}{8} > \frac{7}{9}$; $\frac{7}{8} = \frac{63}{72}$, $\frac{7}{9} = \frac{56}{72}$; $\frac{63}{72} - \frac{56}{72} = \frac{7}{72}$ 12 $1\frac{9}{10} = \frac{76}{40}$; $1\frac{9}{10} = \frac{19}{10} = \frac{76}{40}$; $\frac{19}{10} - \frac{76}{40} = 0$

13 $(\frac{8}{9} - \frac{7}{8}) < \frac{2}{100}$; $(\frac{8}{9} - \frac{7}{8}) = (\frac{64}{72} - \frac{63}{72}) = \frac{1}{72} = \frac{100}{7200}$, $\frac{2}{100} = \frac{144}{7200}$; $\frac{64}{72} - \frac{63}{72} = \frac{1}{72} < \frac{2}{100}$

Page 12

1 $3\frac{1}{2}$ 2 3 3 $3\frac{2}{5}$ 4 $3\frac{1}{3}$ 5 7 6 $8\frac{1}{2}$ 7 $5\frac{2}{7}$ 8 $5\frac{1}{4}$ 9 $6\frac{3}{4}$ 10 $5\frac{1}{2}$

11 $7\frac{4}{5}$ 12 $9\frac{1}{3}$ 13 $8\frac{5}{9}$ 14 $7\frac{1}{7}$ 15 $6\frac{2}{3}$ 16 $10\frac{1}{5}$ 17 $6\frac{1}{20}$ 18 15

Page 13

2 $\frac{4}{15}$ 3 $\frac{5}{31}$ 4 $\frac{8}{57}$ 5 $\frac{9}{32}$ 6 $\frac{8}{65}$ 7 $\frac{5}{46}$ 8 $\frac{8}{43}$ 9 $\frac{4}{31}$ 10 $\frac{6}{41}$

11 $\frac{8}{60}$ 12 $\frac{7}{64}$ 13 $\frac{5}{46}$ 14 $\frac{8}{35}$ 15 $\frac{5}{54}$ 16 $\frac{3}{151}$ 17 $\frac{100}{999}$ 18 $\frac{10{,}000}{990{,}999}$

Page 15

1 p $\frac{3}{4}$; $(\frac{2}{4} + \frac{1}{4})$ 2 h $\frac{11}{12}$; $(\frac{8}{12} + \frac{3}{12})$ 3 e $1\frac{7}{20}$; $(\frac{15}{20} + \frac{12}{20})$ 4 e $1\frac{9}{10}$; $(1\frac{4}{10} + \frac{5}{10})$

5 y 7; $(3\frac{10}{12} + 3\frac{2}{12})$ 6 a $8\frac{1}{8}$; $(5\frac{3}{8} + 2\frac{6}{8})$ 7 u $5\frac{3}{10}$; $(3\frac{7}{10} + 1\frac{6}{10})$

8 o $\frac{17}{72}$; $(\frac{9}{72} + \frac{8}{72})$ 9 r $7\frac{5}{21}$; $(3\frac{24}{42} + 3\frac{28}{42})$ 10 y $1\frac{1}{2}$; $(\frac{2}{8} + \frac{4}{8} + \frac{6}{8})$

11 a $8\frac{1}{21}$; $(4\frac{7}{21} + 3\frac{15}{21})$ 12 e $8\frac{1}{12}$; $(5\frac{3}{12} + 2\frac{10}{12})$ 13 e $1\frac{7}{9}$; $(\frac{6}{18} + \frac{14}{18} + \frac{12}{18})$

14 s $\frac{1}{8}$; $(\frac{18}{24} + \frac{20}{24} + \frac{3}{24} = \frac{41}{24})$ 15 l $\frac{1}{15}$; $(\frac{15}{30} + \frac{10}{30} + \frac{3}{30} + \frac{2}{30})$ 16 b $1\frac{12}{100} = 1\frac{3}{25}$; $(\frac{4}{100} + \frac{2}{100} + \frac{1}{100} + \frac{20}{100} + \frac{10}{100} + \frac{50}{100} + \frac{25}{100})$ Check Yourself Hey, are you asleep?

Page 16

1 $\frac{7}{15}$; $(\frac{10}{15} - \frac{3}{15})$ 2 $\frac{5}{12}$; $(\frac{9}{12} - \frac{4}{12})$ 3 $\frac{7}{20}$; $(\frac{12}{20} - \frac{5}{20})$ 4 $\frac{11}{21}$; $(\frac{14}{21} - \frac{3}{21})$ 5 $\frac{7}{30}$; $(\frac{25}{30} - \frac{18}{30})$ 6 $\frac{1}{24}$; $(\frac{4}{24} - \frac{3}{24})$ 7 $\frac{23}{36}$; $(\frac{27}{36} - \frac{4}{36})$ 8 $\frac{9}{28}$; $(\frac{16}{28} - \frac{7}{28})$ 9 $\frac{4}{9}$; $(\frac{12}{18} - \frac{4}{18})$

10 $\frac{5}{56}$; $(\frac{21}{56} - \frac{16}{56})$ 11 $\frac{17}{42}$; $(\frac{35}{42} - \frac{18}{42})$ 12 $\frac{2}{99}$; $(\frac{11}{99} - \frac{9}{99})$ 13 $\frac{1}{9{,}900}$; $(\frac{100}{9{,}900} - \frac{99}{9{,}900})$

Page 18

1 $7\frac{7}{8}$ 2 $4\frac{1}{2}$ 3 $4\frac{5}{6}$ 4 $11\frac{13}{15}$ 5 $6\frac{17}{20}$ 6 $11\frac{2}{35}$ 7 $5\frac{11}{36}$ 8 $2\frac{25}{42}$ 9 $\frac{7}{24}$

10 $\frac{23}{132}$ $(\frac{12}{11} = \frac{144}{132}, \frac{11}{12} = \frac{121}{132})$

Page 19

1 $\frac{11}{16}$ 2 $1\frac{1}{12}$ 3 $\frac{7}{20}$ 4 $1\frac{5}{24}$ 5 $4\frac{2}{15}$ 6 $\frac{1}{42}$ 7 $1\frac{7}{8}$ 8 $4\frac{1}{45}$ 9 $4\frac{7}{9}$

10 28 11 a > b; $\frac{19}{12} > \frac{17}{12}$ 12 a is $\frac{1}{15}$ smaller 13 $\frac{15}{56}$

14 $6\frac{1}{4} \times 4\frac{4}{5} = \frac{\overset{5}{\cancel{25}}}{\underset{1}{\cancel{4}}} \times \frac{\overset{6}{\cancel{24}}}{\underset{1}{\cancel{5}}} = 5 \times 6 = 30$

Page 21

1 n $\frac{1}{8}$ 2 i $\frac{3}{8}$ 3 n $\frac{3}{7}$ 4 g $\frac{5}{9}$ 5 r $\frac{3}{16}$ 6 a $\frac{2}{3}$ 7 o 1 8 p $\frac{3}{14}$ 9 a $\frac{1}{12}$

10 d $\frac{1}{9}$ 11 a $\frac{5}{3}$ 13 b $\frac{4}{7}$ Check Yourself a grand piano

Page 22

1 $1\frac{7}{8}$, $\frac{3}{4} \times \frac{10}{4} = \frac{30}{16} = \frac{15}{8} = 1\frac{7}{8}$ 2 4, $\frac{4}{3} \times \frac{3}{1} = \frac{12}{3} = 4$ 3 $6\frac{3}{10}$, $\frac{9}{5} \times \frac{7}{2} = \frac{63}{10} = 6\frac{3}{10}$ 4 $\frac{3}{4}$, $\frac{27}{4} \times \frac{1}{9} = \frac{27}{36} = \frac{3}{4}$ 5 $3\frac{3}{4}$, $\frac{3}{2} \times \frac{5}{2} = \frac{15}{4} = 3\frac{3}{4}$ 6 2, $\frac{11}{3} \times \frac{6}{11} = \frac{66}{33} = 2$ 7 $3\frac{3}{7}$, $\frac{22}{7} \times \frac{12}{11} = \frac{2}{7} \times \frac{12}{1} = \frac{24}{7} = 3\frac{3}{7}$ 8 $\frac{13}{24}$, $\frac{1}{4} \times \frac{13}{6} = \frac{13}{24}$ 9 $2\frac{10}{27}$, $\frac{4}{3} \times \frac{4}{3} \times \frac{4}{3} = \frac{64}{27} = 2\frac{10}{27}$ 10 $\frac{2}{3}$, $\frac{1}{2} \times \frac{1}{3} \times \frac{4}{1} = \frac{4}{6} = \frac{2}{3}$ 11 $\frac{10}{101}$, $\frac{101}{10}$ x reciprocal = 1 12 $\frac{12}{7}$, $\frac{7}{12}$ x reciprocal = 1, $\frac{7}{4} \times \frac{1}{3} = \frac{7}{12}$

Page 23

1 $\frac{{}^{1}\cancel{4}}{7} \times \frac{1}{\cancel{4}_{1}} = \frac{1}{7}$ 2 $\frac{{}^{1}\cancel{5}}{\cancel{8}_{4}} \times \frac{{}^{1}\cancel{2}}{\cancel{5}_{1}} = \frac{1}{4}$ 3 $\frac{{}^{1}\cancel{4}}{\cancel{6}_{1}} \times \frac{{}^{1}\cancel{6}}{\cancel{16}_{4}} = \frac{1}{4}$ 4 $\frac{{}^{1}\cancel{3}}{\cancel{4}_{1}} \times \frac{{}^{5}\cancel{20}}{\cancel{30}_{10}} = \frac{1}{2}$ 5 $\frac{{}^{1}\cancel{2}}{\cancel{3}_{1}} \times \frac{{}^{4}\cancel{12}}{\cancel{14}_{7}} = \frac{4}{7}$ 6 $\frac{{}^{1}\cancel{2}}{\cancel{6}_{1}} \times \frac{{}^{6}\cancel{24}}{\cancel{30}_{15}} = \frac{4}{15}$ 7 $\frac{{}^{1}\cancel{5}}{\cancel{4}_{1}} \times \frac{{}^{3}\cancel{12}}{\cancel{20}_{4}} = \frac{3}{4}$ 8 $\frac{{}^{2}\cancel{16}}{5} \times \frac{3}{\cancel{8}_{1}} = \frac{6}{5} = 1\frac{1}{5}$ 9 $\frac{{}^{5}\cancel{25}}{\cancel{6}_{1}} \times \frac{{}^{3}\cancel{18}}{\cancel{5}_{1}} = 15$ 10 $\frac{{}^{7}\cancel{35}}{\cancel{4}_{1}} \times \frac{{}^{2}\cancel{8}}{\cancel{5}_{1}} = 14$ 11 $\frac{{}^{1}\cancel{4}}{\cancel{3}_{1}} \times \frac{{}^{2}\cancel{6}}{\cancel{8}_{2}} \times \frac{{}^{1}\cancel{4}}{\cancel{5}_{1}} \times \frac{{}^{1}\cancel{5}}{\cancel{4}_{1}} = 1$

Page 25

1 3, $\frac{3}{5} \div \frac{1}{5} = \frac{3}{\cancel{5}_{1}} \times \frac{{}^{1}\cancel{5}}{1} = \frac{3}{1} \times \frac{1}{1} = 3$ 2 6, $\frac{4}{1} \div \frac{2}{3} = \frac{{}^{2}\cancel{4}}{1} \times \frac{3}{\cancel{2}_{1}} = \frac{2}{1} \times \frac{3}{1} = 6$ 3 $\frac{5}{6}$, $\frac{5}{2} \div \frac{3}{1} = \frac{5}{2} \times \frac{1}{3} = \frac{5}{6}$ 4 $\frac{9}{10}$, $\frac{3}{4} \div \frac{5}{6} = \frac{3}{\cancel{4}_{2}} \times \frac{{}^{3}\cancel{6}}{5} = \frac{3}{2} \times \frac{3}{5} = \frac{9}{10}$ 5 $\frac{3}{10}$, $\frac{8}{10} \div \frac{8}{3} = \frac{{}^{1}\cancel{8}}{10} \times \frac{3}{\cancel{8}_{1}} = \frac{1}{10} \times \frac{3}{1} = \frac{3}{10}$ 6 $1\frac{31}{35}$, $\frac{11}{5} \div \frac{7}{6} = \frac{11}{5} \times \frac{6}{7} = \frac{66}{35} = 1\frac{31}{35}$ 7 $\frac{5}{24}$, $\frac{7}{40} \div \frac{21}{25} = \frac{{}^{1}\cancel{7}}{\cancel{40}_{8}} \times \frac{{}^{5}\cancel{25}}{\cancel{21}_{3}} = \frac{1}{8} \times \frac{5}{3} = \frac{5}{24}$ 8 3, $\frac{21}{5} \div \frac{14}{10} = \frac{{}^{3}\cancel{21}}{\cancel{5}_{1}} \times \frac{{}^{2}\cancel{10}}{\cancel{14}_{2}} = \frac{3}{1} \times \frac{2}{2} = 3$ 9 $\frac{2}{3}$, $\frac{5}{4} \div \frac{15}{8} = \frac{{}^{1}\cancel{5}}{\cancel{4}_{1}} \times \frac{{}^{2}\cancel{8}}{\cancel{15}_{3}} = \frac{1}{1} \times \frac{2}{3} = \frac{2}{3}$ 10 10, $\frac{1}{10} \div \frac{1}{100} = \frac{1}{\cancel{10}_{1}} \times \frac{{}^{10}\cancel{100}}{1} = \frac{1}{1} \times \frac{10}{1} = 10$ 11 $3\frac{1}{3}$, $(\frac{5}{2} \div \frac{3}{2}) \div \frac{1}{2} = (\frac{5}{2} \times \frac{2}{3}) \div \frac{1}{2} = (\frac{5}{1} \times \frac{1}{3}) \div \frac{1}{2} = \frac{5}{3} \div \frac{1}{2} = \frac{5}{3} \times \frac{2}{1} = \frac{10}{3} = 3\frac{1}{3}$

Page 27

1 $2\frac{7}{8}$, $\frac{3}{2} + \frac{11}{8} = \frac{12}{8} + \frac{11}{8} = \frac{23}{8} = 2\frac{7}{8}$; $\frac{23}{8} - \frac{11}{8} = \frac{12}{8} = 1\frac{1}{2}$ 2 $5\frac{7}{12}$, $\frac{19}{3} - \frac{3}{4} = \frac{76}{12} - \frac{9}{12} = \frac{67}{12} = 5\frac{7}{12}$; $\frac{67}{12} + \frac{3}{4} = \frac{67}{12} + \frac{9}{12} = \frac{76}{12} = 6\frac{1}{3}$ 3 $4\frac{1}{2}$, $\frac{15}{4} \times \frac{6}{5} = \frac{3}{2} \times \frac{3}{1} = \frac{9}{2} = 4\frac{1}{2}$; $\frac{9}{2} \div \frac{6}{5} = \frac{9}{2} \times \frac{5}{6} = \frac{3}{2} \times \frac{5}{2} = \frac{15}{4} = 3\frac{3}{4}$ 4 $1\frac{5}{9}$, $\frac{7}{6} \div \frac{3}{4} = \frac{7}{6} \times \frac{4}{3} = \frac{7}{3} \times \frac{2}{3} = \frac{14}{9} = 1\frac{5}{9}$; $\frac{14}{9} \times \frac{3}{4} = \frac{7}{3} \times \frac{1}{2} = \frac{7}{6} = 1\frac{1}{6}$ 5 $10\frac{17}{30}$, $\frac{20}{3} + \frac{39}{10} = \frac{200}{30} + \frac{117}{30} = \frac{317}{30} = 10\frac{17}{30}$; $\frac{317}{30} - \frac{39}{10} = \frac{317}{30} - \frac{117}{30} = \frac{200}{30} = 6\frac{2}{3}$ 6 $2\frac{11}{35}$, $\frac{13}{5} - \frac{2}{7} = \frac{91}{35} - \frac{10}{35} = \frac{81}{35} = 2\frac{11}{35}$; $\frac{81}{35} + \frac{2}{7} = \frac{81}{35} + \frac{10}{35} = \frac{91}{35} = 2\frac{21}{35} = 2\frac{3}{5}$ 7 $3\frac{1}{2}$, $\frac{9}{4} \times \frac{14}{9} = \frac{1}{2} \times \frac{7}{1} = \frac{7}{2} = 3\frac{1}{2}$; $\frac{7}{2} \div \frac{14}{9} = \frac{7}{2} \times \frac{9}{14} = \frac{1}{2} \times \frac{9}{2} = \frac{9}{4} = 2\frac{1}{4}$ 8 $\frac{1}{4}$, $\frac{28}{8} \div \frac{14}{1} =$

$\frac{28}{8} \times \frac{1}{14} = \frac{2}{8} \times \frac{1}{1} = \frac{2}{8} = \frac{1}{4}$; $\frac{1}{4} \times \frac{14}{1} = \frac{1}{2} \times \frac{7}{1} = \frac{7}{2} = 3\frac{1}{2}$ **9** $1\frac{23}{24}$, $\frac{13}{12} + \frac{7}{8} = \frac{26}{24} + \frac{21}{24} = \frac{47}{24} = 1\frac{23}{24}$; $\frac{47}{24} - \frac{7}{8} = \frac{47}{24} - \frac{21}{24} = \frac{26}{24} = 1\frac{1}{12}$ **10** $2\frac{29}{42}$, $\frac{17}{6} - \frac{1}{7} = \frac{119}{42} - \frac{6}{42} = \frac{113}{42} = 2\frac{29}{42}$; $\frac{113}{42} + \frac{1}{7} = \frac{113}{42} + \frac{6}{42} = \frac{119}{42} = 2\frac{35}{42} = 2\frac{5}{6}$ **11** $5\frac{4}{9}$, $\frac{7}{3} \times \frac{7}{3} = \frac{49}{9} = 5\frac{4}{9}$; $\frac{49}{9} \div \frac{7}{3} = \frac{49}{9} \times \frac{3}{7} = \frac{7}{3} \times \frac{1}{1} = \frac{7}{3} = 2\frac{1}{3}$ **12** $\frac{3}{7}$, $\frac{22}{7} \div \frac{22}{3} = \frac{22}{7} \times \frac{3}{22} = \frac{1}{7} \times \frac{3}{1} = \frac{3}{7}$; $\frac{3}{7} \times \frac{22}{3} = \frac{1}{7} \times \frac{22}{1} = \frac{22}{7} = 3\frac{1}{7}$

13 $\frac{20}{7}$, $(\frac{7}{5} \times \frac{5}{3}) \div (\frac{10}{1} \div \frac{3}{2}) = (\frac{7}{1} \times \frac{1}{3}) \div (\frac{10}{1} \times \frac{2}{3}) = \frac{7}{3} \div \frac{20}{3} = \frac{7}{3} \times \frac{3}{20} = \frac{7}{1} \times \frac{1}{20} = \frac{7}{20}$, $\frac{7}{20} \times \frac{20}{7} = 1$

Page 28

1 1 + □ **2** □ – 5 **3** $\frac{3}{4} \times 12$ **4** □ ÷ 2 **5** $\frac{1}{2} - \frac{1}{3}$ **6** $\frac{1}{3} \times □ = \frac{3}{4}$

Page 30

1 r $\frac{2}{3}$ **2** b $\frac{1}{2}$ **3** e $2\frac{1}{4}$ **4** u $1\frac{1}{3}$ **5** t $3\frac{1}{2}$ **6** o $\frac{1}{6}$ **7** l $\frac{1}{15}$ **8** a $\frac{3}{4}$ **Check Yourself** trouble

Page 31

1a 2 minutes **1b** 50 ÷ 2 = 25 **2a** $1\frac{1}{4}$ pages per hour **2b** $1\frac{1}{4} \times 3 = 3\frac{3}{4}$

3a $1\frac{7}{8}$ minutes each **3b** $1\frac{7}{8} \times 12 = \frac{15}{8} \times \frac{12}{1} = \frac{45}{2} = 22\frac{1}{2}$ **4a** $31\frac{1}{4}$ blocks

i $2\frac{1}{2}$ $(1 \div \frac{2}{5} = 2\frac{1}{2})$ **ii** $31\frac{1}{4}$ $(2\frac{1}{2} \times 12\frac{1}{2} = \frac{5}{2} \times \frac{25}{2} = 31\frac{1}{4})$

4b $3\frac{1}{5}$ hours $(100 \div 31\frac{1}{4} = \frac{100}{1} \times \frac{4}{125} = \frac{4}{1} \times \frac{4}{5} = \frac{16}{5} = 3\frac{1}{5})$

Page 32

1 80 gumballs, 4 dozen = 48. 48 ÷ 3 = 16, which is $\frac{1}{5}$, so $\frac{5}{5}$ = 16 x 5 = 80. Or, 48 ÷ $\frac{3}{5}$ = $\frac{48}{1} \times \frac{5}{3}$ = 80. **2** $1\frac{2}{5}$ hours, $1\frac{1}{20} \div 3 = \frac{7}{20}$ hour (time needed to do $\frac{1}{4}$ of problems) $\frac{7}{20} \times \frac{4}{1} = 1\frac{2}{5}$ hours. Or $1\frac{1}{20} \div \frac{3}{4} = \frac{21}{20} \times \frac{4}{3} = 1\frac{2}{5}$ **3a** 1 hour, $12\frac{1}{2} \div 3\frac{3}{4} = \frac{24}{2} \times \frac{4}{15} = 3\frac{1}{3}$, $3\frac{1}{3} \times \frac{3}{10} = \frac{10}{3} \times \frac{3}{10} = 1$ **3b** $26\frac{1}{4}$ laps , $2\frac{1}{10} \div \frac{3}{10} = \frac{21}{10} \times \frac{10}{3}$ = 7 sets of $\frac{3}{10}$. $7 \times 3\frac{3}{4} = \frac{7}{1} \times \frac{15}{4} = \frac{105}{4} = 26\frac{1}{4}$ laps. **4a** 250 miles, 210 ÷ $10\frac{1}{2}$ = miles on one gallon. $\frac{210}{1} \times \frac{2}{21}$ = 20. 20 x $12\frac{1}{2}$ = 250 miles. **4b** $\frac{21}{40}$ gallons, $10\frac{1}{2}$ out of 20 = $10\frac{1}{2} \div 20 = \frac{21}{2} \times \frac{1}{20} = \frac{21}{40}$ gallons. **5a** 40 trucks, How many $\frac{1}{4}$'s in $3\frac{3}{4}$? For every $\frac{1}{4}$ multiply by $2\frac{2}{3}$ trucks. $3\frac{3}{4} \div \frac{1}{4} = \frac{15}{4} \times \frac{4}{1}$ = 15; 15 x $2\frac{2}{3}$ = 40. **5b** $9\frac{3}{8}$ hours, How many $2\frac{2}{3}$'s in 100? For each of those, multiply by $\frac{1}{4}$ hour. $100 \div 2\frac{2}{3} = \frac{100}{1} \times \frac{3}{8} = 37\frac{1}{2}$. $37\frac{1}{2} \times \frac{1}{4} = \frac{75}{2} \times \frac{1}{4} = 9\frac{3}{8}$ hours.

6 2:40 pm; $20 \div 3 = \frac{20}{3}$; $\frac{20}{3} \times \frac{2}{5} = 2\frac{2}{3}$ hours. Or, $\frac{2}{5} \div 3 = \frac{2}{15}$; $\frac{2}{15} \times 20 = 2\frac{2}{3}$.

Page 33

1 t $1\frac{1}{12}$ 2 r $3\frac{11}{15}$ 3 a $\frac{11}{35}$ 4 e $1\frac{23}{24}$ 5 f $6\frac{1}{4}$ 6 e $\frac{29}{40}$ 7 s 1 8 n $6\frac{3}{7}$

9 d $1\frac{1}{9}$ 10 n $\frac{1}{4}$ 11 a $6\frac{2}{3}$ 12 k $2\frac{2}{7}$ 13 i $\frac{3}{4}$ 14 b $\frac{9}{100}$ 15 r $\frac{7}{25}$

16 m $7\frac{1}{2}$ ($30 \div 4\frac{1}{2} = 6\frac{3}{4}$ feet per hour x $1\frac{1}{8} = 7\frac{1}{2}$ feet) Check Yourself breakfast, dinner

Page 35

1 $\frac{1}{5} = \frac{20}{100} = 20\%$ 2 $\frac{3}{4} = \frac{75}{100} = 75\%$ 3 $\frac{7}{10} = \frac{70}{100} = 70\%$ 4 $\frac{1}{20} = \frac{5}{100} = 5\%$

5 $\frac{49}{50} = \frac{98}{100} = 98\%$ 6 $\frac{2}{4} = \frac{50}{100} = 50\%$ 7 $\frac{4}{5} = \frac{80}{100} = 80\%$ 8 $\frac{10}{10} = \frac{100}{100} = 100\%$

9 $\frac{3}{5} = \frac{60}{100} = 60\%$ 10 $\frac{11}{25} = \frac{44}{100} = 44\%$ 11 $50\% = \frac{50}{100} = \frac{1}{2}$ 12 $30\% = \frac{30}{100} = \frac{3}{10}$

13 $8\% = \frac{8}{100} = \frac{2}{25}$ 14 $15\% = \frac{15}{100} = \frac{3}{20}$ 15 $90\% = \frac{90}{100} = \frac{9}{10}$ 16 $2\% = \frac{2}{100} = \frac{1}{50}$

17 $42\% = \frac{42}{100} = \frac{21}{50}$ 18 $25\% = \frac{25}{100} = \frac{1}{4}$ 19 $3\% = \frac{3}{100}$ 20 $4\% = \frac{4}{100} = \frac{1}{25}$

Page 37

1 y 50% 2 s 35% 3 i 25% 4 u 20% 5 r $12\frac{1}{2}\%$ 6 p $8\frac{1}{3}\%$ 7 s $66\frac{2}{3}\%$

8 o $16\frac{2}{3}\%$ 9 r $11\frac{1}{9}\%$ 10 m $28\frac{4}{7}\%$ 11 o 15% 12 e $83\frac{1}{3}\%$ 13 f 3 years = 3%

14 l $\frac{150}{500} = 30\%$ Check Yourself your promises

Page 38

1 6 ($\frac{1}{4}$ of 24 = 6) 2 \$6 ($\frac{3}{20} \times \frac{40}{1} = \$6$) 3 150 miles (15% left. $\frac{3}{20} \times \frac{1,000}{1} = 150$ miles) 4 \$48 ($\frac{1}{25} \times \frac{1,200}{1} = \$48$) 5 \$120 ($\frac{1}{3} \times \frac{180}{1} = \$60$ off. $180 - 60 = \$120$)

6 \$21 ($\$3.50 = \frac{1}{6} \times \square$; $3.50 \div \frac{1}{6} = \$21$) 7 24 ($\frac{2}{5} \times 60 = 24$) 8 \$1.20 ($\frac{12}{100} \times \frac{10}{1} = \$1.20$) 9 45 ($\frac{9}{10} \times \frac{50}{1} = 45$) 10 200 ($\frac{2}{3} \times \frac{300}{1} = 200$) 11 8 ($\frac{1}{8}$ of 64 = 8) 12 \$1.01 ($\frac{1}{20} \times \$20.20 = \$1.01$) 13 $\frac{27}{100}$ 14 500 ($\frac{1}{2} \times 1,000 = 500$) 15 300 ($\frac{3}{4} \times \frac{400}{1} = 300$)

16 10 ($\frac{5}{6} \times \frac{12}{1} = 10$) 17 28 ($\frac{7}{8} \times \frac{32}{1} = 28$) 18 50 ($\frac{1}{20} \times \frac{1}{10} \times 10,000 = 50$)

Page 39

1 $15 ($\frac{1}{5}$ = $3, so $\frac{5}{5}$ = $15) 2 475 ($\frac{1}{3}$ = 125, so $\frac{3}{3}$ = 475) 3 50 ($\frac{1}{25}$ = 2 minutes, so $\frac{25}{25}$ = 50 minutes) 4 500 (50 = $\frac{1}{10}$, so $\frac{10}{10}$ = 500) 5 80 (☐ x $\frac{3}{4}$ = 60; 60 ÷ $\frac{3}{4}$ = 80) 6 144 ($\frac{1}{12}$ = 12 minutes, so $\frac{12}{12}$ = 144 minutes) 7 21 (7 problems = $\frac{1}{3}$, so $\frac{3}{3}$ = 21 problems) 8 10 ($\frac{3}{20}$ x ☐ = $1\frac{1}{2}$; $1\frac{1}{2} \div \frac{3}{20}$ = 10) 9 256 ($\frac{1}{2}$ of $\frac{1}{2}$ of ☐ = $6\frac{1}{4}$; $6\frac{1}{4} \div \frac{1}{4}$ = 25) 10 2,400 ($\frac{3}{4}$ x ☐ = 1,800; 1,800 ÷ $\frac{3}{4}$ = 2,400 meters) 11 $37\frac{1}{2}$% ($\frac{4}{9}$ x ☐ = $\frac{1}{6}$; $\frac{1}{6} \div \frac{4}{9} = \frac{3}{8} = 37\frac{1}{2}$%)

Page 40

1 25% ($\frac{3}{12} = \frac{1}{4}$ = 25%) 2 $37\frac{1}{2}$% ($\frac{6}{16} = \frac{3}{8} = 37\frac{1}{2}$%) 3 5% ($\frac{\frac{1}{2}}{10} = \frac{1}{20}$ = 5%)

4 25% ($\frac{\frac{3}{4}}{3} = \frac{3}{12} = \frac{1}{4}$ = 25%) 5 $12\frac{1}{2}$% ($2\frac{1}{2} \div 20 = \frac{5}{2} \times \frac{1}{20} = \frac{1}{8} = 12\frac{1}{2}$%)

6 16% ($\frac{8}{50}$ = 16%) 7 32% ($\frac{\frac{4}{5}}{2\frac{1}{2}} = \frac{4}{5} \times \frac{2}{5} = \frac{8}{25}$ = 32%) 8 $16\frac{2}{3}$% ($1\frac{3}{4} \div 10\frac{1}{2} = \frac{7}{4} \times \frac{2}{21} = \frac{1}{6} = 16\frac{2}{3}$%) 9 $33\frac{1}{3}$% ($\frac{80}{240} = \frac{1}{3} = 33\frac{1}{3}$%) 10 $87\frac{1}{2}$% ($84\frac{7}{8} \div 97 = \frac{7}{8} = 87\frac{1}{2}$%)

Page 41

1 20%, Reduced $1 out of $5, ☐% x 5 = 1, ☐% = 1 ÷ 5 = $\frac{1}{5}$ = 20%, 20% of 5 = $\frac{1}{5}$ x 5 = 1 2 $33\frac{1}{3}$%, Increased 1 out of 3, ☐% x 3 = 1, ☐% = 1 ÷ 3 = $\frac{1}{3} = 33\frac{1}{3}$%, $33\frac{1}{3}$% of 3 = $\frac{1}{3}$ x 3 = 1 3 $16\frac{2}{3}$%, Decreased 10° out of 60°, ☐% x 60 = 10, ☐% = 10 ÷ 60 = $\frac{10}{60} = \frac{1}{6} = 16\frac{2}{3}$%, $16\frac{2}{3}$% of 60 = $\frac{1}{6} \times \frac{60}{1} = \frac{1}{1} \times \frac{10}{1}$ = 10 4 $71\frac{1}{2}$%, Decreased $71\frac{1}{2}$° out of 100°, ☐% x 100 = $71\frac{1}{2}$%, ☐% = $71\frac{1}{2}$ ÷ 100 = $71\frac{1}{2}$%, $71\frac{1}{2}$% of 100 = $71\frac{1}{2}$ 5 100%, Up $4.50 from $4.50, ☐% x 4.50 ÷ 4.50, ☐% = 4.50 ÷ 4.50 = 100%, 100% of 4.50 = 4.50 6 $87\frac{1}{2}$%, 21 out of 24 eaten, ☐% x 24 = 21, ☐% = 21 ÷ 24 = $\frac{21}{24} = \frac{7}{8}$ = $87\frac{1}{2}$%, $87\frac{1}{2}$% of 24 = $\frac{7}{8} \times \frac{24}{1} = \frac{7}{1} \times \frac{3}{1}$ = 21 7 6%, Increased 3 inches, from 50

inches, □% x 50 = 3, □% = 3 ÷ 50 = $\frac{3}{50}$ = 6%, 6% of 50 = $\frac{3}{50}$ x $\frac{50}{1}$ = $\frac{3}{1}$ x $\frac{1}{1}$ = 3 (8) 10%, Down $1\frac{3}{5}$ from 16, □% x 16 = $1\frac{3}{5}$, □% = $\frac{8}{5}$ ÷ 16 = $\frac{8}{5}$ x $\frac{1}{16}$ = $\frac{1}{5}$ x $\frac{1}{2}$ = $\frac{1}{10}$ = 10%, 10% of 16 = $\frac{1}{10}$ x $\frac{16}{1}$ = $\frac{16}{10}$ = $\frac{8}{5}$ = $1\frac{3}{5}$

Page 42

(1) $\frac{6}{4}$ = $1\frac{1}{2}$ = 150% (2) $\frac{16}{5}$ = $3\frac{1}{5}$ = 320% (3) $\frac{40}{12}$ = $3\frac{1}{3}$ = $333\frac{1}{3}$%

(4) $1\frac{1}{4}$ x $1\frac{1}{2}$ (150%) = $\frac{5}{4}$ x $\frac{3}{2}$ = $1\frac{7}{8}$ (5) $6\frac{3}{4}$ ÷ $2\frac{1}{4}$ = $\frac{27}{4}$ x $\frac{4}{9}$ = 3 = 300%

Page 43

(1) $\frac{11}{10}$ x $\frac{50}{1}$ = 55 (2) 200% = 2; 2 x 35 = 70 (3) 175% = $1\frac{3}{4}$; $\frac{7}{4}$ x 20 = 35

(4) 4 $\frac{50}{100}$ x 1 = $4\frac{1}{2}$ (5) 140% = $1\frac{2}{5}$; $\frac{7}{5}$ x $\frac{5}{1}$ = 7 (6) $1\frac{2}{3}$ x 900 = $\frac{5}{3}$ x $\frac{900}{1}$ = 1,500

(7) $2\frac{1}{2}$ x $\frac{3}{5}$ = $\frac{3}{2}$ = $1\frac{1}{2}$ (8) 3 $\frac{25}{100}$ = $\frac{325}{100}$ x $\frac{300}{1}$ = 975 (9) $1\frac{1}{3}$ x 600 = 800; 600 + 800 = 1,400 (10) $\frac{23}{20}$ = $1\frac{3}{20}$ = 115% (11) $2\frac{1}{4}$ x □ = 90; 90 ÷ $\frac{9}{4}$= 40

(12) $\frac{110}{20}$ = $5\frac{1}{2}$ = 550% (13) $\frac{1}{10}$ ÷ $\frac{1}{4}$ = $\frac{4}{10}$ = 40% (14) $1\frac{2}{3}$ ÷ $\frac{1}{4}$ = $\frac{20}{3}$ = $6\frac{1}{3}$ = $633\frac{1}{3}$%

Page 44

(1) a, c, d (2) a, c, d (3) d ($\frac{27}{36}$ eaten = $\frac{3}{4}$) (4) a ($\frac{18}{20}$ = 90%) (5) b, c, d (6) a, c, d

(7) e ($\frac{1}{7}$ x $3\frac{1}{2}$ = $\frac{1}{2}$ = 50% of 1) (8) d ($\frac{300}{100}$ x $\frac{5}{3}$ = 5) (9) b ($\frac{1}{8}$ x 4 = $\frac{1}{2}$ = 50%)

(10) b (110% = $1\frac{1}{10}$ x 100 = 110. 100 + 110 = 210) (11) a (63 ÷ 12 = $5\frac{1}{4}$ = 525%)

(12) b (Drop 6 from 16 = $\frac{6}{16}$ = $\frac{3}{8}$ = $37\frac{1}{2}$% sale)

Page 46

(1) e 1.0001 (2) d 3.025 (3) a 0.30 (4) c 26.04 (5) b 1.42

Page 47

(1) r 4.05 (2) w 42.1 (3) e 42.02 (4) d 4.42 (5) t 0.042 (6) a 40.25

(7) h 4.200 (8) i 4.02 (9) s 4.50 (10) h 4.20 (11) o 40.002

(12) r 4.05 ($\frac{25}{100}$ x $\frac{81}{5}$ = $\frac{405}{100}$ = 4.05) (Check Yourself) their shadow

Page 48

1 n 3.72 2 e 0.13 3 a 76.032 4 e 2.01 5 c 126.991 6 f 1.0061

Check Yourself a fence

Page 50

1 a. $\frac{1}{4}$ b. $\frac{11}{25}$ c. $1\frac{3}{5}$ d. $\frac{3}{4}$ e. $\frac{1}{2}$ f. $5\frac{7}{20}$ g. $\frac{4}{25}$ h. $\frac{1}{500}$ i. $3\frac{1}{20}$ j. $\frac{2}{25}$ k. $\frac{17}{20}$ l. $\frac{5}{8}$ m. $\frac{1}{5{,}000}$ n. $1\frac{3}{8}$ o. $\frac{1}{3}$ p. $1\frac{7}{80}$ 2 a. 0.5 b. $0.6\overline{6}$ c. 0.75 d. 1.52 e. 0.06 f. 1.01 g. 0.0032 h. $0.08\overline{3}$ i. 4.3 j. $3.8\overline{3}$ k. 0.12 l. 0.14 m. 12.75 n. $0.8\overline{3}$ o. 0.04 p. 1.0

Page 51

1 $\frac{205}{100}$ and 2.05 2 $1\frac{7}{20} = 1\frac{35}{100}$ = 135% = 1.35 3 $\frac{2}{3}$ x \$24.99 = \$16.66

4 0 + 0 = 0 5 reciprocal of $1\frac{2}{8}$ is $\frac{8}{10} = \frac{4}{5}$ 6 $1\frac{1}{2} \div 6 = \frac{1}{4}$ = 25% 7 $60 \div \frac{3}{4} = 80$

8 $1\frac{3}{4}$ increase $\div \frac{1}{2} = 3\frac{1}{2}$ = 350% increase 9 $10\frac{1}{8} - 4\frac{1}{6} = 5\frac{23}{24}$

10 $10\frac{1}{8} \div 4 = \frac{81}{32} = 2\frac{17}{32}$ 11 $\frac{1}{50}$ x 50 = 1 = $\frac{13}{18} + \frac{1}{6} + \frac{1}{9}$ 12 $\frac{36}{90} = \frac{2}{5}$ = 40%

13 $\frac{1}{4} \times \frac{1}{4} \times \frac{1}{3} \times \frac{1}{2} = \frac{1}{96}$ 14 $\frac{25}{1{,}000} = \frac{2.5}{100}$ = 2.5% 15 decreased 4 out of $4\frac{1}{2} = \frac{8}{9} = 88\frac{8}{9}$%

Page 52

1 Total = 256 □'s. 32 out of 256 = $\frac{1}{8} = 12\frac{1}{2}$% shaded.

(Together, the shaded parts = 2 squares out of 16 = $\frac{1}{8}$.)

2 ◺ = 2.3, since ⧄ ◺ = 3◺'s. So, 2.3 x 5◺'s = 11.5

3 ●●● = 20% = $\frac{1}{5}$ of total. 5 x (●●●) = 15 ●'s x .01 = 0.15

4 Both choices are equal. $6\frac{1}{4} = \frac{1}{16}$ so $\frac{1}{16} \times \frac{1}{5} = \frac{1}{80}$ of 800 = \$10.

$\frac{1}{2}$% of 2,000 = 1% of 1,000 = $\frac{1}{100}$ x 1,000 = \$10.

5 $\frac{24}{25}$ out of 24 hours = $\frac{24}{25} \div 24 = \frac{1}{25}$ of a day = 4%

6

a = $\frac{1}{3}$, b = $\frac{7}{8}$, c = $\frac{3}{8}$, d = $\frac{7}{12}$

a + c	d – a
$\frac{17}{24}$	$\frac{1}{4}$
b + c	b – d
$1\frac{1}{4}$	$\frac{7}{24}$

7

a = $\frac{5}{6}$, b = $\frac{2}{7}$, c = $\frac{1}{8}$, d = $\frac{3}{5}$

a x c	a ÷ d
$\frac{5}{48}$	$1\frac{7}{18}$
b x c	b ÷ d
$\frac{1}{28}$	$\frac{10}{21}$

8 Since $0.0625 = \frac{1}{16}$, then $0.00625 = \frac{1}{10} \times \frac{1}{16} = \frac{1}{160}$, so $\frac{1}{2} \div \frac{1}{160} = 80 = 8{,}000\%$

9 ⊠ $= \frac{1}{9}$. So, ⊠ $= \frac{1}{9}$ and ◺ $= \frac{1}{72}$ so, $\frac{1}{9} + \frac{1}{9} + \frac{1}{72} + \frac{1}{72} = \frac{18}{72} = \frac{1}{4}$

10

3	$\frac{1}{2}$	1	$2\frac{1}{2}$
$\frac{1}{3}$	$2\frac{1}{6}$	2	$1\frac{1}{2}$
$1\frac{5}{6}$	$1\frac{2}{3}$	$1\frac{1}{6}$	$2\frac{1}{3}$
$\frac{5}{6}$	$2\frac{2}{3}$	$2\frac{5}{6}$	$\frac{2}{3}$

Magic sum = 7 (from 3rd column)

Complete the diagonal first.

Page 53

SET A 1 $1\frac{1}{8}$ 2 $1\frac{1}{12}$ 3 $1\frac{13}{30}$ 4 $2\frac{3}{10}$ 5 $4\frac{11}{20}$ 6 $8\frac{2}{15}$ 7 $7\frac{1}{24}$ 8 $1\frac{5}{36}$ 9 $5\frac{1}{28}$ 10 $\frac{47}{60}$ 11 $2\frac{5}{18}$ 12 $3\frac{7}{15}$ 13 $4\frac{3}{56}$ 14 $12\frac{7}{45}$ 15 $11\frac{17}{28}$

SET B 1 $1\frac{1}{2}$ 2 $9\frac{1}{12}$ 3 $3\frac{9}{10}$ 4 $7\frac{1}{6}$ 5 $\frac{16}{21}$ 6 $1\frac{31}{36}$ 7 $2\frac{17}{48}$ 8 $4\frac{11}{12}$ 9 $\frac{13}{24}$ 10 $\frac{29}{30}$ 11 $4\frac{13}{30}$ 12 $\frac{7}{60}$ 13 $5\frac{19}{24}$ 14 $\frac{60}{100} = \frac{3}{5}$ 15 $\frac{23}{60}$

Page 54

SET C 1 $\frac{3}{5}$ 2 $\frac{1}{8}$ 3 $\frac{3}{20}$ 4 $3\frac{2}{3}$ 5 $5\frac{1}{3}$ 6 $16\frac{4}{5}$ 7 $1\frac{3}{10}$ 8 12 9 10 10 $20\frac{1}{4}$ 11 $\frac{1}{8}$ 12 1 13 $7\frac{3}{5}$ 14 $8\frac{2}{5}$ 15 8

SET D 1 $\frac{8}{9}$ 2 8 3 $3\frac{3}{8}$ 4 $2\frac{1}{4}$ 5 $3\frac{1}{5}$ 6 $2\frac{5}{7}$ 7 $5\frac{5}{7}$ 8 $3\frac{1}{2}$ 9 $1\frac{1}{2}$ 10 $\frac{1}{15}$ 11 $1\frac{1}{2}$ 12 12 13 $\frac{1}{5}$ 14 6 15 $1\frac{3}{5}$

Multiplication Table and Hundreds Grid Cut-Outs

Cut out these tables—or a copy of the tables—and paste them onto a file folder or heavy paper to use for demonstration and/or as a hands-on student aid. You can also download these pages (www.CriticalThinking.com/tablefractions) as a PDF to print on heavier paper.

X	1	2	3	4	5	6	7	8	9	10
1	1	2	3	4	5	6	7	8	9	10
2	2	4	6	8	10	12	14	16	18	20
3	3	6	9	12	15	18	21	24	27	30
4	4	8	12	16	20	24	28	32	36	40
5	5	10	15	20	25	30	35	40	45	50
6	6	12	18	24	30	36	42	48	54	60
7	7	14	21	28	35	42	49	56	63	70
8	8	16	24	32	40	48	56	64	72	80
9	9	18	27	36	45	54	63	72	81	90
10	10	20	30	40	50	60	70	80	90	100

1									
2									
3									
4									
5									
6									
7									
8									
9									
10	20	30	40	50	60	70	80	90	100

Fraction Bars Cut-Outs

Cut out these fraction bars—or a copy—and paste them onto a file folder or heavy paper to use for demonstration and/or as a hands-on student aid. You can also download these pages (www.CriticalThinking.com/tablefractions) as a PDF to print on heavier paper.

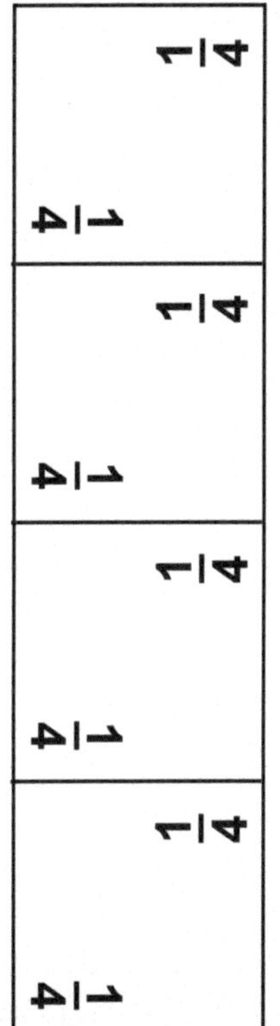

Critical Thinking In Everyday Life

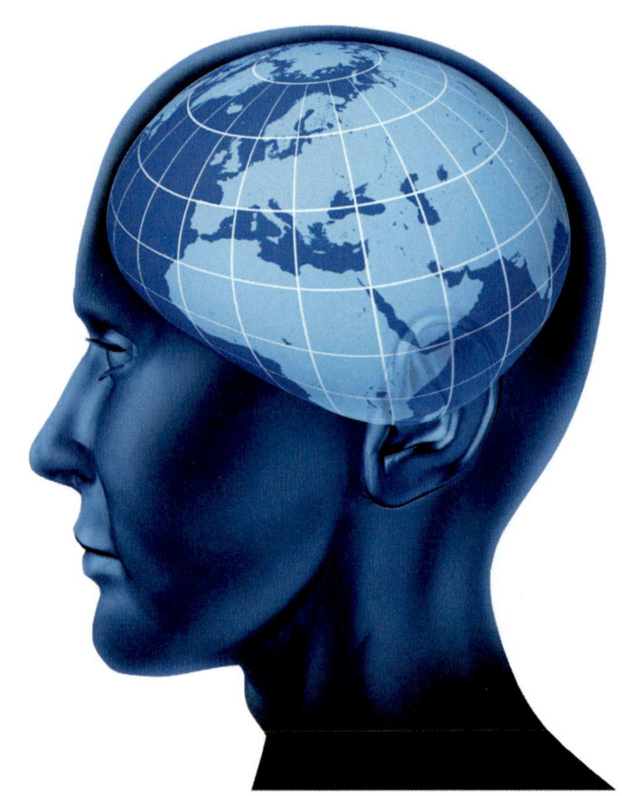

Written by

Robert W. Ridel, Ph.D.

Title: Critical Thinking in Everyday Life
Author: Robert W. Ridel, Ph.D.
Published by: Calm Sky Media
ISBN: 978-0-9863515-0-1

Calm Sky Media, LLC
1928 East Highland Avenue
F-104-478
Phoenix, Arizona 85016

Published in the United States of America

DISCLAIMER

This book is designed to provide information on critical thinking. It is sold with the understanding that the publisher and author are not engaged in rendering legal, accounting or other professional services. If legal or other expert assistance is required, the services of a competent professional should be sought.

It is not the purpose of this textbook to reprint all the information that is otherwise available to authors and/or publishers, but instead to complement, amplify and supplement the academic field of critical thinking and provide a practical guide for understanding the importance of critical thinking in everyday life.

Every effort has been made to make this manual as complete and as accurate as possible. However, there may be mistakes, both typographical and in content. Furthermore, this textbook contains information on critical thinking and global events that are current only up to the printing date.

The purpose of this textbook is to educate and entertain. The author and Calm Sky Media shall have neither liability nor responsibility to any person or entity with respect to any loss or damage caused, or alleged to have been caused, directly or indirectly, by the information contained in this book.

Critical Thinking in Everyday Life

Robert W. Ridel, Ph.D.

Dedication

I dedicate this book to my family.

Acknowledgments

I would like to express my deepest appreciation to the following people for providing the guidance and motivation necessary to complete the textbook:

- My father – who, although deceased, continues to impact my life
- My mother – who, at 99-years of age, remains an inspiration to me
- My brothers – who I respect and adore
- My friend – Bob, whose friendship I treasure and who I hope to always emulate in kindness and integrity
- My friend – David, who was instrumental in producing the textbook and who plays a meaningful role in my life
- My faculty – who provided invaluable comments and suggestions while writing the textbook
- My students – without whom the textbook would never have been written

Preface

The most important requirement to live – other than breathing – is to think. To think critically. This textbook was written with that insight in mind.

My overarching objective is to help you proceed along your critical thinking journey – from being an unreflective or aspiring thinker into becoming a critical thinker. Along that path, the textbook will help you:

- Recognize the need to develop your critical thinking skills
- Identify barriers to critical thinking and devise strategies to modify or replace them
- Assess the reliability of information and evaluate the credibility of people who deliver it
- Understand the origin of and conditions that maintain problems, and apply lessons learned to solve them in your everyday life
- Deepen and broaden your base of knowledge, motivate you to speak your mind, and help you avoid falling back into unreflective habits

I hope you enjoy reading the textbook as much as I enjoyed writing it. I'm honored to participate in the process of you becoming a critical thinker. Serving you in that capacity is an important role in **my** everyday life. I take that responsibility very seriously – just as you should the task of becoming a critical thinker in **your** everyday life.

My sincerest hope is that this textbook will permanently transform you from being an unreflective or aspiring thinker who was susceptible to biases, false assumptions, and unreliable information – into becoming a critical thinker who "demands" research, facts, and answers to questions that you will skillfully pose for the remainder of your life.

Onward – and welcome to your new world of **critical thinking.**

About the Author

Dr. Ridel possesses an educational and business background that spans over three decades. He was schooled in the social sciences (sociology, psychology) and received specialized training in conflict sociology and behavioral psychology. Robert's educational background also includes solid exposure to the humanities, including studies in culture, ethics, philosophy, and (his passion) critical thinking. He earned his degrees, including his Ph.D., through the University of California system.

Dr. Ridel is currently the Dean of Retention at the University of Phoenix – which was his occupational home for over 10 years as Academic Dean, Area Chair, and Lead Faculty. He also served as Lecturer and Department Chair at various universities across the United States and overseas in Europe and Asia. In addition, Robert was associated with the National Institutes of Health (Research Fellow – Laboratory of Brain Evolution and Behavior) and the United Nations (Field Observer – Africa). He also founded a business management and career consulting firm that worked with companies to become more profitable, as well as with professionals to manage and advance in their careers.

Although he has occupied various positions in his professional life, Dr. Ridel's primary interests continue to be focused on the field of educational administration and helping students proceed through their programs of study and develop within their chosen career paths.

Table of Contents

Chapter 1
Critical Thinking:
Welcome To Your New World Of Thinking

To question is to understand.

Robert W. Ridel, Ph.D.

Let me ask you a question. Ready? Here you go:

"What the heck are you doing in school?"

Yes, you read it correctly. No need to rub your eyes or pinch yourself. Let me repeat: What the heck are you doing in school?

Before you answer, let me try to guess.

Hmm, OK – you're in school because you want to learn. Because you have a passion for knowledge. Correct? Nah. That would be great, but such a reason would be most unusual. I've taught tens-of-thousands of students in my educational career – and precious few ever made that claim. At least not seriously.

Let me guess again.

You're in college because you want to land a great job. Make a comfortable salary rather than earn a meager hourly wage. Receive health benefits. Work in a cubical instead of an open space or, better yet, in your own office with a great view. Buy a house. Get out of debt. Send your kids to college. Travel. Ah yes, travel. Am I on the right track? Yes, I figured I was. Yippee.

Now, here's another question:

"How is all that going to happen?"

I mean – really? How are you going to make more money, purchase a home with a glorious, panoramic view, and travel to all those great places in Europe and Asia? Oh – did I mention make more money? Will you magically snap your fingers? Perhaps wish on a four-leaf clover? Or maybe a shooting star? Silly, I know. But really, how is all that going to happen?

Let me make another guess.

You attend classes, read textbooks, listen to lectures, write papers, make presentations, receive grades – and do that over and over again until you get ready to graduate. How cool will that be?

And then, right after your graduation party, the phone will start ringing off the hook with offers for six-figure jobs complete with three months vacation, the office view you desperately want, and a dreamy career trajectory. Yes, that's the answer to the question:

"How is all that going to happen?"

You'll simply graduate from school.

Well, I hate to be the purveyor of bad news, but that just ain't going to happen.

Oh, you can graduate from school – but the money, vacation, view, and career won't magically appear overnight like a pimple on your cheek or friends unexpectedly showing up at your apartment at midnight. No way. Not in your wildest dreams. Forget about snapping your fingers and wishing on four-leaf clovers.

If you want to land a really good job, make more money, buy a neat house, and travel the world – you'll need to possess the skills required by the marketplace. Plain and simple, you'll need to earn the trappings of success. And you can only do that by acquiring skills the marketplace deems important.

"Skills? What skills," you ask.

Good question. The marketplace requires several – some of the most notable being skills related to:

- Communication
- Collaboration
- Information Utilization
- Professional Competencies

No surprise with any of these. None at all. The marketplace is looking for students who are solid communicators, get along well with colleagues, know how to effectively use information, and who possess a strong set of competencies related to their occupational pursuits.

So, have you acquired the skills the marketplace seeks?

Think carefully. Honestly.

One, two, or three out of four won't be enough, at least not to acquire your desired goals in life. It will take four out of four – nothing less. Without all of these skills – you stand a better chance of locating the Holy Grail, winning the lottery, or getting a date with... well, you know what I mean.

But even if you possess all four of these abilities to the nth degree, landing a great job, being richly compensated, and residing in a wonderful home will still be unlikely if you don't acquire skills in another area valued by the marketplace; namely (see Figure 1.1):

- Critical Thinking

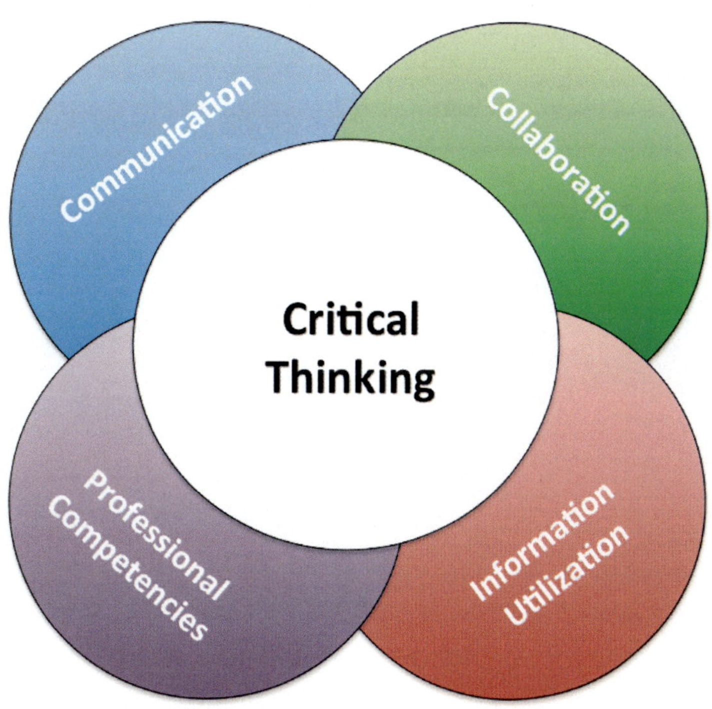

Figure 1.1
Architecture of Employable Skills

Communication, collaboration, information utilization, and professional competencies are important, to be certain – **but your goals will likely remain elusive unless you learn how to think critically.** A car can have comfy leather seats, an awesome quadraphonic sound system, Bluetooth technology, shiny rims, sunroof, and a GPS that can track coordinates on the Moon – but it can't transport you to your desired destination without an engine. Absolutely not. And critical thinking is that engine. It – more than any other skill deemed important by the marketplace, will "drive" you toward your professional goals. Nothing else comes close.

Critical thinking is tremendously important in its own right, of course – but it also:

- Enhances your ability to communicate persuasively.
- Elevates your skill to collaborate with colleagues.
- Improves your ability to search for and apply relevant information.
- Sharpens your skill at developing competencies related to your professional endeavors.

Again, critical thinking is that important.

"Really," you ask?

In a word, yes. And in two words, absolutely yes.

Let me respond to your question more boldly: In the absence of critical thinking skills, you can forget about the money, nice home, view property, traveling, and neat career.

No engine. Goodbye goals. Ain't going to happen.

And that's why you need to read what I'm about to state carefully. Very carefully. I know you're not going to like it. Indeed, most of my students are initially put off by my words.

Ready?

Just promise you won't throw your laptop against the wall, curse my name, or rush to the registrar's office to drop the class. Promise? OK – here you go:

"You're not the critical thinker you think you are."

Ouch.

I can only imagine what you're thinking:

"Who the heck is this guy – telling me I don't think critically?"
How dare he? I think critically all the time."

Well, the unfortunate truth is you probably don't. Indeed, I strongly suspect you're nowhere close to being the critical thinker you believe you are (or can become).

The fact is, believing you're a critical thinker just because you skimmed an article or took a class on the subject doesn't make you a critical thinker. Not at all. Quite the contrary, developing critical thinking skills takes an enormous amount of time, dedication, and patience. And unless you "lived" critical thinking over the course of many years (not days, weeks, or months) – it's unlikely you're the critical thinker you claim to be. Stated frankly, believing you're a critical thinker doesn't make you a critical thinker.

"So," you ask – *"how can I become a better critical thinker?"*

That's an excellent question – and one that, not surprisingly, will be addressed throughout this book. Too early to focus on the "how" question in Chapter 1 – but let me give you a teeny-weeny hint of what's to come.

Every journey has a beginning – which, in the case of becoming a critical thinker, involves admitting you don't yet possess the skills required to actually be a critical thinker. Ironic, isn't it – that you need to acknowledge that you're not the person you think you are in order to potentially become that person; namely, in our case, to become a critical thinker.

Ironic, yes – but it's certainly not unusual for people to overestimate their abilities. Consider the following illustrations – as they relate to the previously identified skills required by the marketplace.

- Jesse proudly states *"I'm a great communicator,"* but he can't string three coherent sentences together.
- Trina confidently believes she's a wonderful team player, even though her colleagues avoid her like she was the bubonic plague.
- Keisha boldly claims to be talented at locating and utilizing information, although she's actually quite inept at all things technical.
- Marco, despite his brash comments to the contrary, lacks several competencies necessary to be successful in his career.

Jesse, Trina, Keisha, and Marco are committed to their points-of-view, to be certain – but that doesn't mean their self-assessments are accurate. For all of them, the facts convince us otherwise – despite what they "think." And that's most unfortunate – because by failing to recognize and improve upon their respective weaknesses, Jesse, Trina, Keisha, and Marco will undoubtedly remain mired in a state of "occupational mediocrity" (or worse) for the duration of their careers.

None will advance – and each will wonder why.

Well – the same outcome is destined for people who mistakenly claim they are critical thinkers when, in fact, they aren't.

- George confidently asserts he can accurately determine the reliability of information and the credibility of people who provide it. But he can't.
- Judy boldly declares she makes decisions and solves problems by skillfully asking questions and evaluating alternative points of view. But she doesn't.

And you know what will happen to each of these so-called critical thinkers, don't you?

Again, none will advance – and each will wonder why.

And that, my good student, is why you're reading this textbook instead of playing cards with your kids, talking to friends at a local coffee shop, napping on the couch, or watching one of your favorite movies. Because educators, like the marketplace, have determined that you need to develop your critical thinking skills in order to acquire your career and financial goals.

Remember what I stated a moment ago – that the first step to becoming a critical thinker involves admitting that you don't yet possess the skills required to be a critical thinker. Unfortunately – Jesse, Trina, and our friends didn't learn that lesson.

Will your name be added to that list? Or will you admit that you have much to learn about critical thinking? I hope the latter.

Everyday Life with David

"Day 1: What If?"

Hi. My name is David, and I'm one of you. I've done a lot of interesting things in my life – teacher, writer, cube dweller, minimum wage earner in college – and through it all, I was at a serious disadvantage. I made some bad decisions early in my life, and it has taken me a couple of decades to catch up. "*What disadvantage*," you ask?

Well, I was a Level 3 critical thinker (on a scale of 1 – 10). That wasn't very good. I didn't question as much as I should have, and was highly susceptible to the influence of my friends and the media. I also didn't follow a structured process when it came to decision-making and solving problems – and as a result, I made some really bad choices. Basically, I "winged it" through life.

I can only imagine what my life would have been like if I possessed critical thinking skills. I probably would have been less vulnerable to being influenced, and I certainly would have made better decisions and solved problems more effectively. And I have to believe I would have been more successful. No question. I just know. No "what if" about it. Sound familiar?

Here's the good news: You have a head start over me. You have an opportunity to learn from my mistakes. Please take advantage of this "second chance." Embrace critical thinking now, and you won't have to wait a couple decades as I did to discover the power of questioning and evaluating, as well as the value of facts and research.

Today is the first day of the rest of my life. I look forward to joining you on this life-changing journey. We have so much to learn together.

DEFINITION OF CRITICAL THINKING

The best place to begin your education on critical thinking is to acquire a clear understanding of what critical thinking means. Let's start with a few popular "academic" definitions.

Consider the words of the legendary John Dewey who defined critical thinking as an:

> *"Active, persistent and careful consideration of a belief or supposed form of knowledge in light of the grounds that support it, and the further conclusions."*

Huh? With all due respect, that definition doesn't make much sense. It's way too confusing, at least for me. How about for you?

A few decades ago, John McPeck defined critical thinking as:

> *"The skills and propensity to engage in an activity with reflective skepticism."*

Okay, that's a little better. The word "reflective" implies that you should think about your surroundings – that's good. And the word "skepticism" implies questioning – which is also good (not to take anything for granted). It's a good start – but there's plenty of content missing.

In a seminal study on critical thinking, Edward Glaser offers the following definition:

> *"The ability to think critically involves three things: (1) an attitude of being disposed to consider in a thoughtful way the problems and subjects that come within the range of one's experiences, (2) knowledge of the methods of logical inquiry and reasoning, and (3) some skill in applying those methods. Critical thinking calls for a persistent effort to examine any belief or supposed form of knowledge in the light of the evidence that supports it and the further conclusions to which it tends."*

What the heck? I can't fathom this definition. Can you?

Finally, let's fast-forward to the 21st Century. What do you think about the below "definitions" of critical thinking found on the Internet?

> *"Critical thinking is the objective analysis and evaluation of an issue in order to form a judgment."*

Pretty basic.

"The awakening of the intellect to the study of itself."

Interesting – but too poetic and "empty" for my tastes.

In an attempt to de-cloak the "secret" of what critical thinking means, let me offer a more straightforward, comprehensive definition that applies to your everyday life. I will refer to it throughout the book (so make certain you integrate the definition rather than simply memorize it). It consists of 25-words (see Figure 1.2):

> ***"Critical thinking is a continuous process of evaluating information, formulating opinions based on facts, and applying learning to effectively solve problems and make sound decisions."***

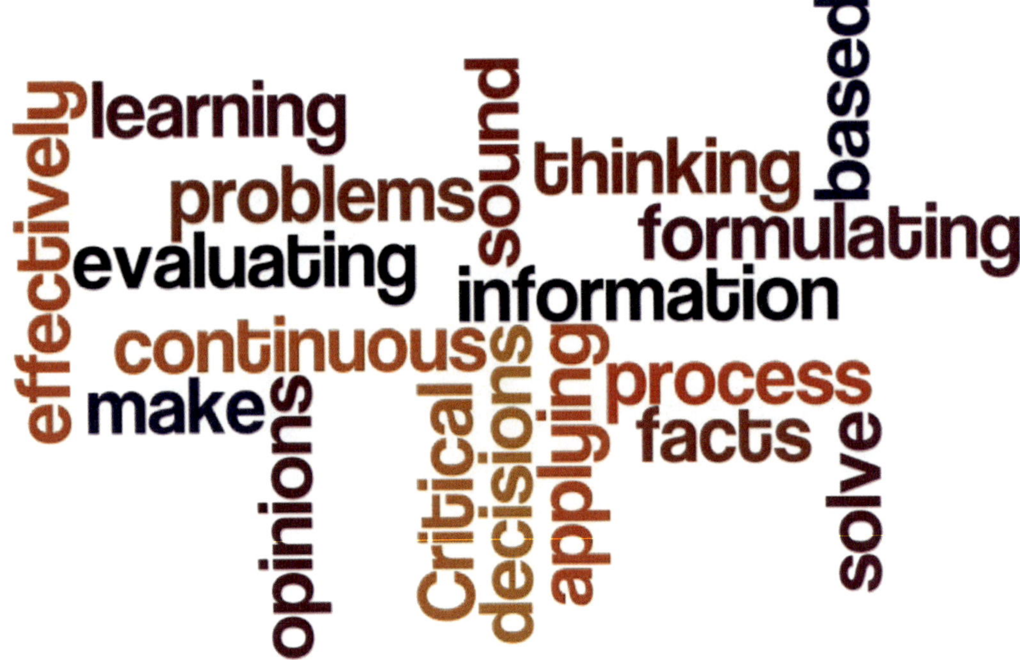

Figure 1.2
Definition of Critical Thinking

Let's break the definition down into its component parts, of which there are three:

- **Critical thinking is a continuous process:**

  Critical thinking is a 24/7/365 endeavor. There's nothing temporary about it. It's a habit. A state of being. Constant companion from the moment you wake up until you drift into slumber.

Nothing and no one is "out of bounds" or off limits for critical thinkers. Every thought, opinion, attitude, value, belief, and behavior is subject to constant review and analysis – all the time. And everyone, including family, friends, acquaintances, and strangers, is "fair game" to be questioned. Again, all the time.

- Critical thinking is a continuous process of **evaluating information and formulating opinions based on facts:**

The reliability of information is an important cornerstone of critical thinking, as is the credibility of the people who deliver it. I mean – would you make decisions based on content contained in fortune cookies or horoscopes? And would you attempt to solve problems based on information offered by cartoon characters or uninformed and overly biased people? Of course you wouldn't. But that's precisely what many people do when they adopt positions based on unsubstantiated information that originates from unreliable sources (i.e. Internet and tabloids) and "non-credible" people (i.e. politicians, actors/actresses, and athletes).

In this context, consider critical thinking as a filter that keeps misinformation and biased opinions out of your reservoir of knowledge (refer to Figure 1.3). Without it, questionable information delivered by non-credible sources would negatively impact (contaminate) your ability to develop sensible, accurate points-of-view. And that wouldn't be good – your reservoir would become absolutely filthy.

Figure 1.3
Waterfall – Critical Thinking As A Filter

- Critical thinking is a continuous process of evaluating information, formulating opinions based on facts, and **applying learning to effectively solve problems and make sound decisions.**

  Life is defined by an enormous number of problems that need to be solved, and a huge array of decisions that need to be made. Not surprisingly, critical thinkers follow a structured process when dealing with them.

  For example, critical thinkers solve problems only after evaluating strategies and ideas advanced by non-biased, "in the know" experts. They also analyze a wide-range of options before making decisions – no matter how unpopular the alternatives might be. And in all cases, critical thinkers emphasize the applied nature of the critical thinking process. For them, the mantra is always "how can I **apply** what I've learned to effectively solve problems and make good decisions."

* * * * *

With this definition securely in your mind, how would you characterize yourself as a critical thinker? Come on – be honest. No stretching the truth, or worse (lying). Actually, answering my question should be relatively easy. Just focus your attention on the three stated subcomponents of my definition – which I'll reintroduce as questions:

- Do you think critically all the time?
- Do you analyze information and develop opinions based on facts?
- Do you apply what you learn from your research when attempting to solve problems and make decisions?

Probably not, or at least not as often as you think.

Now – breathe a sigh of relief. No need to fret if you don't satisfy the criteria of my definition. You're in good company. The vast majority of people seldom (if ever) think critically, at least not according to the above definition. Quite the contrary, they rarely research their opinions or evaluate the information they receive from who-knows-who. And as a result, their opinions tend to be unconfirmed or, even worse, incorrect – which often causes them to make poor decisions and be ineffective when attempting to solve problems.

I'm so confident what I just stated is true, I'll wager you the following: If you placed 100 people in a room and asked them if they could factually substantiate three of their most important opinions – only 12 would be capable of doing so. Would you take the bet? And would you be included in that very special dozen? Check out Figure 1.4.

Let's explore some tangible examples.

How many among the 100 would be able to factually substantiate their points-of-view on climate change? Same for immigration reform, gun control, and capital punishment? And how many really understand what produced the debt crisis and what measures are required to reduce the deficit without causing serious economic consequences?

Not many.

My wager is looking pretty good.

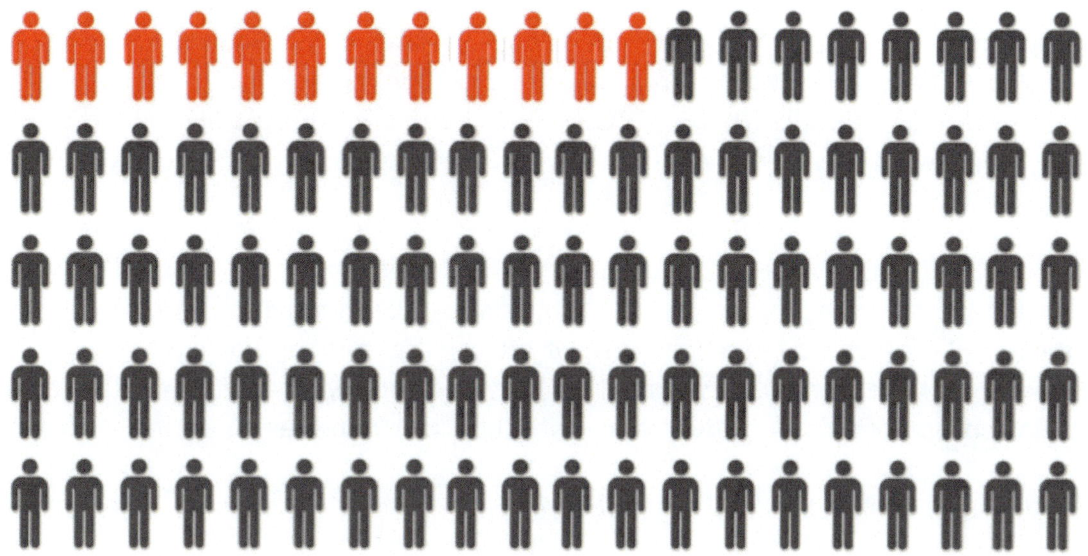

Figure 1.4
A Dozen Critical Thinkers

Have any doubts? If so – just ask anyone who is opinionated about those or other important issues to substantiate their positions. What you'd discover is that most have no clue about what they're talking or writing about – even though they confidently claim otherwise.

Now that I think about it – maybe my estimate of 12 out of a 100 is a tad too optimistic. Maybe the number should be in single digits.

The point is this: Understanding my definition of critical thinking is one thing. It's easy enough to learn. But practicing the three components is another matter, entirely. Becoming a better critical thinker takes more than 2-nano seconds to accomplish. No article, class or, for that matter, textbook will transform you from someone who possesses poor or mediocre critical thinking skills into a person who is a moderate or advanced critical thinker. Just can't be done.

The key is to integrate the components of my definition into your everyday life (hence the title of the book). Begin by evaluating information and formulating your opinions based on facts and evidence. Then, apply your insights whenever you attempt to solve problems and make decisions. And do it all the time (or as frequently as you can).

If you incorporate all of the definitional components into your everyday life – **you will eventually become a critical thinker.**

Promise.

In order to evaluate your progress at becoming a critical thinker – we'll need to establish a baseline of what type of critical thinker you are now. Are you just beginning to develop your critical thinking skills, do you already possess them to a significant degree, or are you somewhere in-between?

Let's find out.

Everyday Life with David

"Day 3: A Habit"

They say you can develop a habit in just 30 days. Exercising, studying, and eating healthy are all great habits. Oddly, nobody ever adds "thinking" to the list.

I wonder why? Just think about it (pun intended) – thinking is at the heart of everything you do, including exercising, studying, and eating healthy. I can't think of another habit more worthy of your attention. Or mine.

Don't get me wrong, I didn't always think this way. In fact, I just started thinking about my thinking a few days ago. But the more I think about it, the more I realize that critical thinking is something worth pursuing – everyday of my life.

With this insight in mind, I will dedicate the next 30 days to developing a habit of critical thinking. I will practice thinking every day – for the duration of the course and hopefully beyond.

How about you? Let's do this together.

DETERMINE YOUR LEVEL OF CRITICAL THINKING

A few moments ago, I asked if you were a critical thinker according to my definition. Well, now I want to ask you to identify what level of critical thinker you are.

Refer to Figure 1.5 for an illustration of the critical thinking distribution. Please note: Everyone is a critical thinker to some degree – ranging from Levels 1 to 10.
In reality, no one operates as a completely unreflective thinker (Level 1) or a thoroughly masterful thinker (Level 10). Those are simply end points on the continuum that don't exist in reality. Everyone falls within a range from Levels 2 to 9, with the vast majority of people occupying the space between Levels 3 and Level 8.

So, where do you think you fall on the critical thinking continuum?

Use the below information as a guide to find out. (The content within each level is simply descriptive – and should be considered for illustrative purposes only.) Again, be honest. It's important because the selected level will be used as a baseline to monitor your progress throughout the textbook.

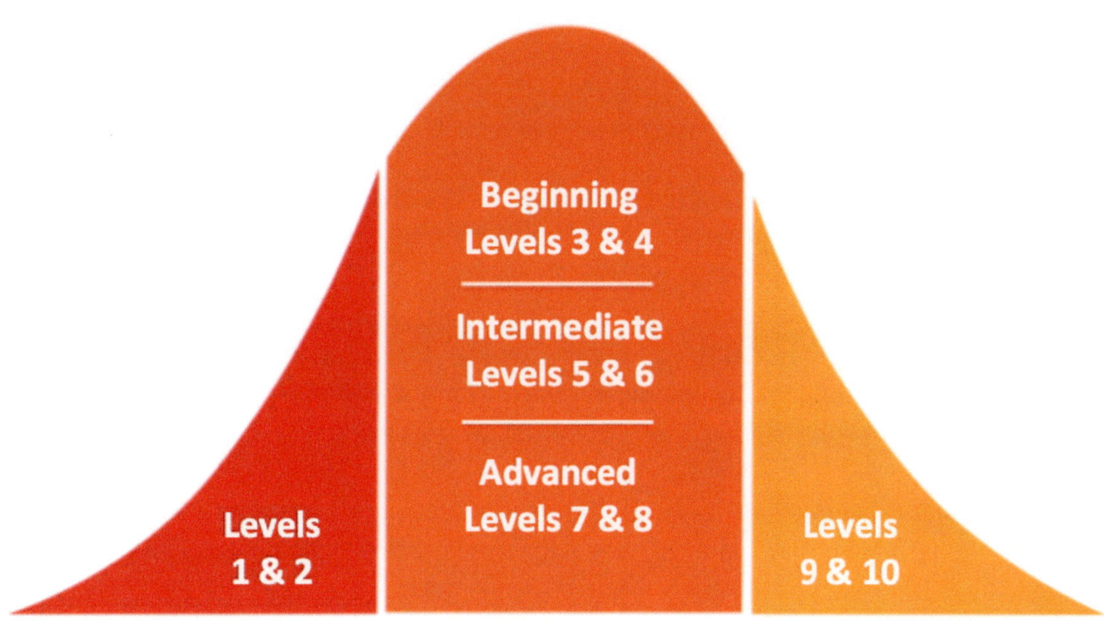

Figure 1.5
Critical Thinking Distribution

Level 3: Beginning Critical Thinker I:

- I don't spend much time thinking about how I think. Critical thinking just isn't a high priority for me.
- I haven't evaluated my behavior, opinions, or values. I simply do things the way I've always done them.
- I like what I think about – and how I do it. Why would I want to change?

Level 4: Beginning Critical Thinker II:

- I guess critical thinking is important, but I don't have any interest in analyzing my beliefs and attitudes.
- I know that I'm biased in a lot of my opinions. However, I'm reluctant to change the way I think about "stuff."
- I tend to follow whatever my family and friends believe in and do. Doing so has worked for me for many years.

Level 5: Average Critical Thinker I:

- I evaluate information for accuracy on occasion – but only when doing so requires little effort. I don't have a lot of extra time to analyze data.
- I want to think critically – I really do. I just need to get motivated to change the way I think.
- I don't always believe what I read – and I'm getting somewhat better when it comes to determining whether people are telling the truth or lying.

Level 6: Average Critical Thinker II:

- I try to be careful before I formulate an opinion – making certain that I thoroughly consider all sides of an issue.
- I understand personal biases distort my view of the world – and I'm trying to eliminate them from my thinking.
- I feel good about my thinking process. I'm getting much better at understanding what stops me from thinking critically and working around my barriers.

Level 7: Advanced Critical Thinker I:

- I apply my critical thinking skills everyday – and as such, I make fewer mistakes when solving problems and making decisions.
- I am getting much better at detecting biases in what I read and hear, as well as addressing and eliminating my own biases.
- I question nearly everything – no matter the source. It's interesting – I get really excited whenever I detect unsubstantiated statements made by other people. And I always think: "I don't believe you. Gotcha."

Level 8: Advanced Critical Thinker II:

- I hesitate to believe anything or anyone until I research and evaluate the information presented and the people advancing it.
- I question everything I hear and read – automatically and all the time. It's a great habit – and I'm glad I developed it.
- I intentionally surround myself with people who have different opinions, attitudes, and values from my own. I embrace diversity – and I'm a better critical thinker for doing so.

So – what level of critical thinking did you select for yourself? C'mon, really. Be truthful. As I mentioned earlier, it's important for you to be honest because the selected level will be used as a baseline to monitor your progress throughout the remainder of the textbook.

BECOMING A BETTER CRITICAL THINKER: AN EIGHT-STEP PROCESS

At this point, you're probably thinking:

> *"OK, I'm convinced – maybe I'm not the critical thinker I thought I was. You captured my attention. I want to develop my critical thinking skills. So tell me, how can I get better? I'm motivated and ready to learn.*
>
> *And don't worry, I'm not going to drop the class, curse your name, or throw my laptop against the wall. I really want to become a critical thinker."*

Am I right – or even close? If so, my response to you would be something like this:

> *"Be patient. Try not to rush the process. Recall what I mentioned earlier – that becoming a critical thinker takes more than 2-nanoseconds to accomplish. No single article, class or, for that matter, textbook will transform you from someone who possesses mediocre critical thinking skills into a person who becomes an advanced critical thinker. Again, be patient – and realistic about what can happen in only one chapter.*
>
> *But rest assured, you're on the right track. Yes, you're off to a very good beginning, indeed."*

The remainder of the book is dedicated to helping you reach your desired critical thinking destination. And it begins in earnest in a moment – when I introduce you to an eight-step process that, if followed, will propel you along your trajectory to become a critical thinker.

I developed the "Eight-Step Process to Critical Thinking" years ago to counter the tendencies most people have to:

- Believe they are critical thinkers when they're not.
- Overlook or actually ignore barriers that inhibit them from thinking critically.
- Employ ineffective methods to modify or replace critical thinking barriers.
- Accept points-of-view without questioning them, evaluating their reliability, and without "demanding" they be substantiated by facts.
- Assign credibility to shaping agents for no justifiable reason other than they're famous, attractive, or wealthy.
- Make decisions without using a structured process to explore options and proactively weigh consequences associated with certain alternatives.
- Deal with problems in a disorganized, haphazard, almost random way – without researching their origins and the conditions that maintain them.
- Forget lessons-learned – resulting in a reversion back to being unreflective thinkers.

Simply (and accurately) put – the above tendencies go a long way to explain why most people don't become critical thinkers. As you'll soon discover, all of them can be overcome by proceeding through the Eight-Step Process to Critical Thinking.

The good news is this: You've already accomplished the most important step to becoming a critical thinker, without even realizing it. And that is admitting you're not the critical thinker you thought you were.

That's Step 1.

- **Step 1: Recognize the need to improve your critical thinking skills**

Admitting you can improve as a critical thinker (Step 1), as uncomfortable as it might be to acknowledge, is a required (and I mean mandatory) precondition for you to actually become a critical thinker. Think about it. How can people strengthen areas of weakness without recognizing that improvement is necessary? (Remember my previous discussion of that point – earlier in this chapter.) Odd – but ever so true, and becoming a better critical thinker is no exception.

But you mustn't rest on your laurels – recognizing that you need to improve your critical thinking skills is one thing, but much more work needs to be accomplished in order to actually become a solid critical thinker. And the process continues by asking the following two questions:

- **Step 2: "What barriers inhibit me from developing my critical thinking skills?"**
- **Step 3: "How can I modify or replace them?"**

I know you want to improve your critical thinking skills. However, before you can proceed – you first have to identify what's stopping you from becoming a better critical thinker (Chapter 2). Recognizing the barriers is a great beginning – but you're doomed to failure if you rely on that observation to transform you from being an unreflective thinker into becoming a critical thinker. What you also need to do is replace and modify the barriers that thwart the development of your critical thinking skills (which will be discussed in Chapter 3).

But there's more. The next phase of advancement requires you to employ your newly acquired critical thinking skills to:

- **Step 4: Determine the reliability of information ("message")**
- **Step 5: Determine the credibility of the source ("messenger")**

Imagine if you were able to determine the accuracy of information. To differentiate fact from fiction. Truth from falsehood and deceit. And pretend you were able to ascertain the credibility of the people who deliver information. To decipher who was genuine and credible, and who was insincere and unworthy of your confidence and trust. **How cool would that be?**

Well – later in the book, I will discuss how you can accurately evaluate the tsunami of information that "drowns" you from the moment you wake up in the morning to when your head descends into the pillows at night. My goal will be to help you differentiate what's real and factual from what's make-believe and fantasy. But I must "warn" you – you'll never read newspapers or listen to television the same way. That will be addressed in Chapter 4.

What's more, I'll also try to help you decode the credibility of the messengers who constantly bombard you with all sorts of information. My objective will be to help you determine who's telling the truth and who is stretching it or downright lying? Again, be forewarned – you'll never listen to politicians and salespeople the same way. I'll consider that topic in Chapter 5.

- **Step 6: Understanding the problem solving process**
- **Step 7: Solving problems in your everyday life**

Now – all of that is fine and good. But what are you, as an aspiring critical thinker, going to do with all your newly acquired insights about informational reliability and source credibility? Stated bluntly, all of your learning about critical thinking will count for naught unless you apply lessons learned when making everyday decisions and solving everyday problems. Failing that – you'll never realize your potential to become a critical thinker. Never.

Such a situation would be most unacceptable – not only for you, but also for your family and friends, me, the academic institution that is educating you, and your community. And that ain't going to happen – at least not if I have anything to do or say about it.

I will discuss the benefits associated with applying critical thinking principles when solving problems in Chapters 6 and 7.

But even if you successfully apply your critical thinking skills when dealing with problems, there's no guarantee you will complete the transition from being an unreflective thinker to becoming a critical thinker. The final, and most important, step is to be a critical thinker "full time" – 24/7/365 until you close your eyes for the last time.

And that point brings us to the final step in the Eight-Step Process to Critical Thinking:

- **Step 8: Critical thinking becomes the essence and defining characteristic of your existence**

Have you ever tried to lose weight? How about stop smoking? If so, you possess first-hand knowledge about how difficult it is to keep weight off and stay away from cigarettes. As challenging as it is to accomplish those objectives – you know the real struggle is to not retreat into old habits.

Well – the same applies to critical thinking. Proceeding through Steps 1 – 7 is demanding enough, but Step 8 is the real test – to not fall back into becoming an unreflective thinker.

In the final chapter of this book (Chapter 8), you'll be given an opportunity to not only reflect on what you've learned, but also to apply your critical thinking skills to your everyday life – today and in the future.

My expectation (hope) is that you'll become permanently transformed from being an unreflective thinker who was susceptible to biases, false assumptions, and unreliable information – into a critical thinker who "demands" research, facts, and answers to the questions you skillfully pose for the remainder of your life. No recidivism (falling back into old habits) for you. Again, the transition must be permanent.

And that, my friend, is the ultimate goal of becoming a critical thinker.

Consider the possibilities (in Figure 1.6).

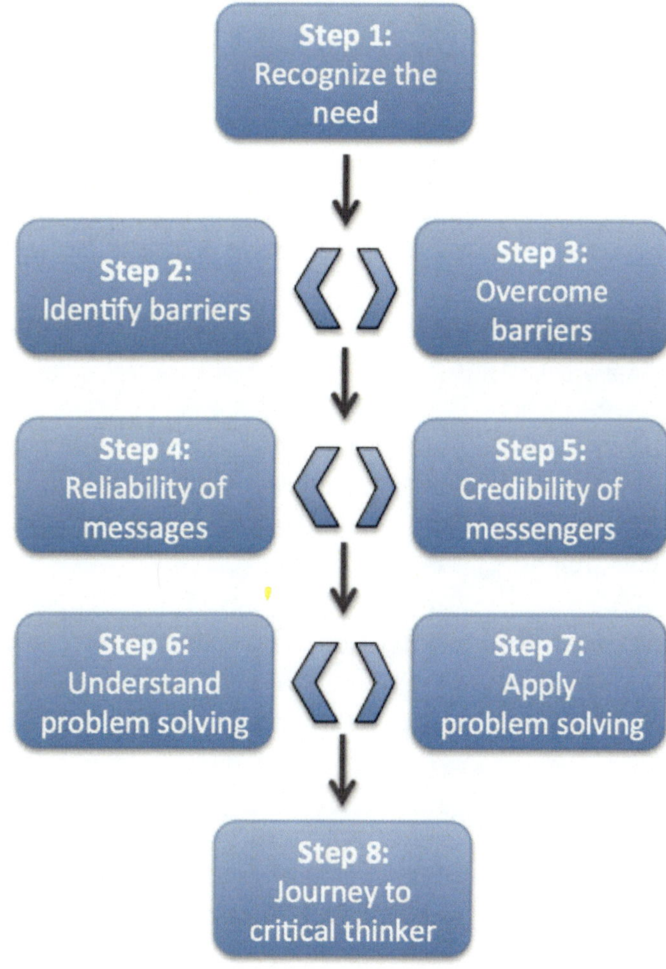

Figure 1.6
The 8-Step Critical Thinking Process

A CONCLUDING THOUGHT

Critical thinkers come in all different shapes and sizes. They can be conservative, moderate, or liberal. Poor, middle class, or wealthy. Religious or not. Adore football and skydiving or fancy opera and poetry. Some are highly educated and started their studies early in life, while others have no formal schooling in critical thinking and only recently embarked on their journey to become critical thinkers.

Yes, critical thinkers represent one of the most diverse populations of people you'll ever encounter – transcending all barriers and boundaries.

That stated, critical thinkers share a wide variety of traits and characteristics. Just as all human beings possess the same genetic constitution, critical thinkers all proceed through their personal and professional lives in the same way.

Unlike other people, who mosey through life guided by common sense and intuition (whatever that means), critical thinkers employ a systematic process when:

- Identifying barriers to critical thinking and devising strategies to modify or replace them
- Evaluating the reliability of information and "sizing up" the credibility of people who offer it
- Attempting to make sound decisions and effectively solve problems

And – critical thinkers employ this systematic process **all the time**.

For critical thinkers – structure replaces randomness. Order trumps chance. And data generated by reliable and credible research takes precedence over unsubstantiated information originating from "who-knows-where" and from "who-knows-who." That's a huge difference from the methods and mindsets that characterize unreflective thinkers.

And to remind you again – critical thinkers adhere to their profile all the time.

Now tell me – do you want to become such a person? Think carefully – just as a critical thinker would.

Let me make your decision a little easier by helping you weigh the disadvantages and advantages of becoming a critical thinker. Below please find some content in each category, with corresponding counter positions.

Disadvantages of becoming a critical thinker:

- You might have to abandon some of your opinions because the facts demonstrate them to be untrue.
    - Counter – identifying and eliminating opinions that are incorrect would be a good thing, no? Why would you want your reservoir of knowledge to be contaminated by false, unsubstantiated points-of-view?
- The time and effort required to become a critical thinker.
    - Counter -- Yes, developing your critical thinking skills won't come easy. But what good things in life ever do? The key deciding factor will be the "Return On Investment" (ROI) you experience from becoming a critical thinker. What value would you place on being successful in your professional and personal life? Recall the extra compensation, desirable office space, vacations, and lovely

home I discussed at the beginning of this chapter. Wouldn't those desired outcomes be worth studying late into the evening and occasionally missing a party? I would think so.

- Some of your friends might be "put off" when you question the opinions they hold dear.
    - Counter – why would you want to hang out with people who possess unsubstantiated and misinformed points-of-view? Just to be accepted? To be popular? Those reasons might be appropriate for an unreflective thinker, but certainly not for someone who aspires to become a critical thinker. Wouldn't you agree?

Advantages of becoming a critical thinker:

- Critical thinking will help you learn by asking specific, relevant questions and considering alternative (even opposing) points-of-view.
    - Counter – none.
- Critical thinking will help you identify the barriers that inhibit you from developing your critical thinking skills – and develop strategies on how to modify or replace them.
    - Counter – none.
- Critical thinking will help you determine the reliability of information and the credibility of people who provide it – making you less vulnerable to people who want you to adopt opinions and behave in ways that advance their interests – not yours.
    - Counter – none.
- Critical thinking will help you make better decisions and more effectively solve problems.
    - Counter – none.
- Critical thinking will help you develop skills related to empathy, integrity, honesty, and being fair-minded.
    - Counter – none.

So – what's it going to be? Become a critical thinker – or not?

The decision, of course, is ultimately yours – it's your life to decide how you want to live it. I can only speak for myself – and I've benefited tremendously from developing my critical thinking skills over the years (as have thousands of my students).

As you will learn in Chapter 2 – I had little or no formal training in critical thinking while growing up. None. I didn't ask questions or listen attentively to people who had the answers. Nor did I evaluate information or weigh options before making decisions or solving problems. I believed whatever I read and whatever I heard from people on television, in the classroom, and from my family and friends. All done automatically – almost without question. **I was about as opposite of a critical thinker as a person could be. Imagine that.**

But something magical and transformational happened to me a long time ago.

It's beyond the scope of this introductory chapter to detail how I was able to depart the heavily populated ranks of unreflective thinkers – and gain entry into the exclusive club of critical thinkers. I will share my story at some point in this book – just hang around long enough to find out. How's that for a tease? And believe me, if I became a critical thinker – you most certainly can, as well. How's that for motivation? Here's my challenge to you.

Seize the moment. Become truly engaged in the process of becoming a critical thinker – rather than being a mere spectator and simply going through the motions. Read this textbook with that purpose in mind, not simply because it's required for your course. Do that – and you'll be deeply rewarded.

Onward – and again, "Welcome To Your New World of Thinking."

Everyday Life with David

"Day 5: My Immediate Plan"

I guess Dr. Ridel was right when he said that I'm not the critical thinker I think I am. Fortunately, I'm an optimist – and I firmly believe I'll steadily improve my critical thinking skills over the next 30 days. Remember, that's how long it takes to develop a habit. And here's how I'm going to accomplish that important goal.

To begin with, I'm going to read the textbook with a high degree of focus and dedication. Second, I'm going to discuss what I learn with my family and friends. Third, I'm going to apply critical thinking concepts to my everyday life. And finally, I'm going to guard against falling back into my old, unreflective ways of thinking.

I don't know about you, but I'm fired up about what's in store for me next. I can't wait to read the rest of the textbook. I hope you feel the same.

One more page, one more chapter, one more step closer to becoming a critical thinker.

Chapter 2
Barriers To Critical Thinking: Who Are They?

Our ability to think critically isn't certain – it's under constant siege by forces that would rather us not.

Robert W. Ridel, Ph.D.

All of us were born human. No question. Imagine how shocked our parents would have been, as well as the delivering physician, if we were born as a baby giraffe, turtle, or monkey. Really – can you imagine the look on their faces if you entered the world as a giraffe? They'd be in shock – and in desperate need of immediate medical attention.

Oh – we were born human, make no mistake about it – and from the very beginning we acted just as we were genetically programmed to behave. We cried for whatever reason, pooped at inopportune times, sucked on any object within reach, and smiled on cue – or so our parents thought. No eating leaves on trees (giraffes), swimming in bodies of water (turtles), or swinging from branches (monkeys) for us. No way. Just didn't happen. Instead, we did a lot of "stuff" infants are supposed to do.

But we didn't "think."

Surprised, aren't you? Come on – admit it, you really believe infants can think. Don't you? I promise not to tell anyone. It will be our secret. Again, promise.

But the fact is, despite what you and some (most?) other people "think" – no bona-fide research exists that demonstrates infants think. None. Forget what your friends or relatives told you, and disregard what the media wants you to believe (to sell magazines and entice you to watch talk shows). From a critical thinking perspective – the belief that infants think is simply not supported by the facts.

And the same can be said about the belief that critical thinking is widespread. Most people think they're critical thinkers, just as you did before completing Step 1 in the "Eight-Step Process to Critical Thinking" outlined in Chapter 1. But they really aren't critical thinkers. Yes, they can think – just not critically. And yes, they have the potential to think critically – but usually don't realize it.

Why?

For a one-word question – you'd think the answer would be easy to figure out. But it isn't.

Indeed, academics have debated the "why" question for decades – and still haven't reached a consensus on why most people are unreflective (rather than critical) thinkers. Some fault biological dysfunctions, while others blame inadequate learning environments. Still another group combines both of these viewpoints to explain why most people don't think critically. And the divergence of opinion continues.

So – where do I stand on this so-called nature-nurture debate?

Well, I studied the "why" question throughout my academic career – and for me, the decision has always been a veritable "no-brainer" (no pun intended).

By way of full disclosure, I wholeheartedly embrace the position that the social environment (as contrasted to its biological counterpart) influences whether people become critical thinkers, or not. Biological functioning is important, to be certain. But in my view, the type of social environment people experience ultimately determines what type of thinker they become – unreflective or critical.

Simply stated:

- If people are raised in learning environments that discourage critical thinking, they will likely become unreflective thinkers.
- If people are raised in learning environments that promote critical thinking, they will likely become critical thinkers.

Duh.

So much for the nature-nurture debate.

The answer to the "why" question is no more complicated than that. Most people are unreflective thinkers because they were socialized in learning environments that thwarted them from becoming critical thinkers. Again, "simple" as that.

My immediate responsibility in this chapter is to help you identify what barriers prevent you from developing your critical thinking skills and then, in Chapter 3, explain how they can be modified and replaced. In essence, my task is to help you understand the "thwarting process" so you can extricate (remove) yourself from it and move down a path toward becoming a critical thinker.

THE PUPPETEER THEORY

Of course, I'd like to take credit for answering the "why" question, but academic ethics compel me to acknowledge the real architect of the solution. Let me introduce you to:

The Puppeteer.

The Puppeteer is the central figure in a theory I developed long ago to address the "why" question; namely, why most people are unreflective (rather than critical) thinkers. It highlights the far-reaching influence the social environment exerts on us when it comes to what we think and whether we think critically, at all. With respect to the "why" question, the Puppeteer Theory advances the notion that shaping agents within the social environment (not biological) serve as barriers that impede people from becoming critical thinkers.

To better understand how the Puppeteer Theory relates to thwarting critical thinking, try to visualize a Puppeteer manipulating a dummy through a series of strings (Figure 2.1). The Puppeteer represents society. The strings represent the shaping agents used by the Puppeteer to prevent critical thinking from taking place. Finally, the "dummy" represents – well, the dummy represents you, me, or any person who lacks critical thinking skills.

Sorry for the unflattering imagery.

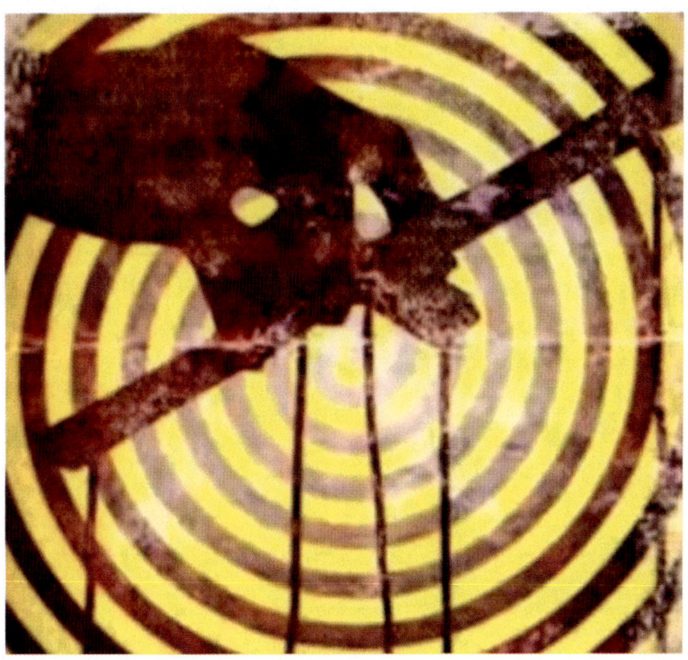

Figure 2.1
The Critical Thinking Puppeteer

Now – I know what you're thinking: "This guy must be out of his mind – thinking that some entity called the Puppeteer actually exists. What's he doing, smoking peyote? Drinking heavily? Or is he just crazy?"

No. No. And hopefully not.

What I'm trying to do is help you understand why most people are unreflective thinkers despite their insistence to the contrary. And I'm utilizing the image of a Puppeteer as a metaphor to bring life to a process that powerfully explains why this happens.

That stated, I understand why you might dismiss the Puppeteer Theory as fantasy or as being downright silly. But you shouldn't. Trust me, the Puppeteer isn't a hypothetical construct or fictional cartoon character manufactured in my imagination.

Quite the contrary, the Puppeteer absolutely exists in your everyday life – influencing not only your ability to think critically, but also other aspects of who you are as a person:

- Consider your opinions on gun control, gay rights, and climate change.
- Think about your attitudes on abortion, debt control, and the New York Yankees.
- Reflect on your values associated with marriage and the family.
- Ponder about your goals associated education and careers.

Where do you think these and other opinions, attitudes, values, and goals come from? A collection of genes located on chromosome #14? The position of stars in the galaxy?

No and no.

According to the Puppeteer Theory, your ability to think critically, like the formation of opinions, attitudes, values and goals, is influenced by your social environment and the collective actions of shaping agents that define it. Some configurations promote you to develop your critical thinking skills – while other arrangements thwart your ability to become a critical thinker. But in all cases, regardless of direction – it's the Puppeteer, acting through its shaping agents, that influences whether or not you become a critical thinker. (Sociologists refer to the process of social influence as "socialization," and psychologists study it under the heading of "social psychology.")

And that's why I selected the image of the Puppeteer to address my original question: **"Why are most people unreflective thinkers?"** I know of no other approach more thought provoking, intuitively appealing, and relevant to address the "why" question than the Puppeteer Theory.

But who are these shaping agents, specifically?

Fortunately, each one has a name – and usually a face to go with it, so identifying them (Step 2) shouldn't pose a significant challenge. Doing so will occupy our attention for the remainder of this chapter.

Once you identify the "who" (and I'm confident you will) – you'll then be in a position to modify and replace some (all?) of your barriers to critical thinking (Step 3, as discussed in Chapter 3) and progress through the remainder of the "Eight-Step Process to Critical Thinking." My hope and expectation is that successfully accomplishing each step will further your transformation from being a thinker into becoming a critical thinker.

Permanently.

But let's not get ahead of ourselves. The next step in the process of becoming a critical thinker involves identifying the "who" – the specific barriers that thwart the development of your critical thinking skills. As you already know – they're represented by the Puppeteer's shaping agents.

In this chapter, I will divide them into two broad categories – external barriers and internal barriers. By "external" I mean barriers that reside outside of you. "Internal" will refer to barriers that originate from within you.

Let's begin by working from the outside in – starting with external barriers to critical thinking and then moving onto a discussion of internal barriers.

EXTERNAL BARRIERS TO CRITICAL THINKING

Given the massive number of people who inhabit the planet (7+ billion) – I would be foolish to broadly generalize about the external barriers that apply to all of them. No way – impossible. An external barrier to someone who lives in Bulgaria or Ethiopia might not apply to a person who resides in the United States or Finland. And an external barrier to someone in Pittsburg might not be an inhibitor to a person living in Los Angeles. What's more, an external barrier to someone in Los Angeles might not be to another person in Los Angeles.

With that caveat in mind, I will discuss four external barriers (shaping agents) that probably hindered you from developing critical thinking skills while you grew up, just as they did for many other people. They are as follows:

- Family
- Friends
- Teachers
- Media

Let me use myself as a case study (when I was a child and adolescent) to briefly illustrate how external barriers can thwart the development of critical thinking skills. Far from providing me with the resources and motivation necessary to become a critical thinker – my family, friends, teachers, and the media comprised a "critical thinking desert" that shaped me into becoming a relatively unreflective thinker while growing up.

External Barrier: Family

My mother (who's still alive at 99) and father were wonderful parents, and my siblings were pretty good, as well. They provided with me a lot of attention and emotional security, as well as all the basics one typically associates with experiencing an excellent childhood and adolescence. However, I can't recall having a single conversation with them about critical thinking. Nothing around the kitchen or dining room table. No quiet chats in the living room regarding the importance of developing critical thinking skills. Absolutely none. **Great family, but not great promoters of critical thinking.**

External Barrier: Friends

I hung out with a "cool" group of peers while growing up. We'd walk to-and-from school together, rode bicycles (and eventually cars) around the neighborhood, played sports on assorted teams, and partied over the weekend like there was no tomorrow. Great memories. What fun. Oh – did I mention partying? But never, let me repeat never, did we discuss critical thinking. Yes, we'd talk about sports (favorably) and school (unfavorably). And about girls, absolutely. But not about critical thinking. Not once. **Great friends, but not great promoters of critical thinking.**

External Barrier: Teachers

I attended public schools while growing up in middle-class neighborhoods, taught by good instructors. History. English. Math (ouch). Social Sciences. You know the drill – I attended class, stared at the clock, daydreamed, and occasionally listened to what my teachers said. But even then, when I was somewhat attentive, I never heard them speak about critical thinking. Heck, if I knew anything about critical thinking at the time (which I didn't), I would have wondered (doubted?) if my teachers possessed any critical thinking skills, at all. **Good teachers, but not great promoters of critical thinking.**

External Barrier: Media

Like most other kids my age, I spent thousands of hours each year watching television – cartoons (Flintstones), game shows (Dating Game), and athletic events (New York Giants). I also enjoyed going to the movies – science fiction (2001: A Space Odyssey), action (007: James Bond), and mysteries (Sherlock Holmes). Unfortunately, although such experiences were entertaining – they hardly stimulated me to develop my critical

thinking skills. I didn't watch the news, nor read newspapers or journals. Never heard of them. No way. **Good media, but not great promoters of critical thinking.**

* * * * *

With the above information in mind – is it any wonder that I characterized my formative years as being a "critical thinking desert?" That I was a relatively unreflective thinker? Again, no surprise – given my profile of family, friends, teachers, and media.

Like other kids and young adults my age, I never asked my parents about critical thinking, and they never discussed the topic with me (even if they were capable of doing so). What's more, I didn't question what I learned from my peers, what I was taught in school, or what I was exposed to in the media. I wouldn't characterize myself as a "robot" that simply absorbed information without any skepticism or doubt. But I also wouldn't depict myself as someone who was a critical thinker. Not even close. (That would change soon – which I will discuss in Chapter 3.)

Mind you, the external barriers in my life (family, friends, teachers, and the media) weren't "bad." Actually, they were pretty decent. But while they produced a "good kid" (namely me), they didn't comprise a social environment that provided me with the resources and motivation necessary to become a critical thinker. I didn't lie, steal, do drugs (well, sort of), or hurt anyone. But I also didn't learn how to think – to really think critically.

And the same probably applies to you. Like me, you likely developed into a fine person who simply lacked well-developed critical thinking skills. That makes perfect sense. I mean – what impact did your family, friends, teachers, and the media exert on you with respect to developing critical thinking skills? Think about it – really think about it. Did you grow up in an "oasis" with flourishing vegetation that yielded the fruits of critical thinking or, like me, in a desert filled with sand, cacti, rattlesnakes, scorpions, and more sand that "chocked out" opportunities for me to become a critical thinker?

My guess – the latter.

Of course, all of this is mere conjecture on my part. Who knows – your situation might have been somewhat or even vastly different from mine. Consider the following possibilities:

- Your shaping agents might have exerted different degrees of influence on you than mine did – at certain stages of your life cycle. See Tables 2.1 and 2.2 (percentages are used for illustrative purposes only).

Table 2.1:
Degree of Influence for Shaping Agents
At Different Stages of My Life Cycle

	2	7	16	25	40	50
Family	90%	50%	20%	10%	10%	10%
Friends	0%	10%	30%	20%	40%	40%
Teachers	0%	20%	20%	40%	30%	30%
Media	10%	20%	30%	30%	20%	20%

Note that my family exerted a significant amount of influence over me during the early stages of my life – but lost impact as I aged. Same for media. On the other hand, the influence of my friends and teachers increased over time.

Table 2.2:
Degree of Influence for Shaping Agents
At Different Stages of Your Life Cycle

	2	7	16	25	40	50
Family	90%	70%	60%	50%	50%	50%
Friends	0%	10%	20%	20%	20%	30%
Teachers	0%	10%	10%	10%	0%	0%
Media	10%	10%	10%	20%	30%	20%

In this illustrative example, note that your family continued to exert significant influence over you during the early and middle stages of your life. Contrast that to the consistent low levels of influence wielded by your other shaping agents (friends, teachers, and the media).

- Your shaping agents might have positively impacted the development of your critical thinking skills – as opposed to mine who were rather "neutral."
  - **Family**: Your family might have emphasized the benefits of evaluating the reliability of information and questioning the credibility of the people who deliver it.
  - **Friends**: Your friends might have discussed the importance of becoming a critical thinker, and also served as role models who inspired you to develop your critical thinking skills.
  - **Teachers**: Your teachers might have lectured about the value of thinking critically and assigned reading material that pertained to the subject.

- **Media**: Your exposure to the media might have included sources that stimulated critical thinking, such as National Public Radio, CSPAN, and the Discovery Channel.

- Your collection of shaping agents might have been different from mine.

  Earlier I identified four external barriers that serve as shaping agents for most people – family, friends, teachers, and the media. However, I also suggested they didn't exhaust all possibilities – that the Puppeteer can enlist the services of other shaping agents to influence how people think, what they think about, and whether they think critically, at all.

  Let me share a story with you that convincingly demonstrates the point that there are other shaping agents besides family, friends, teachers, and the media. It involves the emotionally charged issue of religion.

  Before venturing into that potentially dangerous quagmire – let me clearly and unambiguously state the following: I will not focus on whether God actually exists, or on any particular religion. These topics are well beyond the scope of this textbook (and my expertise). What I'm going to discuss is how the Puppeteer and its shaping agents can influence whether someone **believes** in the existence of God. That's a huge difference from addressing whether God actually exists.

Story From Dr. Ridel

I had the good fortune to live and work overseas for almost a decade – after finishing my Ph.D. Imagine the life – a few years in Europe and several in Asia teaching at various university locations. And if that wasn't enough, I'd travel the world in-between terms and during summer months. Was I living the life, or what?

One of my first trips was to the People's Republic of China. I flew from Tokyo to Shanghai and spent three days there before traveling to Beijing. As luck would have it, I befriended a Chinese lady who served as my tour guide around the city. Interestingly, but not surprisingly, she was a member of the Communist Party. Not knowing much about communism, and being the type of person who adores learning, I peppered her with dozens of questions about politics and economics under the existing communist and socialist system. Great conversations – complete with lots of learning opportunities and confirming evidence that convinced me I was lucky to be an American.

In any event, I was so consumed with her answers, that I didn't think about asking her if she had any questions of me. So the night before I departed Shanghai for Beijing, I invited her to inquire about anything related to the United States – our government,

economy, and general way of life. Believe it or not, she asked me only one question. Can you imagine that – just one question? And it was the following:

> *"How can you Americans be so smart? Landing people on the Moon, winning so many Noble Prizes, and still believe in something that clearly doesn't exist – God?"*

You can imagine how floored I was with the question. I never expected it, although I should have given that "atheism" was (and still is) the official doctrine of the People's Republic of China. I proceeded to answer her question as best I could – and the next morning departed Shanghai for Beijing and other adventures.

Well – I thought about her question for many years (and still do), mostly about how her shaping agents influenced her to become an atheist. The Puppeteer in her life (family, friends, teachers, media – and government) conspired to create a person who simply didn't believe in the existence of God. The process that impacted her thinking made sense to me. And I also understood her confusion about how a great nation (United States), populated by talented people – could possibly believe such "nonsense" to be true?

But that's only part of the story.

I also learned that the same process works in the other direction – that the Puppeteer, operating through its shaping agents, can "create" people who believe in the existence of God. Let me briefly explain.

One of my dearest friends, who lives in Portland, Oregon – is a devotedly religious person. I trust him with the same level of confidence that I assign to the Earth being sound and securely situated on its axis. One day, while we were eating lunch – I experienced an epiphany. An experience of deep insight that dramatically altered my thinking about religion.

Here is a brief excerpt – expressed as comparative questions about the woman I met in Shanghai and my friend in Portland:

- Why were their views on religion so different?
- What conditions prevailed in their respective social environments that produced such different opinions on religions?
- How would their views change if their shaping agents were different?

My "aha" moment came when I realized that my Chinese acquaintance's Puppeteer influenced her in the same way that my American friend was influenced by his Puppeteer – but only in a different direction. Each Puppeteer was effective in

influencing their thinking on the subject of religion – but transformed them into believing radically divergent views on whether or not God existed.

How interesting.

And here's the thought that will forever drive my thinking on the subject of religion. Imagine how different they would have become if they were born and raised in each other's environment? If they were influenced by the opposite Puppeteer? She probably would have become a devotedly religious person, while he would have probably become an atheist.

Interesting, indeed.

Again, the above illustration isn't offered to address the actual existence of God, or focus attention on any particular religion. Rather, I present the story to illustrate that the Puppeteer possesses a vast stable of shaping agents – that includes more than just family, friends, teachers, and the media. As my example clearly demonstrates, religion can also influence what and how we think. And it also demonstrates that government can serve that function, as well.

In other words, **the Puppeteer is an equal opportunity influencer.**
Regardless of whether you're religious or an atheist, a capitalist or socialist, baseball fan or opera enthusiast, or lover of Italian or Thai food – the Puppeteer was, is, and always will be a central figure associated with the development of your attitudes, opinions, values, and goals, just as it was, is, and always will be a significant player when it comes to your ability to think critically. The sooner you learn this lesson – the better off you'll be when it comes to evolving from being a thinker into becoming a critical thinker.

And learn you have.

You now recognize that you need to improve your critical thinking skills (Step 1, as I discussed in Chapter 1), and you also understand that you need to identify the external barriers that inhibit you from developing them (Step 2, as discussed in this chapter). These breakthroughs place you squarely on a path to modifying and replacing some (all?) of your barriers to critical thinking (Step 3, which I will discuss in Chapter 3), and acquiring the skills necessary to continue through the remainder of the "Eight Step Process to Critical Thinking" (Steps 4–8, which I will discuss in Chapters 4–8).

Congratulations – well done. You should feel proud.

Well – not so fast. Hold the applause.

Step 2 is only half complete. Indeed, there's an additional set of barriers that you must identify (and then eventually modify or replace) if you're going to become a critical thinker.

Yes, believe it or not – the Puppeteer has an ally. Another barrier to join forces with its army of external shaping agents. And you'll never guess who it is. Are you ready? OK – here you go:

The Puppeteer's partner in impeding you from becoming a critical thinker is none other than...

YOU.

Read on – if you dare.

Everyday Life with David
"Day 8: My Battles with External Barriers"

Everybody has battled external barriers to critical thinking – and I'm no exception. One of my most meaningful experiences took place when I attended university as an impressionable young man straight out of high school. I encountered a smorgasbord of shaping agents – an intimidating campus, influential friends, unrelenting professors, and a few other unmentionables. Wow – did they do a number on me. It's a miracle I made it through with some degree of sanity.

Regrettably, none of these influences helped me become a better critical thinker.

I now realize that my family, friends, teachers, and media impeded my development as a critical thinker. How could I have been so unaware of their molding and shaping influences? Now that I see them for who they are, I'm much more diligent about filtering out their "puppeteering power" over me.

I look forward to learning how to deal with my shaping agents over the remainder of the course.

INTERNAL BARRIERS TO CRITICAL THINKING

I'm sorry to be the purveyor of unsettling news, but as I suggested a moment ago, you have another adversary to identify and confront in your quest to become a critical thinker. **YOU.** That's right – you read that correctly. Let me repeat: **YOU**.

How ironic – that you must battle yourself, as well as contend with the external shaping agents discussed earlier (family, friends, teachers, and media), in order to become a critical thinker. Ironic, indeed.

I bet you're thinking:

> *"My goodness. Not only do I have to overcome external barriers, but I also have to battle myself? No wonder most people don't develop the skills necessary to become critical thinkers. The cards are really stacked against me – and them."*

If that's what you're thinking, my response would be something like the following:

> *"Yes – developing critical thinking skills won't be an easy, straightforward process. But think about what you've already learned, and consider all the benefits you'll experience by becoming a critical thinker. Stay the course. Remain focused and motivated. And trust me – your return on investment (ROI) for doing so will be worthwhile."*

To help you through the process, I compiled an abbreviated list of internal barriers for you to review. Take a deep breath and prepare yourself for a reality check. My guess is you'll readily identify with each item contained on the list.

While reading the following pages – keep in mind why it's important for you to identify and deal with your internal barriers. Like their external counterparts – they play a powerful role in thwarting your ability to become a critical thinker. As in "war," it's important to know your enemy – even if the "enemy" is you. **The fact is, unless you recognize that you're part of the problem, you'll never be able to reach your objective** – which, in this case, is to become a critical thinker.

<u>Internal Barrier: Rationalizing</u>

Yes, yes – I know, I know. You're a rational thinker (or at least think you are). You make sound, lucid decisions, as well as devise and implement wise, sensible strategies to solve problems. Yes – I get it. But you know me – as a critical thinker, I won't automatically accept your position without challenging it (at least a bit).

So – let me ask you a question:

> *"Have you ever justified your opinions or excused your behavior – even if they turned out to be wrong and damaging? If so – you're rationalizing (as opposed to being rational). And that's a significant internal barrier to you becoming a critical thinker."*

Consider the following examples.

Tom cheats on his wife, falsifies information on his tax returns, steals an expensive sweater from a high-end store, and cheats on the psychology tests he takes in school.

If challenged by others (or himself) – do you think Tom would admit that he desecrated the sanctum of marriage? Confess he broke the law? Concede he's a thief? Acknowledge he violated academic principles of honesty and the student code of conduct?

No – not a chance.
Instead, Tom will justify and excuse (rationalize) his actions on each count – confidently stating the following:

- "An affair will actually benefit my marriage. And besides, everyone else is doing it – including women."
- "Companies lie on their tax returns all the time – and so do my friends. I'm just doing what everyone else does."
- "The store rips me off on other items – I'm just taking back what I overpaid on them."
- "I've seen other students plagiarize and get away with it. Besides, I have to maintain a high GPA otherwise I'll lose my financial aid and will have to drop out of school."

As unacceptable as these rationalizations might be to you and most people – they're perfectly acceptable (rational) to Tom. In effect, he justifies his behavior as an adulterer, criminal, thief, and cheater – so that his behavior isn't in conflict with his thinking that he is a good family man, law-abiding citizen, honest shopper, and ethical student. Far from evaluating his behavior as "wrong," he actually judges his actions as acceptable or even noteworthy.

Psychologists refer to inconsistencies between behavior and thinking as "dissonance" – and theorize that people are motivated to reduce conflict by changing their behavior or modifying how they evaluate it. Seems odd, yes – but the tendency to rationalize is really quite "normal." And it's effective, too – dissonance simply disappears from the minds of those who experience it. **Ah, the games people play in their respective heads.**

Seems like a great strategy for Tom to adopt and implement, doesn't it? By skillfully navigating his way through the psychological waters of self-deception – Tom not only obtains what he wants, but also feels good about doing so. He emerges with a "sexual conquest," extra money, a nice sweater, and better grade – with no sense of guilt or remorse. Tom is free and clear – or so he thinks.

Unfortunately, rationalizing tends to cloud one's ability to rationally evaluate intended actions, especially consequences that will ensue from taking them. People want to maintain favorable self-perceptions so much – that their thinking becomes distorted and short-sighted. Deplorable behavior is perceived as acceptable, if not downright necessary and obligatory – and is vigorously defended with a high-level of delusional creativity. The ends are seen to justify the means – even when they don't. It's a psychological trap that often generates unfavorable outcomes. At some point, reality exposes rationalizations to be untrue and, importantly, penalizes people who employ them.

And that's precisely what happened to Tom – whose heavy reliance on rationalizations ultimately caught up to him:

- His wife filed for divorce
- The IRS is investigating his finances
- He's been charged with shoplifting
- He was recently expelled from the university

A quadruple "ouch" for Tom.

Bottom Line: People tend to be rationalizing, not rational – which seriously compromises their ability to think critically. **That's why rationalizing is an internal barrier.**

Internal Barrier: Emotions

Your state of mind, physical health, and the amount of stress you experience can negatively impact your ability to think critically. But none of these are as consequential as your emotions when it comes to hindering your development as a critical thinker.

Here are two "formulas" to consider:

E > R → BO
R > E → GO

Let me translate them for you:

> "**E**" (Emotions) over "**R**" (Reason) leads to **BO** (**B**ad **O**utcomes)
> "**R**" (Reason) over "**E**" (Emotions) leads to **GO** (**G**ood **O**utcomes)

Mind you -- I'm not suggesting emotions are an unimportant or unnecessary part of your everyday life. Quite the contrary, experiencing feelings and passion is what separates us from all other life forms in the animal kingdom. It's what makes us human. What I am suggesting is that there's a time and place for everything, including being emotional – and some times and some places are not the right times and right places. On those occasions, following one's emotions can be counterproductive and downright damaging.

Consider dating.

Did you ever let your emotions (desires, impulses) get the best of you while "making out" at Lover's Lane or on the couch in the living room? Were you caught up in the heat of the moment? Did you go too far – and regret doing so in the morning?

And think about shopping.

Did you ever purchase something because you absolutely couldn't live without it?

> *"The jeans look so great – I simply have to purchase them.*
> *And the good news – they only cost $250. What a bargain."*

How did you feel the next morning when you experienced an intrusion of reason – commonly known as "buyer's remorse?" Or when you opened the credit card bill later in the month and noticed a balance the size of a small country's national debt?

Of course, "lovers" and marketers strategically understand all of this, and are experts at enticing people to temporarily suspend their reason (and critical thinking skills) and capitulate (surrender) to their emotions. Stated more graphically, manipulators are tremendously skilled at pulling at our "heart strings" and "purse strings" to benefit their own interests and disadvantage our lives.

The point is this: Emotions can suppress critical thinking from taking place. As is the case with rationalizations, they can short-circuit people's ability to carefully evaluate intended courses of action and the consequences that will result from taking them.

Keeping the above scenarios in mind, how do you think life typically ends up for people whose behavior is driven more by emotion than reason? They might live a wonderful, happy, carefree existence – but only for a relatively brief period. Then the penalties induced by emotions would begin to pile up – broken hearts, financial bankruptcy, and

so on. Unfortunately, the negative consequences caused by a lack of reason long outlast the short-term thrills associated with emotionally driven behavior.

Pretty gloomy depiction, isn't it?

Bottom Line: Emotions often win the "mental tug of war" played out with reason, and as such, thwart the development of critical thinking. **That's why emotions are an internal barrier.**

Internal Barrier: Stubbornness

Have you ever noticed that all 16-year-olds have one fundamental trait in common – they're never wrong? Brings back memories, eh? Before you scoff at the notion, consider what you were like at 16 years of age. Your friends were wrong. Your teachers were wrong. And most assuredly, your parents were wrong. But not you – you were never wrong. You were always right, and very stubborn about it.

Are you smiling? I don't know about you – but I certainly am because the point I'm making brings back a lot of memories of me being stubborn when I was 16.
For example, I recall "arguing" with a high school teacher of mine about the importance of math. Day-in-and-day-out we'd debate the point. I'd forcefully state the following:

> *"I'm never going to use this 'stuff' – you'll see, never going to happen. Not a chance."*

Not surprisingly, he would respond:

> *"Wait and see – you'll use math throughout your life, especially in your career."*

Well – guess who was correct?

I was right because I seldom if ever use math in my everyday life. In fact, if you looked at my 10-year old calculator in my office – you'd find the keys practically brand new, except for the addition and subtraction buttons. Admittedly, I use them a lot – but that's about it. My fingers seldom wander over to the multiplication key – and practically never to the division button. Nope – math and I just don't get along. Sound familiar?

But guess what – my high school teacher was correct, as well.

> *"How can that be,"* you ask? *"How could both of you be right?"*

Well – my high school teacher was right because learning math influenced me to think in a certain way – with structure and diligence. Indeed, as it turns out, I'm very organized in my thinking, as well as meticulous, attentive to detail, and obsessively compulsive about "things adding up" (pun intended). I'm also a dogged fan of preparation, tremendously systematic in my approach to life (generally defined), and on a good day/evening logical. Yes – as it turned out, studying math dramatically improved the way I think today.

So we were both right.

"But what does all of that have to do with stubbornness as an internal barrier to critical thinking?" you ask.

Another good question.

Here's my answer.

Even though I wasn't a great critical thinker at the time, I was "smart" enough (even in high school) to realize that my teacher was probably correct – that learning math would improve my problem solving and decision making skills and eventually influence the way I would live my life. But did I agree with him? Yield to his position? Take additional math classes that would have advanced my ability to think? No way – absolutely not. I was stubborn – in the truest sense of the word. I became defensive (emotional) and dismissed all the good points my teacher raised. I simply dismissed (rationalized away) his reasoning. Instead of admitting I was wrong, I stubbornly remained committed to my point of view – even though, deep inside, I knew his position was solid.

Who knows what I would have accomplished if I took his advice seriously. My goodness – he was correct. My goodness – wasn't I a stubborn 16-year-old?

Let me provide you with another example of how being stubborn can thwart the development of critical thinking skills.

I encounter stubbornness on the part of many students when teaching introductory critical thinking courses (like the one you're taking now). The first week is usually challenging for several of them. No – they don't throw their laptops against the wall, curse my name, or march down to the registrar's office and drop the class (at least I hope not). But they do push back when I challenge their perceived ability to think critically (recall the information I presented in Chapter 1).

And why shouldn't they be stubborn on that point? After all, most students arrive to class believing they're already critical thinkers – probably because no one was candid enough to inform them otherwise. Certainly not their family, friends, teachers, or media (remember my discussion of external barriers to critical thinking offered earlier in this

chapter). With that in mind, it makes perfect sense that my students would stubbornly believe they are critical thinkers.

Fortunately, many of my students eventually realize they need to develop their critical thinking skills. And when that moment comes – it's magical. Absolutely magical.

For a split nanosecond, they stop drinking their lattes and eating their pizza, as well as cease reading whatever non-classroom material is displayed on their laptops. Instead, they start thinking about the need to develop their critical thinking skills. Nothing pleases me more, and I mean nothing, than noticing that look in their eyes – that "ton of bricks" gaze of realization. Epiphany. Breakthrough. Eureka. For them – stubbornness (on critical thinking, at least) is a thing of the past.

It's something I hope you experience many times while reading this textbook and proceeding through your education.

But sadly – some of my students never get it. I can see the opposition (stubbornness) in their body language that conveys the following non-verbal signals of stubborn resistance:

> *"What's he talking about? I've been thinking critically for my whole life. I'm free to think whatever I want to think. Do whatever I want to do. Nobody influences or controls me. I can't wait for this class to be over."*

Instead of concentrating on what I'm discussing in class, they happily return to their lattes and pizza, e-Harmony.com (or other Internet dating websites) on their laptops, and stare not so subtly toward the clock as if forcing the minute and hour hands to move more quickly. For them – it's game, set, and match. They lose. An important opportunity to learn has been missed – which means they'll likely remain doomed to a life of unreflective thinking defined by all the penalties and disappointments that come with it.

Sad, indeed.

Bottom line: A "know-it-all" mentality and misplaced arrogance makes the development of critical thinking skills virtually impossible. **That's why being stubborn is an internal barrier to critical thinking.**

Internal Barrier: Biases

Life, as we experience it, certainly isn't neutral or impartial. Whether we're dealing with relatively mundane issues or matters of extreme importance, our observations and impressions are never fully objective. Never. Being biased is simply the "baggage of life." It's a defining characteristic of our existence – just like the air we breathe.

"Really – how can that be?"

Good question – just what you should be asking as an aspiring critical thinker.

The fact is everyone acquires biases from their own unique life experiences. Our understanding of everyday life is ultimately created and fine-tuned by several factors, most notably by the social interactions we have with other people. And they, more than any other factor, bias our opinions and points-of-view – making it virtually impossible for us to remain completely objective in our thinking.

Pretty interesting, eh?

Even more interesting (unsettling) is the fact that biases often develop without the informational infrastructure to support them. Indeed, people tend to be biased for or against "this and that," even though they possess precious little understanding about "this and that." Consider:

- Climate Change:
  - Some people believe industry and human expansion are destroying the environment, while other people believe that climate change is a natural part of the Earth's cyclical evolution.

- Government Support:
  - Some people believe that Federal and State assistance programs (i.e. housing subsidies, unemployment benefits, food stamps) represent the country's greatest "call to action," while others believe that social programs are leaches on the U.S. economy.

- Terrorism:
  - Some people believe the global terrorist threat isn't real – that the danger is exaggerated to justify war in the Middle East, while others believe that terrorism is a real threat to the U.S. homeland and we need to strike terrorists preemptively.

- Healthcare:
  - Some people believe that access to affordable healthcare should be a right of every U.S. citizen, while others believe that healthcare is a drain on U.S. taxpayers, eliminates choice, and is simply broken and ill conceived.

Now, let me ask you: How many of these people truly understand the issues they support (or reject)? My guess, if it means anything, is probably not many. Just ask them and I'll wager you'd be unimpressed by their answers. And still, they remain cemented to their biased opinions – vigorously supporting (rationalizing) them and stubbornly refusing to consider alternative points-of-view.

And if that wasn't enough, the situation worsens when biased opinions are intensified by shaping agents (think of politicians) who purposely distort "facts" in order to promote actions that benefit them, not us. Misinformation. Half-truths. Downright lies. Mind you, it doesn't matter what side is "making a pitch" – both offer questionable information to further our commitment to their points-of-view. It happens all of the time – and massively weighs the "baggage" we carry as we proceed through our everyday lives.

All of that reminds me of a story I'd like to share – it's pertinent and I think you'll enjoy learning about it.

I had the good fortune to live overseas for nearly a decade (Europe, Asia). No Internet existed in those times, and I was mostly reliant on the radio to get my daily fix of the news. I would go to bed each night with an AM radio nearby – listening to Radio Moscow, China Radio International, BBC, Armed Forces Radio, and Voice of America discuss various political and economic issues. I was amazed how each presented dramatically different spins for the same story. The Soviets and Chinese had one slant, while the British and Americans had another – each offering radically divergent points-of-view. Talk about biased reporting.

Interestingly, I encountered a similar situation when I returned to the United States. I listened to the radio (and watched television) – and was intrigued with the different slants Republicans and Democrats had for the same story. And that "spin divergence" continues today. Talking heads tell me (and you) about "this" on FOX, while commentators provide information about "that" on MSNBC – with CNN occupying someplace in the middle (or so they claim). Biased reporting, again – on the same story.

What an unbelievable "war of biases."

The problem isn't that all of us have opinions. Opinions, in general, are fine. Opinions become problematic when they lack factual foundation, and when people vigorously support them by kowtowing (yielding) to the not-so-subtle influence exerted by their shaping agents. That's when mere opinions cross the line and become biases.

Bottom Line: Unsubstantiated opinions block the fundamental tenets of critical thinking, such as questioning and evaluating. **That's why biases are an internal barrier to critical thinking.**

* * * * *

So be honest – how many of the before mentioned internal barriers apply to you? None, some, several, all? Before you answer, let me inform you that the "gig" is up. The question is only rhetorical – because I already know the answer. If you're honest, it has to be that all of them apply to you. As they do to me – and everyone else. Remember what I said at the beginning of this section – that **YOU**, as the internal barrier, represent a substantial impediment to becoming a critical thinker. In order for you to achieve that goal, your tendency to be rationalizing, emotional, stubborn, and biased need to be modified and replaced, just like the external barriers I discussed earlier (family, friends, teachers, and the media).

So – are you up for it? Can't hear you. Ah – just as I thought. Good. Let's proceed.

A CONCLUDING THOUGHT

The best way to conclude this chapter is to return to the beginning. Do you remember my opening quote?

> *"Our ability to think critically isn't certain – it's under constant siege by forces that would rather us not."*

Does that statement make better sense now? It should – given what you learned about external and internal barriers, and how they influence whether people develop their critical thinking skills.

That stated, I'm not convinced that you've integrated the meaning of the quote – at least not entirely (you know us critical thinkers – always questioning what people claim). After all, the position I'm advancing is considered utter heresy by many of my students – and I can't expect a textbook, much less one or two chapters, to counter what took them decades to learn and believe – that they're critical thinkers. And you're probably no different.

As such, I want to drive the point more forcefully.

You can believe in leprechauns, but that doesn't mean they actually exist. You can believe that 3 + 5 = 14, but that doesn't mean it does. Yes, you can believe whatever you want, even that fictional creatures exist and that you're a whiz at mathematics. But that doesn't mean your beliefs and opinions are true.

And the same applies to the belief that you're a critical thinker.

As I've emphasized several times, people are powerfully influenced by external shaping agents who reinforce unreflective thinking and, if that wasn't enough, by internal forces that thwart the development of their critical thinking skills. Recall the inhibiting influence exerted by family, friends, teachers, and the media. And you mustn't forget the counterproductive consequences associated with being rationalizing, emotional, stubborn, and biased. The barriers that define your everyday life collectively represent a "double whammy" that's not easily overcome – no matter how strongly you believe that you're a critical thinker.

The good news is that, given time, many of my students entertain the possibility that external and internal barriers impede their ability to become critical thinkers. Importantly, after reaching that conclusion – most of them become committed to doing something about it. Good for them.

How about you?

Have you accepted the fact that external and internal shaping agents impede your development as a critical thinker? And if so, are you equipped to apply your newly acquired skills to modify and replace them? If you're not certain, consider the following cautionary note:

> *"Unless you act, all of the important skills you learned will drift into limbo. They'll count for naught. Without action – you won't become a critical thinker, nor will you achieve the desired goals I alluded to in Chapter 1, including working in a wonderful career, travelling the world, purchasing a comfortable home, and earning desirable compensation. Remember?"*

My challenge is in place. You know what the "whammies" are – now it's time for you to act. Are you up for it? I hope so.

Ready, set, **ACTION**.

Everyday Life with David

"Day 10: My New Puppeteer"

This critical thinking journey has taught me so much already.

As I reflect on my life, I realize that my external and internal barriers have caused a lot of chaos for me, including disrupting the development of my critical thinking skills.

Even more powerful is the unexpected and sudden realization that I am one of my own worst enemies. As an internal barrier myself, I stand in the way of achieving my dreams – a better career, nicer home, and opportunities for travel. Completely unacceptable.

My eyes have been opened to the influence exerted by the shaping agents of the Puppeteer – and that is a staggering realization. Mind you, that's not bad. It's an important realization to make. With that recognition in mind, I'm motivated to take **action** – to overcome my barriers.

How about you?

Chapter 3
Barriers To Critical Thinking: Replacing And Modifying Them

While anything is possible, nothing is believable until the possible is supported by evidence.

Robert W. Ridel, Ph.D.

Try as you might – there's just no getting away from the Puppeteer, even if you disappear into the deserts of Africa, outback of Australia, rain forests of South America, and jungles of Asia – or hang out with penguins in Antarctica. And I would know. Other than hob-knobbing with penguins, I've visited all of those places and simply couldn't rid myself of my Puppeteer. Its influence, exerted through my shaping agents, followed me wherever I went – no matter how hard I tried to escape.

And the same probably applies to you in your everyday life.

Indeed, once the strings of the Puppeteer become connected to you, it's virtually impossible to completely free yourself from them. And for good reason. I mean – how could you, me, or anyone counteract or override learning histories that were decades in the making? That would be a lot of influence – and powerful shaping agents – to overcome.

Let me use my father as a quick illustration.

- He was a political independent (rare during his era) – and influenced me to become one, as well.
- He was a fiscal conservative (raised during the "Great Depression" in an "orphanage") – and influenced me to become one, as well.
- He was a social liberal (again, atypical during his time) – and influenced me to become one, as well.
- He was a devoted father (despite never knowing his) – and influenced me to become one, as well.

My father's favorite food was Italian – guess what mine is? His favorite sport was football and his beloved team was the New York Giants – guess what mine are? He was generous, impatient, and sarcastic. Guess how my friends would describe me. Yup – generous, impatient, sarcastic.

Heck – I even yawn like my father yawned.

And there you have it – a grand **"perpetuation of sameness"** at the hands (pun intended) of my Puppeteer.

My father was also a fervent advocate for education – and influenced me to become one, as well (just ask my children and students). The method he used to convince me about the importance of education was as creative as it was effective – and is worth offering for our immediate purposes to demonstrate the influential power of shaping agents.

Consider the following story as an example.

Story from Dr. Ridel

It was a late Friday afternoon, and I was a high school senior getting ready to go out on a date. Well, it actually wasn't going to be a real date – I just needed a story to tell my friends on Monday morning. I had an image to uphold, you know. Come on – you probably stretched the truth when you were younger, as well.

In any event, my father was home from work uncharacteristically early that day, and I needed to speak with him about a decision I reached earlier about not wanting to start college the following year. I decided that college wasn't for me – I didn't know what I wanted, but I was certain it wouldn't involve school. My father listened patiently as I explained my decision. And that was the end of that. I was liberated. No more school. Or so I thought.

So I left the house and went on my "date." I headed home around midnight and placed my key into the lock to open the front door. And guess what? Yes – you're correct. The darn key didn't fit.

> *"What the heck is going on,"* I thought to myself. *"Was I at the right house?"* Yes. *"Did I drink anything that night?"* Nothing. *"Consume any hallucinogenic substances?"* No comment (just kidding).

Yup – I was at the right house.

I wasn't much of a critical thinker back then, as I readily admitted in Chapters 1 and 2, but my reasoning ability was decent enough to figure out that my father changed the lock to the front door. And that's exactly what happened. He expressed his disagreement with my decision in a stroke of pure genius – informing me that he would "disown" me if I decided not to attend college – toss me out of the house and write me out of the family will (not that it contained much). His message was loud and clear.

And guess what? While I slept outside that evening – I thought to myself:

"You know, going to college wouldn't be such a bad idea."

Yes, my father influenced (coerced?) me to value education – and as matters turned out, I will forever be grateful to him for knocking some sense into me.

Great story, right?

Yes – my father was the quintessential (classic) shaping agent. His influence had considerable staying power with me – and still does (even though he died almost 25 years ago). But what my father wasn't – was a critical thinker.

And why should he be? After all, my father was simply a product of his social environment – just I was a product of the social environment that he (and my other shaping agents) created for me while I was growing up. In both cases, his and mine, critical thinking wasn't on the "learning menu." We unknowingly conformed to what our respective shaping agents taught us. We just didn't know any better, or never thought to ask questions about what we were being socialized to think. Stated simply (but accurately), we thought as we were raised to think; in a word, unreflectively.

Now – I'm not suggesting the social environment cements people into being unreflective thinkers (even though it frequently does). We aren't mere robots always following the dictates of our Puppeteer. To be certain, there are several examples that clearly demonstrate people can distance themselves from their shaping agents when it comes to thinking. Yes – people can change from being unreflective thinkers into becoming critical thinkers. Indeed they can.

Which begs the following question:

"How can that transition actually take place?"

At least two methods come to mind:

- Replacement of External Barriers
- Modification of Internal Barriers

Let me discuss each in turn.

EXTERNAL BARRIERS: REPLACING YOUR SHAPING AGENTS

To the extent that external barriers to critical thinking are difficult (if not impossible) to modify – you'll need to search elsewhere for a method to free yourself from their influence. Boldly stated, my suggestion is to "replace" them with shaping agents who promote (rather than inhibit) critical thinking. Yes, you read that correctly – to replace them.

There are at least two approaches to replace shaping agents:

- Self-directed
- Societal-directed

Let's consider each of these methods – highlighting how you can apply them to change the "shaping landscape" of your everyday life.

Self-Directed Replacement

Imagine if you could replace your Puppeteer. Substitute the shaping agents (external barriers) who hold you back from developing your critical thinking skills. You know – (figuratively) exchange them for other shaping agents who would actually facilitate you to become a critical thinker. How cool would that be?

I refer to that process as self-directed replacement – because the process is initiated by you.

In this form of "barrier replacement," you purposefully decide to "escape" your shaping agents and seek out alternatives who encourage you to develop your critical thinking skills. For example, you might "trade in" your parents for new ones. Not literally, of course – but you might seek out influential people (such as mentors) who take you "under their wings" to become a critical thinker, such as teachers, friends, or other members of the community.

And that's precisely what I did.

> *"OK, OK – enough of the tease, Dr. Ridel. Will you please tell me how your transformation actually took place – so I can apply what you (and others) learned to change my shaping landscape and continue my journey to become a critical thinker?"*

My pleasure – here you go.

Story from Dr. Ridel

After experiencing the "door-lock" incident I shared with you a moment ago – I needed to decide what university I would attend to continue my schooling. (Remember – getting disowned by my father wasn't an option for me. Besides, sleeping on a bench wasn't very comfortable.) My friends elected to enroll at a school located a short distance from where I lived – and everyone figured I would join them.

But for some reason, which I still can't understand, I decided not to follow my friends. My thinking, driven by whatever limited critical thinking skills I possessed at the time, must of went something like this:

> *"My family and friends shaped who I was, and I wanted to change (remember, I was a teenager at the time) – so why would I remain in a situation that directly exposed me to the same Puppeteer that exerted tremendous control over my thinking throughout my life? That wouldn't make sense."*

Fortunately, I realized I needed to get away from my Puppeteer (and its shaping agents) if I was going to have any chance of changing. Again – not a bad conclusion to reach for someone who at the time possessed limited critical thinking skills. But how would I break away from my shaping agents? The answer – I would move and attend a university in another location, which is precisely what I did.

And low-and-behold – that change in geography produced a corresponding change in me. I started to become a different person, especially when it came to critical thinking. Of course, I didn't change overnight – but the process gradually chipped away at the "old" me and progressively produced a "new-and-improved" me.

The changes I experienced became especially apparent whenever I returned home to visit family and friends. Interestingly, the closer I got to my destination – the more I reverted back to being my former unreflective thinking self. Heck, by the time I arrived home – I had almost completely metamorphosized back into the person I once was. The me of old. I found myself saying things without thinking. Offering unsubstantiated points-of-view. Not asking questions. Accepting suggestions offered by people who knew little more about a topic than I did (and maybe even less). **It was as though the Puppeteer of my youth sprang on the scene and recaptured me, again.** Which I guess it did – to an extent.

It's also interesting to note that I started to become the "new" me again – just as soon as I left my family and friends and traveled back to my new home. In the blink of an eye, as soon as I threw kisses and waved "goodbye" to them – the person who had temporarily disappeared began to resurface, again.

One other interesting observation to offer before closing this illustration.

Over the years, I noticed that visiting family and friends no longer changed me. It seems the new me finally took permanent hold. My transformation was complete (or nearly so). I must admit that I felt bad ("guilty") about distancing myself from my "shaping agents" of old, from the people who shaped my life for so many years. But if that's what I needed to do in order to become a critical thinker – so be it.

Ah – the critical thinker I was rapidly becoming.

The above story strongly supports what I stated earlier in this chapter about the social environment and how it influences the development of unreflective thinking and critical thinking. In my situation, the key was for me to replace old shaping agents who facilitated "blah-blah-blah" thinking with new shaping agents who motivated me to become a critical thinker.

In my new environment, which was populated by people who were themselves critical thinkers, I was encouraged to question and scrutinize my opinions, as well as seek out data and facts before I became committed to them. I also became receptive to other points-of-view, and applied what I learned to make better decisions and more effectively solve problems in my life. (Recall that all of these changes represent some of the defining characteristics of critical thinking – as I discussed in Chapter 1.) Importantly, I also stopped acting like a sheep who automatically believed what my friends said, "talking heads" stated on television, and what I read in the popular press.

Figure 3.1
Self-Directed Replacement

No longer would I be a "baa-baa-baa" (not to be confused with "blah-blah-blah" ☺) to my shaping agents. That type of "sheepish thinking" was being replaced with critical thinking. Review Figure 3.1 for an illustration of self-directed replacement of external barriers to critical thinking.

What it doesn't clarify is how my transformation actually took place? Specifically, what the heck happened to me when I moved away from home that changed the trajectory of my critical thinking?

Let me briefly provide some detail.

- I **replaced** my family with mentors who figuratively became my "parents" – people who guided me on how and why I needed to think critically, as well as provided me with the resources needed to improve my critical thinking skills.

- I **replaced** my friends of old with new friends who shared my interest in critical thinking. Conversations no longer revolved around memories and past experiences; instead, interactions focused more on how critical thinking will improve the quality of my life.

- I **replaced** my teachers of old, who seemed more interested in simply "going through the motions" of teaching, with professors who were "in the know" about the critical thinking process, and who willingly helped me identify my path to become a critical thinker.

- I **replaced** my media of old, which consisted mostly of game shows, sporting events, and rock-'n-roll radio stations – with viewing reputable (trustworthy) news shows, listening to award-winning radio broadcasts and, believe it or not, reading widely respected newspapers and academic journals.

In summary, I found myself under the "spell" (influence) of two radically different Puppeteers. It was an epic battle – a classic mental tug of war between them. Mind you, I didn't eliminate one Puppeteer for another – as much as I **replaced** one that thwarted the development of my critical thinking skills with another that motivated and taught me how to think critically. See Figure 3.2.

And what a difference it made (and still makes).

Figure 3.2
Puppeteer Tug-O-War

Something magical and transformational happened to me (just as I referenced at the end of Chapter 1). I was leaving the ranks of non-critical thinkers and was rapidly gaining a "toe-hold" into the world of critical thinking. With all due respect to my shaping agents of old, especially my family – I'm pleased with my "upgrade."

The transformation I underwent, by replacing my Puppeteers can be imagined as a modified version of the Puppeteer Theory discussed in Chapter 2. Critical thinking can metaphorically serve as a pair of scissors for you to "cut" the strings that attach you to your Puppeteer.

"Free at last." Pretty cool, eh?

Yes – that all makes sense, but I suspect you're wondering how in the world does the process of replacing shaping agents apply to you? I can imagine you thinking:

> *"I can't leave my family and friends. I have two young children who need my ongoing attention and I have no desire to move away from my community. Besides, I can't stop working – after all, I have a lot of bills to pay."*

Let me be clear in response.

I'm not suggesting that you disown your parents. Not at all. What I'm proposing is that you consider reconfiguring your Puppeteer so it's represented by encouraging – rather than inhibiting – shaping agents. **That's what self-directed replacement is all about.** The key will be for you to select shaping agents that motivate you to develop your critical thinking skills – and that provide you with the resources necessary to accomplish that important objective. After all, in essence, that's what I did. Nothing more, nothing less.

Now it's YOUR Turn.

Here are some possible methods to modify your external barriers without actually replacing them:

- **Family**: Encourage your parents and siblings to promote critical thinking – to emphasize the value and benefits associated with evaluating information and questioning sources. Imagine how motivating it would be to have conversations around the dining room table or on the living room couch about critical thinking. You could discuss events related to the economy, politics, and education instead of the usual fare – reality TV, pop culture, and who's dating whom. This way, you can encourage everyone in your family to think critically – which is just the type of social environment required for you to develop your critical thinking skills.

- **Friends**: Urge your friends to participate in conversations and activities that involve critical thinking – just like you did with your family above. And, like with them, doing so can go a long way to produce a social environment that encourages critical thinking. Who knows – you might be able to mentor some of your friends to become critical thinkers, themselves. Of course, another way would be to become friends with people who already are critical thinkers – or

who are at least interested in developing their critical thinking skills. Psychologists refer to this process as "social facilitation" – when other people's competencies in particular subjects or skills cause you to "raise your game." This is a great way to develop your critical thinking abilities – and do so rather quickly.

- **Teachers**: Ask your teachers to structure their learning environments around critical thinking, whenever possible. Encourage them to discuss critical thinking concepts in class, and present multi-media resources that clearly illustrate the benefits associated with asking questions and analyzing data. Teachers who offer topics, objectives, assignments, and reading material that highlight the fundamentals of critical thinking will facilitate your transition from being an unreflective thinker into becoming a critical thinker. In addition, you should consider enrolling in critical thinking classes to continuously improve your skills. Of course, doing so will expose you to shaping agents (teachers and peers) who will empower you to develop your critical thinking skills.

- **Media**: Choose your media carefully. You might not be able to change the media, per se – but you can certainly be more selective in what you watch and read. For example, make sure everything you watch on television is trustworthy, fair, and objective. You also need to exercise care when it comes to reading newspapers and magazines that promote mindless unsubstantiated dribble. That means continually evaluating the reliability of the information and the credibility of the people who deliver it. In all cases, avoid "empty calorie" television shows, movies, and magazines.

To slightly re-phrase an old adage, "*You are what you watch.*" Well, in critical thinking terms, you're also who you grow up with (family), who you hang out with (friends), and who you learn from (teachers). If your family, friends, teachers, and media are thought-provoking – you will become thought-provoking. However, if your family, friends, teachers, and media exhibit "dummy-like" tendencies – you will become a … (well, you get the point).

Now that you've learned how to initiate self-directed replacement of your external shaping agents, it's time to turn your attention to the other method of replacement; namely, societal-directed replacement. In the next section, I'll discuss how "macro" changes in society can jumpstart your critical thinking development – in much the same way as your "micro" (self-directed) replacements can.

<u>Societal-Directed Replacement</u>

The method of self-directed replacement I just addressed worked wonders for me – insofar as launching my journey to become a critical thinker. I questioned as never before. I evaluated as never before. And I was pleased with myself as never before.

But the influence my shaping agents exerted on me, albeit potent, was weak in comparison to the powerful impact I experienced from another method – which I refer to as societal-directed replacement. In this form of "thinking transformation," social movements **change the way people think** as they transform the very fabric of society. And my goodness – they certainly changed me, hugely building on the critical thinking foundation initiated by the self-directed replacement of my shaping agents.

Indeed, my world – and that of many other people my age, served as the perfect petri dish for the development of critical thinking skills. Like many other adolescents and young adults of the time (1960's and 1970's), I rebelled against my immediate shaping agents (i.e. family, friends, teachers, and the media) – and also with what was taking place in politics, education, health care, and in the prevailing economy.

It was a time when an enormous number of people were questioning and evaluating the:

- Prejudicial and discriminatory state of race relations
- Number of poor people
- Gender inequality in the workplace and at home
- State of environmental deterioration
- War in a far-away place (Vietnam)

And I joined them for the ride of my life.

Yes – moving away to school initiated the development of my critical thinking skills. But that was only the beginning. Participating in various social movements significantly propelled me forward as a critical thinker – transformed the old me (unreflective thinker) into the new me (critical thinker). Like "Miracle Grow" spurs the growth to plants, they deepened my roots (pun intended) as an aspiring critical thinker.

Now it's YOUR turn.

I suspect you're wondering how in the world does my participation in social movements decades ago apply to you? I can imagine you thinking:

> *"That's an interesting lesson in history, Dr. Ridel – but none of those social movements exist today, in my era. Yes, we still have challenges related to such areas as race relations, the environment (climate change), and poverty – but nothing like what you experienced when you were my age. How can I participate in social movements to develop my critical thinking skills when none exist?*

Au Contraire (quite the opposite) – let me respond in two ways.

First of all, there are some notable parallels between 21st Century challenges and the before-mentioned 20th Century challenges. Consider the following:

- The state of race relations.
  - While I no longer confront the National Guard and occupy administration buildings to support advances in race relations – what are you doing about racially based violence and discrimination in American cities – big and small, today?
- War.
  - While I no longer shut down freeways and squat in the middle of airport runways to protest military conflicts – what are you doing about the lingering military action in Iraq and Afghanistan, today?
- Increased poverty rates in the nation.
  - While I no longer sleep on park benches and in refrigerator boxes along with the homeless – what are you doing about rampant (widespread) poverty that exists throughout the nation (especially among children), today?
- Women's rights.
  - While I no longer march to bring attention to gender rights – what are you doing about such gender-related issues as earning inequality in the workplace and domestic violence in and around the home, today?
- Poor condition of the planet.
  - While I no longer participate in protests to save the environment – what are you doing about climate change, polluted air, and water-borne diseases, today?

Looks like my social movements of the 1960s and 1970s are evidenced today – only in a modified form. Yes, it's true – they aren't spotlighted on headline news like they used to be – but the conditions necessary to give birth to social movements are alive and well.

My second response to your quote that social movements don't exist today would be the following: The social media revolution of the 21st Century can empower you to participate in the social movements in ways that I could never have imagined in my era. Nothing like it existed in the 20th Century. Nothing. In my time, I connected with just a few people using paper cups and strings, carrier pigeons, rotary telephones, manual typewriters, and "snail mail." Heck – you have more communication power in your smartphone than NASA provided Apollo 11 astronauts during the landing on the Moon in the 1960's. Yes – that's right, in your smartphone. Imagine that.

You, on the other hand, as an aspiring critical thinker of the 21st Century – can communicate in real-time with anyone and anywhere you want. Social media effectively creates a 24x7x365 link between you and literally millions of people. New York. Tokyo. Moscow. Sydney. London. And even with people inhabiting villages in Nigeria and igloos in Antarctica. In the early morning and late in the evening. Indeed, a minute doesn't go by without you engaging with your mobile device – whether you're standing in line at

the grocery store, eating lunch at a café, or working at the office, on the train, or in the classroom.

What does all that mean?

The point that I'm trying to make, to counter your earlier quoted thinking, can be summarized in this way:

- The issues and causes that existed during my era (1960s and 1970s) are still here today, and you can participate in them as actively as I did.
- Social media can be your vehicle to engage in the social movements of your time – you don't have to confront the National Guard or shut down an airport.

Again – social media in the 21st Century can provide you with innumerable (countless) opportunities to develop your critical thinking skills, just as social movements did mine decades ago in the 20th. All that's required is for you to get involved.

Now it's YOUR turn.

Any doubts? If so, consider how social media paves the way for you to become a critical thinker:

Facebook – is the largest social media site on the planet, with over 1 billion members. This social media ecosystem allows you to connect with millions of people to ask questions and learn about varied ideas and points-of-view. All of that is important to develop a diverse collection of opinions and, as such, overcome the influence exerted by your narrow group of shaping agents. Facebook offers you tremendous growth potential – and that's what critical thinking is all about.

Twitter – is a micro-blogging site that allows you to read and share news ("tweets") in real-time. This 24x7x365 data feed can enable you to not only connect with your family and friends – but also to instantaneously collaborate with strangers about important issues. For example, Twitter allows social activists to share information about politics and economics, and gives impetus (propulsion) to coordinate their rallies and protests. In fact, Twitter has been acclaimed (praised) to be one of the forces that toppled the Mubarak regime in Egypt and the Khadafy government in Libya ("Arab Spring").

Google+ – is the second-largest social media site in the world where you can create a central identity and interact with other enhanced services in a virtual version of "Your World." This social media domain offers you the opportunity to produce – not just consume – information about an entire universe of topics, including (for our purposes) race relations, poverty, gender inequality, climate change, and war. Sounds familiar, doesn't it? In that way, Google+ empowers you to get involved in the social movements that are important to you and affect the world around you.

Word Press – is the most popular blogging platform on the web with more than 60 million websites. This social media platform provides you with a virtual stage from which you can share your views, opinions, and ideas with the rest of the world. Importantly, blogging provides you with many more critical thinking "at bats" (opportunities) to influence your way of thinking and bring about social change throughout the world. Through collaboration and the sharing of ideas, we all learn from one another – and surpass the centralized, unreflecting influence of traditional media.

In addition to these four social media behemoths (giants), there are countless other online tools you can use to develop your critical thinking skills. For example, briefly consider the following:

- **LinkedIn**
  - LinkedIn is the largest business-oriented social media service for professional networking. This type of occupational interaction opens doors to a large variety of learning opportunities and encourages you to engage with like-minded critical thinkers.
- **YouTube**
  - YouTube is the largest video-sharing website on the planet. This personalized and mobile research tool gives you complete control over what you create, see, hear, and believe. But be careful, with this great power comes a greater responsibility to enact your critical thinking filter and scrutinize the message and messengers more carefully.
- **Yelp**
  - Yelp is the most popular crowd-sourced local business reference site on the web. This powerful feedback tool delivers a simple interface to evaluate opinions, ideas, and products at anytime from anywhere – allowing you to critique, collaborate with others, and be skeptical of perfection.
- **MOOCs**
  - MOOCs are Massive Open Online Courses. This online education tool supercharges your critical thinking development by providing you with a larger, more diverse collection of mentors, including other students.

Each of these social media tools, in addition to the ones discussed above (Facebook, Twitter, Google+, Word Press), provides opportunities for you to develop your critical thinking skills.

Now it's YOUR turn.

The above information, albeit (although) briefly developed, clearly supports the position I advanced earlier; namely, that social media can serve you in the same way that social movements served me to become a critical thinker. No longer is the content of your thinking restricted (as it might have been) to certain shaping agents. Quite the contrary, because of social media – the world can become your playground for unencumbered (unrestricted) thought, questioning, reflection, and pondering.

Again, let me repeat: Social media can serve as a **potential change agent for you to become a critical thinker – just as social movements did for me decades ago.**
Yes – I stated "potential." For good reason.

Stated bluntly, you probably won't realize that potential if you restrict your usage of social media to what most people do. For example, discuss where to find a good painter for your house (Yelp), share pictures with Aunt Gertrude (Facebook), meet your friends for dinner (Twitter), and take a course on underwater basket weaving (MOOC). That's all great stuff – but it pales in comparison to the benefits you'd experience if you really unleashed the power of Twitter, Google+, Word Press, You Tube, and so on. Do so, and you'll stand a good chance of furthering your potential to become a critical thinker:

- No more "Yelping" only for dinner – use **Word Press** to write a blog discussing your position on race relations, as well
- No more "LinkedIn" only for resumes – use **Facebook** to find like-minded critical thinkers and debate climate change, as well
- No more "YouTubing" only for your pet's antics – use **Twitter** to join an organized rally and express your views on the war in Afghanistan
- No more "MOOCing" only for a class on your favorite hobby – use **Google+** to volunteer at a center for victims of domestic violence

Again, this is your moment to shine. Like me, you can experience something transformational and magical. Truthfully. Social media can be a change agent for you, as social movements did for me. But first, you must utilize the 21st Century "gifts" that are literally at your immediate disposal – via the smartphone, laptop, and tablet that are in your hand at the moment or certainly close to you. Ignore those possibilities – and you run the real risk of remaining in a prehistoric mode – metaphorically (symbolically) relying on Dixie cups and strings, carrier pigeons, and manual typewriters that defined my era for you to become a critical thinker.

Now it's YOUR turn.

Everyday Life with David
"Day 13: Bring Down the Wall"

Sometimes walls are built to keep people in and at other times to keep people out. For example, the Great Wall of China was constructed to protect a nation and keep the Huns from invading the country. The wall succeeded because of its intimidating size. To those on the outside, the Great Wall of China is insurmountably huge. So huge – it can be seen from space. Amazing.

While the Great Wall was constructed for the protection of Chinese territory, other walls end up causing a lot more harm than good. The Berlin Wall, for example, was erected to divide the country of Germany into East and West. For many years, it became a symbol of communism, tyranny, and the manipulation of a nation – tearing families apart.

The symbolism between these two famous walls and my barriers to critical thinking is powerful. As I read this textbook, I feel my "Berlin Wall" of unreflective bricks crumbling. I destroy a brick every time I demand facts and evidence from biased messengers, and when I replace an external shaping agent with one that encourages critical thinking.

It's as if Pink Floyd's famous album, "The Wall," has materialized in my everyday life. But it doesn't stop there. The more I read and the more I act, the more I construct my own "Great Wall of China" – brick by brick – around my reservoir of knowledge. I'm committed to protecting my points-of-view from the Huns of unsubstantiated opinions and non-credible messengers.

"All in all it's just another brick in the wall."
- Pink Floyd

INTERNAL BARRIERS: MODIFYING YOURSELF

Congratulations, again – for not only identifying the external barriers that impede your ability to develop as a critical thinker (Chapter 2), but also for understanding the strategies necessary to overcome them. Again, kudos to you on both counts. Such learning will serve you well as you progress along your path from being an unreflective thinker to becoming a critical thinker.

But it's too premature to celebrate – because you've only addressed one side of the process; namely, the external. Recall there's another that needs to be dealt with – the internal, represented by YOU. Focusing on one set of barriers without attending to the other is a losing formula to become a critical thinker. It will require you to address both.

My focus in this section will be to help you accomplish precisely that; namely, to concentrate on yourself as an internal barrier.

So be prepared for a battle of epic proportions – with YOU.

To lay the foundation, I will address the four internal barriers discussed in Chapter 2. Recall, if you will:

- **Rationalizing –** clouds people's ability to accurately and honestly evaluate the consequences of their behavior.
- **Emotions –** promotes people's impulsive actions that yield unwelcomed and counterproductive results.
- **Stubbornness –** stymies people's ability to modify misguided opinions and eliminate unacceptable behavior.
- **Biases –** blocks people's receptiveness to alternative points-of-view on how best to make decisions and solve problems.

Each of the above internal barriers negatively impacts your ability to think critically – and the cumulative influence of them can be absolutely devastating. Let me take a moment to consider them more extensively – and propose some methods to minimize their impact on your critical thinking.

Modifying Internal Barriers: Rationalizing

Rationalizing, as you learned in Chapter 2, exerts a negative influence on people's ability to think critically. In this unreflective mode, rationalizers tend to excuse their behavior and opinions, even if they are disputed by facts and lead to harmful consequences. And that's not good.

Plain and simple – rationalizing involves justifying what would otherwise be unacceptable actions and opinions. It's a defense mechanism people use to cope with behaving badly and possessing beliefs that contradict their perception of being good, smart, decent people. After all, they "can't" perceive their actions as being unacceptable or their self-conceptions as being "delusional." Doing so would produce an undesirable state of "psychological unpleasantness" (imbalance) – which would motivate them to distort (rationalize) their reality so it conformed to their desired perceptions of "self" (good, smart, decent). In essence, rationalizers deceive themselves into believing their behavior and points-of-view are acceptable – even if doing so involves lying to themselves.

The sad irony is the following: Even though rationalizations seem to help people cope with psychological imbalances – they tend to accomplish the opposite. Indeed, people who habitually engage in self-deceptions (rationalizations) often live very frustrated, damaged lives because they're deeply out of touch with reality and behave accordingly.

Consider the following examples:

- Meet Michael – who plays practically every gambling game known to humankind, including craps, poker, roulette, and keno. That might be acceptable if he was betting within his means. However, his gambling escapades (sprees) have placed the health and well being of his family into considerable jeopardy. Unfortunately, Michael is on the brink of bankruptcy – and doesn't have enough money to pay for his family's medical bills and children's education. Because of his rationalizing orientation, he justifies his gambling with internal dialogs such as "I can skip a few medical appointments for my kids" and "Just one more win and I can provide my wife with everything she wants." By allowing rationalizations to inhibit his critical thinking, Michael is rolling the dice on his family's future.

- In contrast to Michael, who is driven by rationalizations, let me introduce you to Juanita who is rational when it comes to budgeting her household finances. Although she'd rather buy her kids all the neat technology they want (i.e. iPhone, PlayStation, Android tablet, and Gear watch) – Juanita decided to take a second job to make ends meet and save for her family's future. To her credit, she recognized that the short-term sacrifice she makes (not spending time with her family) will pay substantial dividends later in life – such as being able to pay for her family's health care and afford tuition for her children's college education. No dice, cards, or lotteries for Juanita, as would be the case for Michael. Her "addiction" is providing for her children.

Unselfishness trumps rationalization.

> *"So, Dr. Ridel,"* you ask. *"What can I do to defend myself from rationalizing?"*

Good question – just what you should be asking as an aspiring critical thinker. Here are several ways you can advance as a critical thinker by modifying your tendency to rationalize:

- Stop making excuses to justify your poor decisions.
- Adopt the perspective of other people (known in sociology as "role taking") when deciding what opinions to embrace and behaviors to express.
- Integrate the quote, "To Question is to Understand."

Michael didn't take responsibility for the negative consequences associated with his gambling addiction, nor did he consider the well-being of his family when playing cards with his paycheck or rolling the dice with his life savings. Michael has no one to blame but himself – but you'll know better as a critical thinker.

Bottom Line: In order to become a critical thinker, you must learn to identify and modify your tendency to rationalize your behavior and opinions.

Modifying Internal Barriers: Emotions

Your state of mind, physical health, and the amount of stress you experience can negatively impact your ability to think critically. But none of these are as consequential (important) as your emotions when it comes to hindering your development as a critical thinker.

As you remember from Chapter 1, critical thinking is all about the acquisition and application of knowledge. Well – you can acquire information easily enough, but successfully applying it is another matter. Stated bluntly, the application of knowledge is greatly hindered when the "heart rules the head." You can simply forget about making sound decisions and effectively solving problems when emotions win the "mental tug of war" played out with reason (which often happens). Again – forget about it.

Consider the following examples:

- Meet Chen – he's a "hot head" with a short anger fuse. Not surprisingly, such an emotional state negatively impacts his ability to think critically when it comes to dealing with decisions and problems. For example, Chen recently had too many drinks at the local bar – and became embarrassed when he realized it. His friends encouraged him to take a cab home, but Chen's embarrassment turned to anger and he erupted in an angry fit at their suggestion – yelling "I can drive home, myself." Chen, allowing emotions to get the better of him, decided to drive home. He got behind the steering wheel, placed the key in the ignition, and began a twisting, turning journey that resulted in disastrous consequences.

- Conversely, Jackie uses reason – not emotion – when she makes decisions and offers opinions. In fact, she doesn't have an emotional bone in her body. To her credit, Jackie thinks through the consequences of every decision she makes. For example, if Jackie was at the bar with Chen and had too many drinks, she would have considered her options before deciding to drive home. Unlike Chen, who made a hasty (sudden) emotional decision, Jackie would have recruited a designated driver or called for a cab. As it turns out, regardless of the option she selected, Jackie had a much better evening than Chen. Importantly, she woke up the next morning safe and sound. Unfortunately – Chen didn't.

Reason trumps emotion.

> *"So, Dr. Ridel,"* you ask. *"What can I do to defend myself from emotions?"*

Good question – just what you should be asking as an aspiring critical thinker. Here are several ways you can advance as a critical thinker by controlling your emotions:

- Recognize your emotional state before you act.
- Avoid emotional "highs" and "lows" whenever you're making decisions or trying to solve problems.
- Rely on reason and factual evidence (not emotions) when evaluating your behavior and opinions.

Chen's life would have been different (and longer) if he had thought matters through carefully and critically before he acted. If he had evaluated the consequences of his intended actions before getting in his car, the night would have ended very differently. Chen has no one to blame but himself – but you'll know better as a critical thinker.

Bottom Line: In order to become a critical thinker, you must learn to listen to your head – not your heart.

Modifying Internal Barriers: Stubbornness

Being stubborn is not only an internal barrier to critical thinking, it's also a sure-fire way to upset your family, alienate your friends, and compromise advancement in your career. Don't get me wrong – sometimes "standing your ground" (being stubborn) is justified. After all, our behavior and opinions can't always be unsound and incorrect (can they?). But when they are, it's best to rethink your actions and points-of-view – rather than foolishly (stubbornly) defend them.

Like rationalizations and emotions – stubbornness can shut down social interactions and delay learning from taking place. And that's only the beginning of a "slippery slope" that befalls (happens to) unreflective, closed-minded thinkers. Before they know it, stubborn people begin dismissing (rationalizing away) other people's reasoning while they defensively (emotionally) cling to their misinformed actions and opinions. That's when stubborn, "know-it-all" tendencies interfere with people's ability to make rational decisions – and that's when stubborn people accelerate down their "slippery slopes" and experience negative consequences associated with their stubbornness.

Consider the following examples:

- Meet Serena – she's an up-and-coming marketing assistant for a young cosmetics company. She was recently given an opportunity to write an advertisement about the firm's new line of facial cream. When she discovered the facts didn't support her exaggerated claims, she fabricated her own evidence. Ouch. Making matters worse, when she was confronted about the legitimacy of her claims – she obstinately (stubbornly) defended her fabricated evidence and overall weak position. Serena's boss, who knew better, gave Serena an opportunity to come

clean and admit her mistake. Unfortunately, she foolishly stuck with her position. In the end, she was dismissed when the company discovered that her "evidence" was indeed fabricated.

- In contrast to Serena, Ahmed doesn't have a stubborn bone in his body. Instead, he relies on objectivity and impartiality (fairness) when making decisions and solving problems. As a research consultant, Ahmed learned long ago that facts and evidence trump personal opinions and stubbornness when deciding whether to promote a product or service. If Ahmed was in Serena's position, he wouldn't have endorsed the firm's new facial cream in light of disconfirming evidence. Most other professionals would have simply ignored the data and proceeded to endorse the product. Not Ahmed – no way – not with his high level of professionalism.

Research trumps stubbornness.

> *"So, Dr. Ridel,"* you ask. *"What can I do to defend myself from stubbornness?"*

Good question – just what you should be asking as an aspiring critical thinker. Here are several ways you can advance as a critical thinker by modifying your tendency to behave like a stubborn "know-it-all:"

- Focus on objectivity – facts and evidence are all that matter.
- Avoid sticking with a stubborn position, especially when you are confronted with evidence that it is weak and unsupported by data.
- Don't fabricate (make up) data to support your claims.

Serena made three mistakes: She invented data to advance her marketing material (strike one), lied about it (strike two), and stubbornly defended her lies (strike three). Serena should have been more diligent in investigating the research and, if she had been willing to admit her mistake, she probably would have received a second chance. Serena has no one to blame but herself – but you'll know better as a critical thinker.

Bottom Line: In order to become a critical thinker, keep an open mind and resist the urge to be a stubborn "know-it-all."

Modifying Internal Barriers: Biases

Your unique life experiences (and lessons learned from them) define who you are – and how you think. Biases provide the raw material for rationalization, they control your emotions, and "justify" your stubborn opinions. As a result, your unsubstantiated opinions and pre-conceptions about your everyday life can form a very strong barrier to critical thinking. Now that's power. A strong internal barrier, indeed.

And the situation can get even dicier (riskier). Biases are often intensified by the persuasive influence exerted by researchers, journalists, politicians, and sales people – and it's common for unreflective thinkers to be out-maneuvered by them. Many nefarious (despicable) shaping agents will try to take advantage of people's vulnerability by making promises of happiness, security, power, wealth, health, and beauty – all things that most people desperately hope for and dream about. The problem is that they don't ask questions or evaluate the information provided to them. Those biased oversights set them up as easy targets to be manipulated and cheated.

Consider the following examples:

- Steve is a racist. He was raised in a racist family, and as a result, he developed unsupported biases regarding the intellectual inferiority of minorities. When Steve is confronted about his unsubstantiated beliefs, he responds with biased, unreflective explanations such as "I believe this because that's the way it is" and "This is what my parents and friends say is true" and "Look at all the problems caused by minorities, they must be intellectually inferior." It's bad enough that Steve's opinions lack factual foundation, but to make matters worse, he stubbornly supports them even in the face of contrary evidence. Steve's deep-rooted biases hinder his ability to accept contrary data – this is a significant barrier to critical thinking. In summary, Steve is biased by fiction, hearsay, and nonsense.

- In stark contrast, consider Sally – who doesn't have a biased bone in her body. Instead, she relies on facts and evidence to determine her opinions. Such a non-biased approach serves her well when people like Steve claim that minorities are intellectual inferior. Instead of belittling (ridiculing) them, she stays calm in the face of their bigotry and responds with evidence such as: "Research in monogenism proves that all races originate from the same gene pool, and as such, we are intellectually identical" and "Your argument is based on flawed, disproved studies of scientific racism." Sally's ability to use data-centered research to refute unproven, downright silly claims inoculates her from the internal barrier that infected Steve. In summary, Sally is biased by facts and evidence – not fiction and nonsense.

Evidence trumps biases.

> *"So, Dr. Ridel,"* you ask. *"What can I do to defend myself from biases?"*

Good question – just what you should be asking as an aspiring critical thinker. Here are several ways you can advance as a critical thinker by modifying your tendency to make biased decisions:

- Evaluate your own opinions continuously.
- Believe in claims that use scientific methods and problem solving processes rather than hearsay and biased generalizations.
- Beware of un-credible people who compare "apples and tire irons" or appeal to authority figures and celebrities to make their case.

Steve ignored the facts and evidence when confronted about his unsubstantiated beliefs – instead relying on generalizations and biases to form his argument. He should have considered the facts and evidence before jumping to biased conclusions. Steve has no one to blame but himself – but you'll know better as a critical thinker.

Bottom Line: Make up your own mind – a mind that hasn't been manipulated by the testimony of others.

A CONCLUDING THOUGHT

Have you ever seen, read or listened to something that seemed too good to be true? You know, claims that prompt you to scratch your head, drop your jaw, and widely open your eyes in disbelief.

Consider the following examples:

> *"Triple your money quickly – with no risk."*
>
> *"Congratulations – you just won an all-expenses paid trip to Paris. We just need your credit card number to hold the reservation."*
>
> *"Be your own boss, work from home, make thousands of dollars a week."*
>
> *"Lose 10 pounds in 10 days."*

STOP.

Don't proceed if any of the above claims seem even remotely likely to you. Before you continue, re-read the first three chapters of this textbook or, shudder the thought, remove yourself from the class, entirely. Just kidding.

Seriously, don't feel badly if you've ever been tempted by, or fallen victim to, such claims (or ones just like them.) Quick-and-easy paths to one's goals are incredibly alluring – especially when they're "sold" by trained, professional marketers (manipulators). "Getting sucked in" happens to everyone. Everyday. I get it – I really do. Frankly, I've been victimized by such trappings, as well.

Ok, now consider the following claim:

> *"Identify what's stopping you from becoming a critical thinker, modify or replace the barriers, and voila – you'll become a critical thinker."*

PAUSE.

I know this claim seems a lot more credible than the other assertions. But alas – it's only partially correct. Simply put – becoming a critical thinker won't be that easy (as the above statement implies). Indeed, becoming a critical thinker will require considerable effort and unwavering dedication.

BUT (and that's a big "but"), identifying, modifying, and replacing barriers won't be enough. That's only the beginning.

Recall the 8-Step Process to Critical Thinking – which I introduced in Chapter 1. Identifying, modifying, and replacing barriers comprise only one segment of the overall process, Steps 2 and 3, respectively.

Now – math isn't one of my strengths, but according to my calculations, that leaves 6 more steps to learn. 8 – 2 chapters = 6. Subtract Step 1 (recognizing the need to improve your critical thinking skills), which you already completed in Chapter 1 – and that leaves 5 steps remaining for you to become a critical thinker. 6 – 1 = 5. Um – I guess I'm better at math than I thought.

OK – enough kidding around. Here's a brief preview of what's to come.

I will identify two of the remaining 5 steps in Chapters 4 and 5 – when I discuss the importance of determining the accuracy of information ("messages," Step 4) and credibility of sources ("messengers," Step 5). I will then explore two additional steps in Chapters 6 and 7 – applying critical thinking principles when making decisions (Step 6) and solving problems (Step 7).

Finally, in Chapter 8, I will introduce the last step in the 8-Step Process to Critical Thinking, which will deal with overcoming recidivism (Step 8 – in our case, the tendency of people to revert back to their unreflective thinking habits.)

Completing the remaining 5 steps, to go along the 3 you've already accomplished – will complete the bridge from the old you as an unreflective thinker to the "new" you as a critical thinker in your everyday life. Your evolution from an unreflective "cave-person" to a modern critical thinker is depicted in Figure 3.3. How exciting.

PROCEED.

Figure 3.3
Evolution of a Critical Thinker

Everyday Life with David
"Day 15: Now What?"

This chapter has had a profound impact on the way I think about traditional and social media. I feel like blinders have fallen from my eyes and I can now see the world much more clearly. Not only do I recognize the influence of shaping agents in my life, I now find myself pursuing facts and evidence to substantiate my new, more-reflective opinions and ideas.

For example, I became engrossed in a front-page newspaper article just the other day about climate change. Nobody was more surprised than me. Frankly, before reading this book, I would have automatically skipped past the front page and grabbed the sports section.

The story referenced a special news report on the alarming effects of climate change – which I watched on YouTube – and it motivated me to research the subject more

thoroughly on the Internet. I zeroed in on a Word Press blog about carbon emissions from automobiles and the economic impact of our dependence on fossil fuels.

This got me thinking about the environmental value associated with electric cars and the carbon footprint of my own "gas guzzler." I explored the real life experiences of several electric car owners by reading their reviews on Yelp, followed them on Twitter, and researched their Facebook posts. This led me to visit three different car distribution websites to explore the possibility of trading in my old fuel-based car for a new electric one.

I now feel much more in control of my life, regardless of whether I buy an electric car, or not – and I'm fired up about what I'm about to learn in the coming weeks.

Now it's YOUR turn.

Chapter 4
Messages:
Embrace Or Reject?

Fact, fiction, and uncertainty: What's a critical thinker to think?

Robert W. Ridel, Ph.D.

We live in a time that's defined by information – more so than at any other era of human existence. We're bombarded with data, ideas, facts, and opinions all the time and in all places. Like the superhero cartoon character Chickenman – whose tagline was "He's everywhere. He's everywhere!" information is all around us, as well – on television and radio, in newspapers and magazines, and on our computers and tablets. Twitter, Facebook, Google+. There is simply no way to escape from the "Bing" sound emanating from our smart-phones and laptops – unless we travel to Nepal and inhabit a small, remote village nestled deep into the Himalayan mountain range. But even there – information would find its way to penetrate our lives. No doubt about it.

Yes – like the air we breathe, information is everywhere.

That could be a good situation – but it could also be bad. The benefits are easy enough to identify. I mean – how cool is it to obtain unlimited access to whatever type of information you want – whenever and wherever you want it. The downside, on the other hand, is not as easy to detect, even though it's not any less important to recognize.

Consider all the information that engulfs your everyday life and all the people who are trying to sell you this and influence you to believe that – and ask yourself the following straightforward questions:

- "How do you know the information (messages) you read and view is reliable?"
- "How do you know the people (messengers) delivering the information are credible?"

The answer to both questions is: You probably don't know, at least not for certain.

The fact is – we're constantly exposed to fraudulent data, unsubstantiated ideas, questionable "facts," and biased opinions that are advanced by untrustworthy, disingenuous, and uninformed people.

Sadly, the facts also demonstrate that most people (unreflective thinkers) accept unreliable, inaccurate messages as being true – and consider dishonest and uninformed messengers (i.e. politicians, actors/actresses, and athletes) as being credible.

And that's troubling.

Of course, "informational gullibility" isn't unique to our era. Indeed, people have mistakenly accepted half-truth messages and erroneously believed unscrupulous and uninformed messengers for decades, centuries, and millennia. But what we're witnessing today is something different – something hugely different. Why?

Access and speed.

We live in an age when anyone can publish and broadcast anything to everyone – and do so instantly. Ironically, even though informational reach and velocity are hallmark technological achievements of the 21st Century – being exposed to immense amounts of information can place us in harm's way if the messages we hear and read about are inaccurate, and if they're delivered by biased, unprincipled messengers. A double-edge sword if ever there was one.

Given that you consume gigabytes of information on a daily basis – you need to become exceptionally adept at protecting yourself from inaccurate information and the untrustworthy people who deliver it. You need to guard your reservoir of knowledge – lest it become contaminated with misinformation that's presented as "facts" by charlatans (imposters) who attempt to capture your money and votes. And the best method to keep your reservoir of knowledge pure and untainted is for you to become a more discerning and sharp consumer of information, as well as a more astute and perceptive evaluator of the people who deliver it.

What's needed is for you to become a solid critical thinker.

Ah – if only the process was that easy. But as we know – it isn't. Which begs the question: How can you, as a developing critical thinker, protect your reservoir of knowledge from the ongoing assault from misinformation and non-credible messengers? The answer is "simple." You'll need to rely on other protectors to shield it – until you're capable of defending it yourself.

Who might they be?

PROTECTORS OF THE RESERVOIR: KNIGHTS IN SHINING ARMOR

The 21st Century presents you with an ironic "Catch-22" (no-win situation) regarding the availability of information and the cleanliness of your reservoir of knowledge:

> *"We value information and always want more – but the more we get, the less it's worth."*

A "Catch-22," indeed.

The fact is – the more ubiquitous (ever-present) information becomes, the harder it is for you to validate all the content you see and read. Inevitably, some of it will eventually pass through your filter that ends up contaminating your reservoir of knowledge. So I ask again: How will you, as a developing critical thinker, protect yourself from unreliable information and the persuasive influence peddled by "false prophets" – people who skillfully present lies as truth and misrepresent truth as lies?

Let me address that question by discussing three potential "knights in shining armor" that might keep misinformation and uninformed, disingenuous messengers at bay (away):

- Traditional Media
- Government
- Social Media

Let me briefly consider each in turn.

Traditional Media

Traditional media have provided us with some level of protection over the years. For example, editors for newspapers scrutinize and validate informational sources for reliability before publishing content. And executive producers for television evaluate and vet the credentials of so-called experts before placing them on the airways. Examine and confirm. Calculate and investigate. That's all good.

By placing safeguarding measures into operation, such as checking the reliability of messages and assessing the credibility of messengers, traditional media have kept us somewhat safe when reading newspapers and magazines, listening to the radio, and watching television. We feel fairly confident that the messages we read, hear, and view, as well as the messengers who deliver them to us, are at least somewhat reliable and credible. In this way, traditional media have served as our "la-la blanket" to keep us safe.

But be careful.

The above paragraphs read so smoothly and contain such positive, hunky-dory (appealing) content – that I bet you're tempted to believe what I wrote to be true. Well – let me tell you a secret: The traditional media aren't as squeaky clean as those paragraphs suggest. The fact is – they're not the knights in shining armor they pretend to be when it comes to providing accurate messages (information) that's delivered by credible messengers.

Surprised?

If so – consider that the power brokers who own television networks, newspapers, and radio stations actually "control the news." Wealthy beyond imagination and heavily biased in their opinions, many of them predictably use their narrow, profit-driven perspectives and personal agendas to determine what we (the public) watch on television, read in newspapers, and listen to on the radio. And that's unsettling – because doing so denies us important opportunities to read about, listen to, and view varied points-of-view.

That strikes of censorship.

Let me provide you with a couple of quick examples to drive my point.

In 2014, almost one million people marched in New York City (and elsewhere) to protest climate change and the widespread, irresponsible use of fossil fuels. Shockingly, none of the major news outlets covered the march.

Why?

Simple answer – media owners concluded that the protests challenged the vested interests of their advertisers (multi-national energy companies) – and as such, decided to silence the passionate messages expressed by nearly a million voices. Simply stated, although the march was newsworthy – the "plug was pulled" because the messages promoted by the protesters weren't judged supportive of the corporate bottom line – profit.

The Occupy Wall Street protests in New York City (2011) represent another example of censorship. While the activists chanted, "We are the 99%" near the New York Stock Exchange, the traditional media fought back by using a tried and proven method – simply ignore the protester's negative portrayal of the wealthy 1% who worked on Wall Street. For several weeks, there was no television, no newspaper, and no radio coverage of the protests. None at all. The traditional media simply operated by the age-old motto: "What the public doesn't know can't hurt us." It's as though the protests and marches never took place.

By keeping people in Des Moines, Pittsburg, and San Diego, as well as inhabitants of rural Kentucky and North Dakota uninformed – the traditional media effectively neutralized the Occupy Wall Street movement. The voice of the protesters never had an opportunity to surface and spread. Out of sight – out of mind, and the movement eventually became irrelevant and ultimately died away. All that remained was the extreme inequality the activists tried in vain to educate the public about.

(While literally typing the above paragraph, Public Broadcasting Service reported that the top 85 people in the world possess the same amount of money that almost 3.5 billion people collectively have around the world. Amazing – just what the 99% movement was preaching.)

Before leaving this section – I want to emphasize an important point.

I don't mean to imply that media brokers are "bad" people with horns growing out of their heads. I'm sure they love their mothers, believe in God, eat their vegetables, and read their children bedtime stories at night – kissing them on the forehead and reassuring them that there's no "boogiemen" or gremlins hiding in the closet or under the bed. These exceptionally wealthy and powerful people are simply doing what they are supposed to do – and that doesn't involve protecting your reservoir of knowledge. Quite the opposite – they're motivated to maintain and grow their wealth and power.

That might be disappointing – but it shouldn't be surprising. In fact, this situation has a name – it's called the "corporatization of media."

So – where does this leave you? If the traditional media aren't a knight in shining armor, who can you turn to for protection while you develop as a critical thinker?

Government

Some people suggest that government regulation is the answer. That bureaucratic agencies should monitor the flow of information directed at its citizens and, when necessary, regulate content judged detrimental to the "normal" functioning of society (from the government's biased perspective, of course). Seems like a possible knight in shining armor, doesn't it? Government would simply protect us from information it deemed unreliable and from people who it determined lacked credibility. But is government intervention a good idea?

Governments have tried to suppress speech and written forms of communication since the times of Socrates and Plato. Books have been burned (as well as people), peaceful rallies prohibited, and movies removed from distribution – all under the guise (excuse) of protecting society. Even more shocking, governments have killed countless protesters in an attempt to extinguish their ideas before they had a chance to capture the imagination and incite (provoke) the "riot" of their fellow citizens.

As an example, consider how the government in the People's Republic of China cracked down on pro-democracy protests in Tiananmen Square (1989) – resulting in the deaths of who-knows how many people. The protests were triggered by a new generation of Chinese citizens who desired such liberties as freedom of the press and speech. But the Chinese government wanted none of that – and condemned the marches as counter-revolutionary. Not surprisingly, government regulation won out over free access to and the application of information.

For a more recent illustration of government regulation, let's again focus on People's Republic of China – but this time on its confrontation with the world's largest distributor of information on the Internet – Google. In 2006, Google caved (yielded) to government pressure and agreed to censor its search results in order to operate in the country. Never feeling completely comfortable with its decision, Google eventually reconsidered its position and in 2010 opened its search engine to unfiltered information. The Chinese government responded quickly and decisively, blocking Google's operations in China. Government regulation won out over free access to and the application of information. Once again.

Not surprisingly, the Chinese government isn't the only bureaucracy that has attempted to censor information from its people. For example, Egypt, Libya, and Iran also tried to control the distribution of content within their borders, especially during the turbulent political period known as the "Arab Spring" (2013). Millions of people were denied access to information and, sadly, thousands were killed during protests to change their respective governments. Still another illustration of government censorship involves such countries as Saudi Arabia, Kuwait, and Qatar. Citizens in those nations might be rich with oil-generated wealth – but they're relatively impoverished when it comes to free access to information.

Lest we think censorship is restricted to the other side of the globe, there's a plethora (excessive amount) of evidence suggesting that restrictions also occur in the United States. Even though our country was founded on principles of freedom of speech and the press, political forces have been known to restrict access to vast amounts of information and act against people who advocate for its release.

Case in point – consider that the United States ranks 46th in the 2014 World Press Freedom Index – which highlights governments that restrict the free flow of information to their citizens. Hard to believe, isn't it? Some recent examples of censorship include:

- The U.S. government cracked down on student and federal employee access to documents on the international, journalistic website "WikiLeaks." The website includes thousands of files that the government determined should be removed from the "public domain" (our collective reservoir of knowledge.) Must be pretty important stuff, huh? So why not share it with the public? Is the targeted

information truly sensitive for the security of the nation – or is it possible the government simply wants to keep the content a secret for political reasons?

- An American system administrator from the Central Intelligence Agency (named Edward Snowden) was chased out of the United States by the Department of Justice for sharing information regarding government surveillance programs by the National Security Agency. The charges filed against him fueled debates about the delicate balance that exists between free access to information and the government's right to regulate content to protect national security.

- Public school districts around the country regularly censor curriculum by removing lessons that teach "controversial" topics, such as evolution, abortion, and climate change. Denying students access to diverse opinions undermines their prerogative (right) to make up their own minds – as well as thwarts their overall development as critical thinkers.

All of the above illustrations seems like censorship to me.

So – let me ask you: Is that the type of filter you want for your reservoir of knowledge? Or is the so-called solution (government intervention) worse than the problem it's designed to solve; namely, free access to unfiltered information?

Social Media

So, where does this leave us?

Unfortunately, the first two so-called protectors – traditional media and government – turned out to be more like "emperors without any clothes" than knights in shining armor. Instead of protecting your reservoir of knowledge – they actually restrict the flow of information into it. In reality – they design, construct, and maintain your reservoir of knowledge to advance and protect their own purposes and advantages, not necessarily to fill it with content that benefits you.

(Who does that remind you of? Think carefully. Yes, that's correct – the Puppeteer and his shaping agents.)

Again, where does this leave us?

Let me suggest that you think about the situation from a different perspective. Instead of permitting traditional media and government to fill your reservoir of knowledge with censored, biased information – why not keep it open to all sorts of opinions and points-of-view? Yes – how about unraveling several informational hoses, placing them into your reservoir of knowledge, turning the valves wide-open, and filling it up with free, unfettered (unrestricted), and uncensored information? All at your choosing. For free.

What an awesome paradigm shift (change in thinking).

And what source does that bring to mind? Yes – Google. The ultimate informational hose.

Recall that Google battled censorship in the People's Republic of China for years – a clash reminiscent of the biblical confrontation between David (Google) and Goliath (People's Republic of China). Talk about being overmatched. But you know what? Google might have lost the initial battle – but in my educated guess (even though speculation is a no-no in critical thinking), Google will ultimately win the war, not just in the People's Republic of China but elsewhere around the globe.

Why?

Because Google recognizes that people want free, open access to information – not to censored opinions and points-of-view. And that's precisely what Google and other social media companies (Facebook, Twitter, Word Press, You Tube) do – they provide the public what it wants rather than restrict the flow of information.

Come to think about it – didn't David eventually vanquish Goliath?

☺

My goodness – can all of this be true? I mean, is it possible that social media, if not a knight in shining armor – might turn out to be the cavalry that protects your reservoir of knowledge? Have you located your champion?

Maybe.

But wait a moment. Not so fast. I have a concern here (just as you would expect from a critical thinker). Recall the old adage (saying): "If something seems too good to be true, it probably is." Well – is it possible that social media comes with a downside? Can unlimited hoses and all of the information that flows from them actually threaten your reservoir of knowledge? Again, that's my concern.

Let me briefly explain.

While traditional media and government rely on order (censorship) without freedom – social media offer people the opposite: Freedom without order. In a world dominated by social media – everyone is a producer and consumer of information. 24/7/365. Seems great on the surface – but think more critically about a situation defined by "freedom without order." In a situation where information is everywhere (remember Chickenman) – how do people decide what content to accept as fact and dismiss as

fiction? And who do they trust delivering it? Again, is it possible that too much of a "good" thing (information) might not be so "good," after all?

The broader, more comprehensive (wide-ranging) question is the following: Is censorship and control preferable over freedom with accompanying chaos? Or vice versa?

If you ask me (please do), I'm concerned about both ends of the "access continuum." Censorship without choice can produce robotic, manipulated ways of thinking – but freedom without order can lead to overload and confusion. So if you really want to know about my preference – I'd confidently state that I favor neither of the options. Instead, I side with an adage (saying) I learned long ago:

> *"The best option among competing alternatives usually falls somewhere in-between opposing endpoints on a spectrum."*

I believe the same insightful conclusion applies to the dilemma associated with informational access and whether control is preferable over freedom – or vice versa. The best option probably falls somewhere in-between control and freedom.

That stated, let me take a moment to make the case against social media when it comes to protecting your reservoir of knowledge – just as I did a moment ago for traditional media and government. After all, the fundamental tenets of critical thinking require me to be fair and balanced, especially when critiquing (evaluating) opposing points-of-view on issues and problems of importance.

Consider how each of the following social media threatens (rather than protects) your reservoir of knowledge:

Facebook – is the largest social media site on the planet, bar none. Billions of opinions, ideas, and experiences continuously traverse (travel) the world of cyberspace – with no downtime, at all. But there's also no control. How can people, as consumers of information, validate the reliability of billions of messages and the credibility of billions of messengers sending them? No can do. Impossible.

No – Facebook isn't the cavalry.

Twitter – is a micro-blogging site that millions of people visit to gain instantaneous access to news, gossip, and "facts." But as is the case with Facebook, how can you differentiate fact from fiction on a 24x7x365 content delivery platform? Twitter provides huge volumes of unfiltered information with absolutely no oversight (control) – making it virtually impossible for people to distinguish reliable facts from untrustworthy fiction.

No – Twitter isn't the cavalry.

Google+ – is the second-largest social media site in the world. Unfortunately, its massive online community offers enormous amounts of un-vetted information that is produced by countless numbers of misinformed, biased content creators. Such a situation makes it virtually impossible for people to know what's true and what's false, or what's right and what's wrong. Sound familiar? Think of Facebook and Twitter.

No – Google+ isn't the cavalry.

Word Press – is the most popular blogging platform on the web – with almost 100 million "digital journalists" sharing their views, opinions, and ideas with the rest of the world. What's troubling is that blogs, like tweets, often contain lies, exaggerations, and hyperbole (overstatements) that come across as reliable and "proven."

No – Word Press isn't the cavalry.

Are you detecting a pattern among the above referenced social media? You should – because each of them, by offering uncontrolled access to a universe of un-vetted information, actually jeopardizes the cleanliness of your reservoir of knowledge. The informational hoses associated with them are filled to the brink with tsunami amounts of content. But what's true and factual, if anything? Is that commentary or this documentary supported by evidence – or is the information fabricated? Can the writer or speaker be trusted, or do they have vested interests in the position being advanced?

And the onslaught of unsubstantiated information doesn't stop with these four social media goliaths. The list also includes countless other online tools that assault your reservoir of knowledge with unreliable messages offered by non-credible messengers. Consider the following:

- **LinkedIn**
  - LinkedIn is the largest business-oriented social media service for professionals. The challenge with LinkedIn is that it promotes quantity of connections rather than quality. The fact is – professionals don't really know most (any?) of the contacts in their networks, even though they claim to be "connected" to them.

- **YouTube**
  - YouTube is the largest video-sharing website on the planet that continuously streams video content – ranging from singing cats and talking babies to people discussing politics and economics. The problem is that YouTube doesn't vet (evaluate) any of its content for accuracy. Everything goes (streams) – whether the information is accurate or deceitful.

- **Yelp**
  - Yelp is the most popular crowd-sourced local business reference site on the web where millions of people from all over the globe rate products, services, and ideas. Although crowds can potentially provide a collective wisdom that yields solid ideas – it's still important to remain suspicious about the reliability of unsubstantiated ratings and the motives of the people who offer them.

- **MOOCs**
  - MOOCs are Massive Open Online Courses. While Yelp utilizes crowdsourcing for product reviews, MOOCs leverage crowdsourcing for learning. Unfortunately, MOOCs don't adopt the rigorous vetting process found in traditional higher education – and without stringent accreditation (oversight), instruction is often unstructured and level-inappropriate.

* * * * *

So – it seems we're 0 for 3.

We "struck-out" with traditional media, government, and social media. None of them qualify as a knight in shining armor or the cavalry when it comes to protecting our reservoirs of knowledge. None.

I bet you're surprised – but you shouldn't be. I'm certainly not.

Let me be clear and unambiguous on this point – you're supposed to be 0 for 3. Believe it or not, traditional media, government, social media aren't designed to protect your reservoir of knowledge. Quite the contrary – they're motivated to look after their own profit-driven interests. If you rely on them for safeguarding – you're thinking unreflectively and wishfully.

Indeed, if you've learned anything from the last several pages – it should be that you need to look elsewhere.

So who, then, is going to scrutinize the information that is published and aired? And who is going to evaluate the so-called "experts" who deliver it? The answer is obvious enough – but it's also daunting to consider. Ready? The answer is:

YOU.

Yes – in order to protect your reservoir of knowledge, you'll need to monitor the information you read and view, as well as evaluate the people who are attempting to influence your opinions and behavior. The solution will have to come from you. You'll need to become your own knight in shining armor. You'll need to become a member of your own cavalry. Again, you.

The remainder of this chapter will be devoted to helping you do just that – to learn how to rely on yourself to protect your reservoir of knowledge. To achieve that learning outcome, I will structure the content around the following three questions:

- **Are facts always true?**
  - The fact is (pun intended), things aren't always as they seem. What appears to be true might actually turn out to be false. History provides us with numerous examples when so-called "truths" crumble under the weight of evidence, no matter how popular the facts are.

- **For that matter, is fiction always untrue?**
  - A similar switcheroo can occur when it comes to fiction becoming fact. On these occasions, sound ideas and points-of-view that were originally dismissed by the popular opinion of the time turn out to be true and accurate upon further research.

- **And what about those occasions when there isn't enough evidence one way or another to determine fact from fiction?**
  - If the above scenarios weren't intriguing enough – think about all the debatable issues that currently lack certainty one way or the other. Who knows? Sometimes we just don't know what's right or wrong – at least not yet.

What's a critical thinker to think?

The key will be for you to learn how to distinguish fact from fiction, fiction from fact, and how to postpone judgment until enough evidence is gathered. Doing so will help you apply lessons learned to protect your reservoir of knowledge from inaccurate information and the people who try to deliver it.

For now, let's begin with a consideration of "fact becomes fiction," and then develop the other options in turn ("fiction becomes fact" and "who knows").

FACT BECOMES FICTION

Fact becoming fiction describes historical and contemporary issues that people think are true, but they turn out to be untrue. In these cases, critical thinking serves as a magnifying glass that exposes the inaccuracies of generally accepted points-of-view. Just because a position is popular doesn't make it correct and true. Indeed, many opinions crumble under the weight of evidence that reveals them to be little more than myths lacking substance and a factual basis.

Consider:

- **The View that the World is Flat –** Greece, 850 B.C. Homer was a Greek philosopher and one of the very first scientists in history. He believed that the earth was a flat disk floating on the sea. Check out Figure 4.1. Homer made unsound statements like "The Earth is definitely flat" and "If you sail to the horizon you will fall into space." Interestingly, he was actually a decent critical thinker who thought he was reaching solid conclusions. However, no evidence existed to support his analysis – leaving Homer only to guess. Of course, it made sense for him to think the world was flat given what little he knew about the Earth – but as time would eventually reveal, Homer was dreadfully wrong. Surprise, surprise – our home in the galaxy isn't flat.

Figure 4.1
Homer's Flat World

- **The Practice of Drilling Holes in People's Heads –** Rome, 129 A.D. A doctor named Galen believed that drilling holes in a patient's head would cure headaches by allowing demons to escape. He even had a name for the procedure, "trepanation." Galen was an advanced scientist (for his day), but he jumped to conclusions without gathering any supporting evidence or facts – which was a significant breakdown of the critical thinking process. As a result, he developed ineffective methods to treat headaches which would have been less painfully and more effectively cured by certain types of herbs. Like Homer, Galen was thinking "rationally" given the state of knowledge that existed about neurology almost 2,000 years ago. And again, as was the case with his Greek counterpart, time judged him to be in error.

- **The Salem Witch Trials –** Massachusetts, 1692 A.D. Several courts in colonial Massachusetts unjustly accused hundreds of women (and a few men) of practicing witchcraft. The false judgments became one of the world's most notorious cases of mass hysteria, social extremism, and lapses in due process. Case in point, some of the evidence offered to determine ("prove") a witch's identity included dogs eating cakes, blindfolded touch tests, and hearsay (rumor, gossip).

  An even more ridiculous practice involved strapping the accused into a harness and dunking the person into a deep body of water for a few minutes. If the person didn't drown, s/he was burned at the stake because surviving the experience was considered proof that the person was, in fact, a witch. And what do you think happened if the accused didn't survive the dunking? Simple enough. An apology was offered to the corpse – something like: "Sorry, I guess you weren't a witch." Some consolation, eh? Imagine how a "witch" would feel just before being submerged into water? S/He would be dead either way. Talk about a no-win situation.

- **Weapons of Mass Destruction –** Iraq, 2003 A.D. The United States invaded Iraq based on the "factual" argument that Saddam Hussein possessed Weapons of Mass Destruction (WMD). A large coalition of countries – including the United States, Britain, and Australia were convinced that the volatile government in Baghdad would use WMDs for terrorist actions (domestic and international). And they went to war with Iraq. Think about how surprised and angry the allies were when the U.S. Central Intelligence Agency released a report in 2005 stating that no WMDs were found in Iraq.

  Oops.

  Imagine how history would have been different if the United States and its coalition partners didn't intervene? Consider how many thousands of lives would have been saved? How many hundreds of billions of dollars wouldn't have been wasted? Again, another illustration of fact becoming fiction.

Refer to Table 4.1 for a summary of the content of thought and the process of critical thinking as it pertains to my examples of fact becoming fiction.

Table 4.1
Fact Becomes Fiction: The Content and Process of Critical Thinking

SUBJECT	CONTENT of Thought	PROCESS of Critical Thinking
Homer	The world is flat	I have been here all day The sun moved, not me
	If you sail to the horizon, you will fall into space	We only see one side of the moon as it moves in the sky
Galen	Spirits trapped in the brain can cause headaches	Pressure can cause nerve pain – and the brain is full of nerves
	Trepanation will release spirits trapped in the head	Drilling holes in the skull releases head pressure
Salem Witch Trials	Sudden convulsions are caused by supernatural forces	If a "witch" touches a victim during a convulsion, the fit will stop
	Supernatural forces have control over some people (witches)	A "witch" will survive; an innocent woman will drown
WMD	Iraq has Weapons of Mass Destruction (WMD)	Saddam Hussein has the resources and evil intentions to create WMD
	Saddam Hussein is a terrorist and will use WMD	Financing for terrorists has been traced to Iraq and Saddam Hussein

The above examples clearly demonstrate that there is nothing sacrosanct (sacred) about "facts." Here today and gone tomorrow. Of course, many facts withstand the test of time (i.e. Newton's Law of Gravitation and Einstein's Law of Relativity) – but some don't and are simply retired to the "garbage dump" of history. The important lesson for critical thinkers to learn is not to become cemented (married) to anything or anyone unless research and the data generated by it support what they believe to be true. Opinions and behavior shouldn't be driven by popularity or complacency; rather, the fuel that propels points-of-view and actions must be evidence and data.

The proverbial bar must be set high – otherwise you run the risk of contaminating your reservoir of knowledge by accepting unsubstantiated messages and being influenced by non-credible messengers. I know adhering to the above requirement can be challenging – but it simply must be honored otherwise any attempt to become a critical thinker will be futile and met with defeat.

Everyday Life with David
"Day 17: Science Fiction"

The lessons I learned on fact and fiction remind me of my love for science fiction. It's true. I'm a science fiction nut. Always have been and always will be. How cool would it be to journey into time, fly to another planet, acquire super powers, and travel the universe via a space transporter?

But now – I wonder if I've become too fixated on the fiction element in the phrase "science fiction." As I learn more and more from Dr. Ridel, I'm beginning to think that I need to focus more on what I'm learning about message reliability, and less about the possibility of traveling at warp speed. I need to spend more time in the library and less at science fiction conventions.

People who are into science fiction (futurists like me) are always looking for ways to remove "fiction" from the phrase "science fiction." As I learn more and more from Dr. Ridel, I need to become more committed to applying what I'm learning to real life and less prone to "escaping" into fictional worlds of aliens and hobbits.

What matters is what's in front of me. If something can't be applied for 100 years, who cares? There are plenty of pressing issues that need to be addressed in the next 100 days. I need to get my head out of science fiction and focus on what's going on now.

I need to be more mindful of Dr. Ridel's concept of the reservoir of knowledge, and become more skilled at protecting mine from unreliable messages and non-credible messengers.

The bottom line is there is a time and a place for science fiction. It's a great hobby, but I'm not in school to further my hobby. I'm in school to develop myself as a person, and become a business professional – which requires a higher level of critical thinking.

FICTION BECOMES FACT

Fiction becoming fact describes points-of-view that are originally dismissed by popular opinion but, upon further research, actually turn out to be true. Opposition to new beliefs is often driven by superstition, heresy, or downright "stupidity" – not by disconfirming facts and evidence. To slightly paraphrase what I just mentioned in the section on facts becoming fiction – just because a position is unpopular doesn't make it incorrect or untrue.

Consider:

- **Leonardo Da Vinci's Invention of Manned Flight –** Italy, 1505 A.D. Four centuries before people became untethered from the Earth (first human flight), Leonardo da Vinci wrote a revolutionary design manual titled, "*Codex on the Flight of Birds*." In the manual, Leonardo produced more than 35,000 words and 500 sketches dealing with bird flight, the nature of air, and flying machines. At the time, Leonardo was described as absolutely "crazy" by unreflective thinkers. But regardless of what they thought, Leonardo's detailed blueprints of flying machines would ultimately become the basic prototypes (blueprints) for airplanes in the early twentieth century. Review one of his illustrations in Figure 4.2.

Figure 4.2
Leonardo Da Vinci's Codex on the Flight of Birds

- **The View that the Earth Revolves Around the Sun –** Italy, 1615 A.D. One of Galileo's greatest discoveries was his theory that the Earth revolves around the sun (called "heliocentrism"), not the other way around (called "geocentrism"). As it turned out, Galileo was right – the Earth really does orbit the sun – even though leaders in the Roman Catholic Church during the 17th Century concluded that Galileo's theory was contrary to scripture (they believed the sun revolved around the Earth).

  Bad luck for Galileo, who was placed under house arrest for the rest of his life – even though the "evidence" used against him was far less factual than the proof he provided to support his theory. Ironically, Galileo created some of his greatest scientific contributions (theory of gravity, invention of the telescope) while under house arrest. I guess sometimes good things can come from the worst of circumstances.

- **The Discovery of Cholera from a London Water Pump –** London, 1849 A.D. Not that long ago, a disastrous outbreak of cholera took place in the London district of Soho. Hundreds of lives were lost. A physician named John Snow provided evidence that the epidemic was caused by water flowing from a specific pump on Broad Street. However, the existing district council believed otherwise – concluding that ghosts and spirits ("miasma") brought about the outbreak of cholera. Unlike the council members who relied on gossip, rumor, and vivid imaginations – Snow reached his valid but unpopular conclusion based on scientific evidence. Which side do you think won the "battle of ideas?" Yes – that's correct, Snow was overruled by the unreflective thinkers sitting on the district council, even though time would eventually demonstrate that his "fiction" was actually fact. Surprise, surprise – ghosts and spirits did not produce the cholera.

  Note the difference between Snow's position and the ideas advanced by Homer and Galen. His conclusion was founded on facts, while their points-of-view were based on incomplete and inaccurate evidence. He was right and they were wrong. Ah – the power and value of critical thinking.

- **Travel from the Earth to the Moon –** France, 1865 A.D. In the mid-19th Century, Jules Verne published a novel about people flying to the moon in a rocket fired from a gigantic "space gun" (as shown in Figure 4.3). To accompany the novel, he released rough scientific calculations to demonstrate the viability (feasibility) of his vision. Amazingly, Verne's figures were fairly accurate, even though little or no hard data about extraterrestrial (space) travel existed at the time. Of course, the general population considered his work pure fiction and scoffed at the idea that anyone could ever leave the Earth, much less fly to the Moon. Fast forward to 1961 – when the first astronaut (Gagarin) journeyed into space, and to 1969 when astronaut Neil Armstrong stepped onto the surface of the Moon. At long last, Verne's beliefs were vindicated.

Figure 4.3
Jules Verne's "From the Earth to the Moon"

Refer to Table 4.2 for a summary of the content of thought and the process of critical thinking as it pertains to my examples of fiction becoming fact.

Table 4.2
Fiction Becomes Fact: The Content and Process of Critical Thinking

SUBJECT	CONTENT of Thought	PROCESS of Critical Thinking
Leonardo Da Vinci	Birds have a unique aerodynamic design for flight	A Flying Machine can be built using bird aerodynamics
	Man can fly in an airborne machine	If a small-scale model can fly, so can a man-sized machine
Galileo	Mathematics can predict the movements of the Earth and Sun	Based on mathematics, the Earth revolves around the Sun
	The positions of the Sun and Moon change with seasons	If the Sun revolved around the Earth, seasons wouldn't change
John Snow	127 people in Soho, London died of Cholera in one day	There is a consistent link between Cholera and the Broad Street pump
	Water is a better conductor of contagions than miasma	If it's miasma, more inmates would have had contracted Cholera
Jules Verne	A gigantic cannon can fire a man in a space projectile to the moon	Mathematical calculations prove that a space cannon can achieve escape velocity
	Space has no resistance; one can cheat gravity with escape velocity	If a 12-foot cannon can fire a lead ball; a 900-foot cannon can reach the moon

People don't usually embrace what they don't know, or accept anything that contradicts what they understand and deeply believe to be true. Such inertia (resistance to change) can be extremely costly when it thwarts the development and implementation of remarkable ideas, concepts, products, and achievements like airplanes, the Internet, and the polio vaccine. Stated bluntly, just because a lot of people disavow (reject) a point-of-view doesn't make it wrong or fictional. Data are the final arbiters (judges) when it comes to deciding what's worthy of acceptance and what's deserving of rejection – not popularity or social convention.

Lesson learned: Don't underestimate the power of humankind to turn fiction into fact. Think of the matter this way – science fiction can turn into science.

FACT, FICTION – OR WHO THE HECK KNOWS?

Recall the old adage (cliché): "Rush to judgment." This is an unacceptable behavior for critical thinkers.

Unfortunately, many people tend to rush to judgment when they fixate on facts being facts and on fiction being fiction. As I've just discussed, it's not always the case. The problem is that they decide too quickly on what's fact and fiction – before enough data are available to make such evaluations.

But the fact (no pun intended) remains – uncertainty abounds when it comes to many of the contemporary issues we're struggling with today. Are they fact or fiction? Flip a coin. Play eeny-meeny-miny-moe, or rock-paper-scissors. Again, we just don't know – at least not yet. Only time will tell.

But the fact remains, we don't have the luxury of waiting too long before we act – decisions have to be made soon if we're going to have any chance of effectively dealing with these dilemmas. Delay too long and they may worsen and become unsolvable problems.

Consider:

- **Climate Change –** Today. The world's climate is in a dramatic state of flux (change). Temperatures are rising. Ice caps are melting and crashing down into the oceans. Bodies of water are rising – threatening coastal towns and cities. Many scientists believe that humankind has caused these problems and that temperatures are destined to rise further and potentially doom human civilization. Others believe this is a natural, long-term cycle – and that there's nothing to be concerned about. See Figure 4.4 for an illustration of how climate change is affecting the Earth.

  How will climate change play out in the future? Who's right? What action should be taken? We just don't know – yet.

Figure 4.4
Climate Change

- **Affordable Care Act –** Today. The jury is still out on the possible success or failure of the Affordable Care Act (also known as Obama Care). Proponents claim that it will save lives and dramatically reduce the meteoric (rapid) rise in health care costs. In contrast, detractors complain that it places undue (excessive) pressure on the fragile U.S. economy and denies patients the right to choose their physicians.

  How will the Affordable Care Act (Obama Care) play out in the future? Who's right? What action should be taken? We just don't know – yet.

- **Fossil Fuel –** Today. For decades, many people have questioned our reliance on flammable dinosaur remains (otherwise known as oil) to heat and cool our homes, run our factories, and transport us around town and the globe. It's costly, finite in supply and, perhaps worst of all, pollutes the environment. On the other hand, some people believe that oil is the only energy source available that can support the needs of a huge proportion of the world's population (7+ billion people). After all, they state, less than 15% of our energy requirements are satisfied by renewable sources – wind, solar, hydro, and nuclear. What would happen to the infrastructure of our society, and the huge number of people served by it, if fossil fuel (oil) went bye-bye?

  How will our dependence on fossil fuel play out in the future? Who's right? What action should be taken? We just don't know – yet.

- **Radio Waves from Mobile Phones –** Today. Cellular phones use the same radio wave technology as microwave ovens. Over 1 billion cell phones are in use around the world and most people hold them next to their brains. Some health experts worry that cell phone "radiation" might increase the frequency of brain cancer in millions of people – while others point to research reports that show no evidence that cell phone use causes nerve damage.

  How will the health risks of cell phone use play out in the future? Who's right? What action should be taken? We just don't know – yet.

- **United States Debt Crisis –** Today. The United States is mired (stuck) in a seemingly insurmountable debt crisis. The national debt currently sits at roughly $18 trillion (that's 12 zeroes) – or $55,217 per person (man, woman, and child) in the country. Amazingly, in the time it takes you to read this paragraph (30 seconds), the national debt will have increased by approximately $32,400. Again, in 30 seconds. Check out the scary chart in Figure 4.5.

  The question is: What's the best way to get our nation out of debt? Some believe we should spend our way out of it – print more money and have consumers do what they do best (consume) to stimulate the economy. Others prefer implementing strategies that would cut expenses and introduce "across the board" austerity measures to bring the rising debt situation under control.

Figure 4.5
Your Piece of U.S. National Debt

How will the debt crisis in the United States play out in the future? Who's right? What action should be taken? We just don't know – yet.

These are only a few examples of the uncertainty that exists in the fact versus fiction debate. Will climate change be as devastating to the Planet as many scientists would have us believe – or will their concerns be the equivalent to a passing fad? And is all the attention afforded to the debt crisis deserving, or is it blown way out of proportion? Without a time machine to take us 50 years into the future – most people are only guessing.

Guessing?

No way – as you've learned, guessing isn't permitted from a critical thinking perspective.

A CONCLUDING THOUGHT

Well – wait a moment.

What if a time machine actually did exist and you were able to transport yourself 50 years into the future – or even 10, for that matter?

You could look back into the past (our present time) and determine what would've been the best methods to solve some of today's most challenging issues, such as climate change, health care, and the national debt. How cool would that be? You wouldn't have to guess or wait for history to reveal the most effective solutions. You would already know.

Dreaming, aren't I? In literal terms, yes – but not figuratively. Let me explain.

Critical thinking can serve as that time machine.

Indeed, critical thinkers have the potential to utilize their evaluative skills to carefully glimpse into the future – to cautiously predict what it holds for many of today's issues. They don't have to depend on unsubstantiated and biased information to guide their forecasts of how certain events will play out. Instead, critical thinkers can rely on facts and data to guide their expectations of what might actually happen. For them, predictions would be driven by research – evaluated rationally, (not through rationalizations), reasonably (not through emotions), flexibly (not through stubbornness), and objectively (not through bias). In other words, they wouldn't be "sucked in" by the internal barriers discussed in earlier chapters.

Seems too good to be true? I think not. Just consider all the people who used their critical thinking skills as a time machine to predict future events and circumstances – and then acted on those expectations.

- People who accurately predicted the housing and stock market bubble a few years ago – and profited enormously during a time that almost brought the nation to its financial knees.
- People who accurately predicted the outcome of military conflicts in Iraq and Afghanistan.
- People who accurately predicted the world-wide acceptance of such technological breakthroughs as the printing press, steam and mechanical powered vehicles, the telephone, radio, television, computers, Internet, iPods/iTunes, WiFi.
- People who accurately predicted the power of social media – Facebook, YouTube, and Twitter.

Again – these people, and many others like them, used their critical thinking skills as a time machine to figuratively travel into the future and accurately predict what was going to happen in present time. Importantly, they applied their knowledge to make billions of dollars and, in the process, change the world.

Wouldn't you like to be one of them? I know I certainly would. How neat would it be to predict the future and, like critical thinkers before you, position yourself to take advantage of upcoming changes? Even as most other people remain unaware of them? What a competitive advantage you'd possess – to see what was invisible to so many other people and beneficially act on those perceptions. Again, how cool would that be?

Any takers?

Actually, you're already making progress in building your very own time machine (check it out in Figure 4.6.) Consider what you've learned in the previous chapters:

Chapter 1: You recognized the need to improve your critical thinking skills (Step 1). That's the equivalent of the titanium body frame in your time machine.
Chapter 2: You discovered that barriers inhibit you from developing your critical thinking skills (Step 2). That's the equivalent of the communication system in your time machine.
Chapter 3: You learned how you could replace and modify your external and internal barriers (Step 3). That's the equivalent of the holographic, 6-D, digital control panel in your time machine.

And now – in this chapter, you acquired the skills necessary to determine the accuracy of information ("message"). Well – that's the equivalent of the oscillating over-thruster in your time machine.

Great – your time machine is nicely taking shape. Now it's time for you to add another important component to it – by exploring the second question identified at the introduction of this chapter: "How do you know the people (messengers) delivering the information are credible?" The answer to that question, and the next piece for your time machine, will be found in Chapter 5.

Ready for your heat shield?

Figure 4.6
Critical Thinking Time Machine

Everyday Life with David

"Day 20: My Vision of the Future"

Critical thinking would be a lot easier if I had a time machine. Then I would know for certain how today's dilemmas are going to play out in the future. Wouldn't it be cool to discover the true source of climate change, understand the benefits of the Affordable Care Act (Obama Care,) uncover whether or not we're truly dependent on fossil fuels, and learn the truth about the health risks of mobile phone radiation?

Um – perhaps Dr. Ridel is onto something. That critical thinking is a time machine, of sorts. For example, I don't know with complete certainty what's happening to the Earth's climate. But what I do know is that ninety-six percent of credentialed, bonafide scientists believe that a relationship exists between human behavior and the extreme weather conditions taking place around the globe. That's pretty compelling evidence, at least for me. I wonder why the whole world hasn't caught on?

I guess they haven't discovered the critical thinking time machine, yet. Instead, they seem firmly cemented to their biased, unsubstantiated opinions. Outdated like an old, rusted, dented car with ripped seats, an AM radio, wobbling steering wheel, flat tires, and a tired, sputtering engine. What an advantage I have in my sleek, streamlined, supercharged critical thinking time machine.

Ha – that reminds me of my Aunt Gertrude. She believes climate change is part of a natural cycle. That's great for her – but I'm not at all persuaded by her opinion. With all due respect to my aunt, who makes great apple pie – I'm siding with the scientists on the issue of climate change.

Of course, when it comes to Thanksgiving dessert, Aunt Gertrude wins – hands down.

Chapter 5
Messengers:
Who's Telling The Truth, Stretching It, Or Downright Lying?

Don't believe what people say – believe only what they do.

Robert W. Ridel, Ph.D.

"Trust, but verify."
"Doveryai no Proveryai." (Russian)

That's the famous line expressed by former President Reagan to the ex-leader of the Soviet Union, Mikhail Gorbachev – during disarmament negotiations between the two superpowers (1980s). Reagan meant no disrespect – he was just being candid and cautious. Essentially, he informed Gorbachev that he would trust what his counterpart was promising (warhead reductions) – **but** wanted verification (proof) that the Soviets were actually disarming their nuclear stockpiles.

Ah – a critical thinker after my own heart.

Despite what many Democrats thought then (and some think now) – President Reagan (who was a Republican) was no fool, at least not on this particular issue. He understood that people shouldn't be trusted automatically – regardless of their stature (rank) or no matter how sincere they seemed to be. To his credit, Reagan knew enough about history to realize that nations have been damaged and even conquered by unfulfilled promises or "guarantees." And he wasn't about to let that happen to the United States on his watch. Not a chance.

"Trust, but verify."
"Doveryai no Proveryai." (Russian)

Sage advice, indeed.

I don't know if President Reagan was a critical thinker (according to our definition in Chapter 1) – but I do know that critical thinkers habitually doubt the truthfulness of what they hear and read (at least initially). It's not that they automatically reject what other people say and write – it's just that, like Reagan, critical thinkers require verification. No ifs, ands, or buts.

Contrast that orientation to the approach taken by unreflective thinkers. Easily duped and deceived – they tend to be naïve (gullible) when it comes to believing messengers. For unreflective thinkers – the distinction between fact and fiction becomes blurred. Statements are accepted at face value with no questions asked and no research performed. Making matters worse – unreflective thinkers hastily judge messengers based on limited, biased information.

That's a prescription for failure.

Not so for critical thinkers – who are disbelievers by "nature." Always researching and evaluating options – they continually question messengers about the reliability of their information and the integrity of their motives. "Whatever you say" is not in their vocabulary. Indeed, no statement, whether spoken or written, is beyond a critical thinker's demanding line of questioning.

To demonstrate the point – consider the following questions and related cultural proverbs that are built into the fabric of a critical thinker's vocabulary:

- Is the information reliable?
    - "If it sounds too good to be true – it probably is"
- Has it been vetted?
    - "Seeing is believing"
- Why were certain actions taken, while others weren't?
    - "Actions speak louder than words"
- Did the messenger present all sides of a position?
    - "Walk the talk"
- Was the person biased in anyway?
    - "Talk is cheap"

Now – that's a prescription for success.

Again, I'm not suggesting that critical thinkers automatically doubt a messenger's credibility. Not at all. What I am saying is they reserve judgment until they've had an opportunity to evaluate whether messengers are knowledgeable, trustworthy, and relatable. Critical thinkers are, if nothing else, cautious and suspicious– and it's extremely difficult for messengers to earn their trust and respect.

And for good reason.

The world is, after all, populated by messengers who seek to separate people from their money and manipulate their opinions. Any doubts? If so, watch the news. Read newspapers. Listen to stories told by your friends and colleagues at work. Heck – think about your own experiences related to being fooled, conned, deceived, and

bamboozled. Darn – those unscrupulous messengers. Ripping off people time-and-time, again.

Of course, the world is also home to many people who are in fact knowledgeable, trustworthy, and relatable. Fortunately so. But that doesn't invalidate the suspicion critical thinkers have about the reliability of information and the integrity of the messengers who deliver it.

So – what differentiates credible messengers from non-credible messengers? As it turns out, there are three "credibility factors" that separate them. Refer to Figure 5.1.

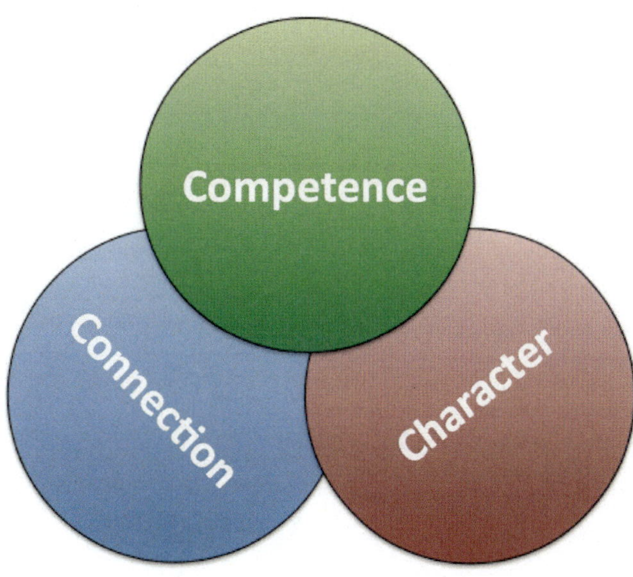

Figure 5.1
Three Factors Of Messenger Credibility

As Figure 5.1 depicts – competence, character, and connection comprise the profile of all messengers. To varying degrees, they establish the level of a messenger's credibility, whether it's low, moderate, or high.

What follows is a brief description of each of them:

- **Competence** – the degree to which messengers are perceived as being experts in their fields. Are they truly subject matter experts (credible) or phony baloney, "know-it-alls" (non-credible)?

- **Character** – the degree to which messengers are perceived as being trustworthy. Are they ethical and fair (credible) or unprincipled and biased (non-credible)?

- **Connection –** the degree to which messengers are perceived as being linked to other people when interactions take place. Are they relatable and approachable (credible) or disconnected and off-limits (non-credible)?

Importantly, all of the above credibility factors (competence, character, and connection) are represented in three types of messengers – credible, quasi-credible, and non-credible. I'll refer to people who score high on these factors as being credible messengers, people who score moderate as being quasi-credible messengers, and people who score low as being non-credible messengers. Again, that's important – because learning about credibility factors (competence, character, and connection) will inform you who's credible and who's not. It's that "simple."

OK – learning the process won't be that easy.

But imagine if you could decipher the "credibility fingerprint" of messengers based on their unique configuration of competence, character, and connection. The benefits would be huge. Immeasurable. Heck – you could even answer the question I posed in the title of this chapter:

"Who's telling the truth, stretching it, or downright lying?"

Would that process be worth learning about? You betcha.

I'll focus the remainder of this chapter on helping you understand the fundamental components associated with each of the credibility factors discussed above. I'll also help you apply lessons learned to understand who's credible and who isn't in your everyday life.

Let's begin with credible messengers, and then I'll follow up with information on quasi-credible and non-credible messengers.

CREDIBLE MESSENGERS

So – what makes up a credible messenger?

As I stated above, credible messengers score high on all of the factors that define credibility – competence, character, and connection. Let's examine each in more detail.

- **Competence –** credible messengers are subject matter experts. Of all the factors, competence is the most important measure of credibility because it confirms the reliability of delivered information. Credible messengers know their content areas and, as a result, people believe what they say and write about to be true (credible).

- **Character –** credible messengers are principled and honest. At its most fundamental level – character is a measure of a person's trustworthiness. If competence means "I believe you," then character means "I trust you." Here are three elements that contribute to the character of a credible messenger:

  - **Ethics** measure character by conveying principles of "right" and "wrong." Credible messengers have high character because they possess a strong moral foundation that contains values related to being fair, decent, and just.
  - **Integrity** measures character by denoting consistency. Credible messengers have high character because they persistently express and defend their core values vigorously – even in the face of considerable opposition.
  - **Truthfulness** measures character by reflecting honesty. Credible messengers have high character because they consistently "do what they say" and "say what they do" – with considerable candor, openness, and confidence.

- **Connection –** credible messengers are relatable and approachable. A high priority is assigned to building genuine relationships based on being engaged, sincere, and friendly. Credible messengers listen to other people with undivided attention and reach out to them earnestly and thoughtfully for all the "right reasons."

Summarizing – credible messengers are defined by high levels of competence, character, and connection. Levels on each of them are always high – relative to their quasi-credible and non-credible counterparts (which I will discuss below).

* * * * *

To help you develop your skill at determining credibility, I'm going to figuratively place you in a real-life situation that involves someone struggling with a controversial decision. You'll be the proverbial "fly on the wall" as you observe the scenario unfold.

In an attempt to assist you further – I'm going to equip you with a top-secret pair of "Truth Goggles" to enhance your observations. While wearing them, you'll acquire the power of invisibility and the ability to determine the credibility fingerprint of the primary character – who I'll call "Senator Stevens."

Put on your Truth Goggles.

INSIDE SENATOR'S OFFICE – WASHINGTON, D.C.

It's Tuesday morning inside Senator Stevens' office. Tuesdays are voting days in the U.S. Senate and today's vote is especially controversial – it deals with the Petroleum Production Bill. The Senator is joined by his Chief of Staff and two senior advisors. There's also a television in the room that's broadcasting a news show.

SENATOR STEVENS
Let's go over the pros and cons of the Petroleum Production Bill one more time.

CHIEF OF STAFF
Yes, Senator – did you get a chance to review the detailed briefing our advisors prepared for you?

SENATOR STEVENS
I read it thoroughly. Thank you. I also conducted some research of my own that substantiates a link between oil production, carbon dioxide gas emissions, and global warming.

The Senator rises from his desk and walks over to the television. He turns if off.

SENATOR STEVENS
(returning to his desk)
On the other side of the coin, there's a strong link between oil production and economic health – especially in our home state.

The Senator reaches into his pocket, removes his mobile phone, and turns it off.

CHIEF OF STAFF
Look Senator – it's pretty clear. Your largest campaign contributor, United Petroleum Association, needs a "Yes" vote on this bill to expand oil production in the Gulf and increase their profits.

SENATOR STEVENS

I understand what they want. But what's right for the country – and the planet? I've studied the research. It raises a lot of questions on both sides of the bill.

CHIEF OF STAFF

It's an easy call, Senator. Your survival in the Senate depends on you securing funding from the oil industry.

ADVISOR #1

Senator, allow me to remind you that next year is an election year. And you're currently behind in the polls.

SENATOR STEVENS

Thanks for the reminder.

Senator Stevens stands up from his chair and deliberately walks over to a window. He glances at a large grove of trees and notices the first signs of Spring. He watches a tour group from his home state walk by the window.

SENATOR STEVENS

How credible are the sources regarding the environmental impact of increased oil production?

ADVISOR #2

It depends who you believe. Scientists from the petroleum industry are certainly experts, but I question their trustworthiness. They claim the impact will be minimal.

(shuffling papers)

On the other hand, the Environmental Protection Agency is an objective government organization with no private funding. Scientists on their staff state that increased oil production will lead to higher levels of damaging greenhouse gases.

Deep in thought, Senator Stevens paces the room for a moment and stops next to the sofa where Advisor #2 is sitting. He sits down on the sofa and looks her in the eye.

SENATOR STEVENS

How's your son doing?

ADVISOR #2

Um ... thanks for asking. He's enjoying his freshman year at college. He's studying political science.

SENATOR STEVENS

Good. How would he vote?

CHIEF OF STAFF

I don't see why that matters, Senator.

SENATOR STEVENS

(shooting a serious look at his Chief of Staff)

He's the future. We are trusted with protecting the planet for his generation. **It's all that matters**.

ADVISOR #2

I suppose he would question why we continue to invest in antiquated fossil fuel technology when the climate is already choking on greenhouse gases.

Senator Stevens rises from the sofa and confidently strides back over to his desk. He turns and addresses the room with passion and emotion.

SENATOR STEVENS

(The Senator nods at Advisor #2)

I trust the Environmental Protection Agency. Their research is more rigorous and unbiased than the data reported by the petroleum industry.

(The Senator looks at Advisor #1)

And yes – I understand that I need "oil money" to win next year's campaign.

(The Senator addresses his Chief of Staff seriously)

But I must vote my conscience – not politics. This bill is bad for the environment and, as such, it mortgages the future of our children.

CHIEF OF STAFF

A press conference is scheduled later this afternoon, Sir. What are you going to tell them?

SENATOR STEVENS

Before the press conference, I want to conduct an impromptu town hall meeting with the tour group from our home state. I'll share the evidence and we'll decide together. It's democracy, right?

CHIEF OF STAFF

Are you sure about this Senator? The United Petroleum Association isn't going to be happy.

SENATOR STEVENS

Yes – I'm sure. The choice is crystal clear. I'm voting "No" on the Petroleum Production Bill this afternoon.

FADE OUT:

Remove your Truth Goggles.

Refer to Figure 5.2 for an illustration of Senator Stevens' credibility fingerprint.

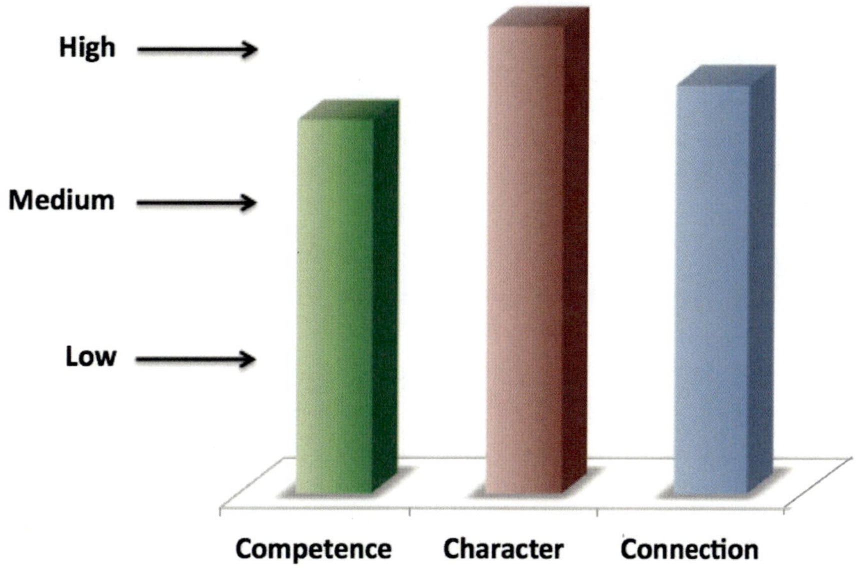

Figure 5.2
Credibility Fingerprint

In summary – Senator Stevens exhibited the following characteristics of a credible messenger:

- **Competence –** the Senator exhibited high competence because he was knowledgeable about the bill and the research associated with it – including data from the petroleum industry and from the Environmental Protection Agency. Importantly, the Senator also conducted some of his own research regarding the strengths and weaknesses of the Petroleum Production Bill – and invested additional time to verify the credibility of all data sources.

- **Character –** the Senator displayed high character when weighing the competing priorities in play – funding his re-election campaign versus protecting the environment. He was unbiased and fair in his assessment of the alternatives. Instead of capitulating (surrendering) to the seductive desire of winning re-election, the Senator decided it was more important to protect the environment for future generations.

- **Connection –** the Senator demonstrated high connection with members of his staff while considering his voting options. He was relatable and approachable during all of his interactions – sensitively engaging with Advisor #2 and professionally interacting with Advisor #1 and his Chief of Staff. He eliminated all distractions (namely, the television and his mobile phone) and was wholly focused on the members of his staff during the entire meeting. He even invited the tour group from his home state to participate in the pre-vote town hall meeting.

Overall Rating: Senator Stevens is a credible messenger.

QUASI-CREDIBLE MESSENGERS

Wouldn't it be great if everyone was deeply competent, possessed high character, and connected well to other people? Unfortunately, we don't live in a world that's populated by an overwhelming number of people who possess those noble characteristics. To the extent that credible messengers are rare – the "next best thing" is to interact with people who are quasi-credible messengers.

But what the heck do I mean by "quasi-credible?"

As straightforward as that question seems – it's not an easy one to answer. Basically, quasi-credible messengers are a mix of credible and non-credible messengers. On occasion they can be credible (knowledgeable, truthful, and interactively adept), but at other times they can be non-credible (ill-informed, untrustworthy, and interpersonally distant).

As I did for credible messengers earlier, let me briefly focus on the three factors that define credibility for quasi-credible messengers – competence, character, and connection:

- **Competence –** quasi-credible messengers can be knowledgeable about some content areas, but typically lack subject matter expertise in most fields. Unfortunately, they don't apply the phrase "I don't know" in situations that are beyond their capabilities. As a result, they cross the "line of credibility" and deliver inaccurate and misleading information as though it is factual and true.

- **Character –** quasi-credible messengers can be trustworthy in situations that require integrity – but they can also be deceitful if the circumstances benefit them. In essence, they teeter on the "character fence" and flip-flop from one side (honest) to the other (dishonest) depending on the defining characteristics of the situation.

- **Connection –** quasi-credible messengers can be approachable or "stand-offish." The type of connection they have with other people ultimately depends on the situation. Some settings promote them to be attentive and respectful in conversation, while others encourage them to be distant and disrespectful to the people around them.

Refer to Figure 5.3 for an illustration of the credibility spectrum and the placement of quasi-credible messengers on it (compared to credible and non-credible messengers).

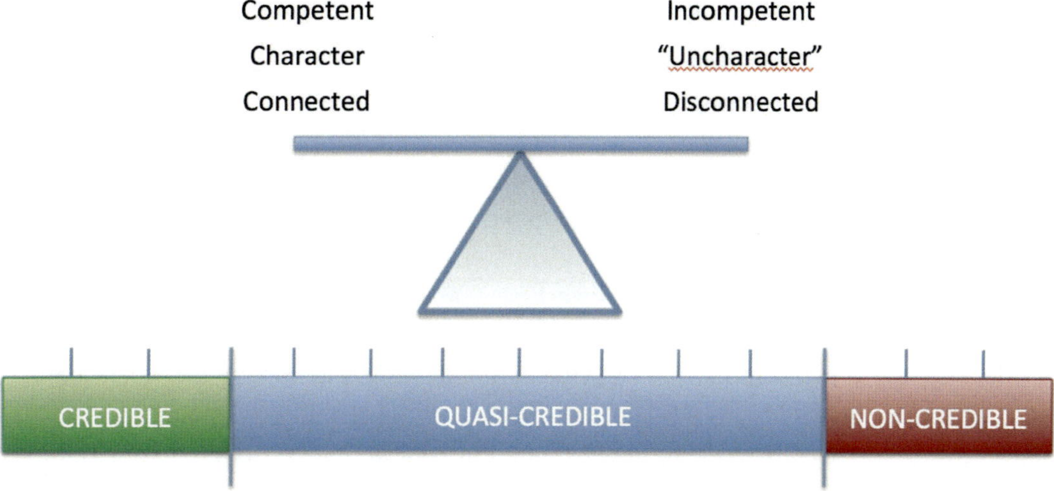

Figure 5.3
Quasi-credible Messengers

Summarizing, quasi-credible messengers are bound by situations – which influence them to be credible or non-credible. Compare that to credible (and non-credible) messengers who conform not to settings, per se – but rather to the defining characteristics of "who they are" as people.

* * * * *

Now, let's use the Truth Goggles to observe the Senator Stevens scenario unfold once again.

Put on your Truth Goggles.

INSIDE SENATOR'S OFFICE – WASHINGTON, D.C.

It's Tuesday morning inside Senator Stevens' office. Tuesdays are voting days in the U.S. Senate and today's vote is especially controversial – it deals with the Petroleum Production Bill. The Senator is joined by his Chief of Staff and two senior advisors. There's also a television in the room that's broadcasting a news show.

SENATOR STEVENS

Let's go over the pros and cons of the Petroleum Production Bill one more time.

CHIEF OF STAFF

Yes, Senator – did you get a chance to review the detailed briefing papers our advisors prepared for you?

SENATOR STEVENS

I glanced at them. But I didn't fully understand the link between oil production, carbon dioxide gas emissions, and global warming. There seems to be a lot of conflicting data.

The Senator turns away from his staff and fixates on the news coverage coming from the television.

SENATOR STEVENS

I wonder how the other senators are voting?

The Chief of Staff walks over to the television to turn it off.

CHIEF OF STAFF

That's not the point, sir.

SENATOR STEVENS

(raising his voice)

Leave it on!

The Chief of Staff stops in his tracks, shakes his head, and frowns. He returns to his chair.

CHIEF OF STAFF

Your largest campaign contributor, United Petroleum Association, expects a "Yes" vote on this bill to guarantee it passes.

SENATOR STEVENS

That makes sense.

(turning to Advisor #2)

I noticed some data in the report showing a strong link between oil production and economic health – especially in our home state. Is that true?

ADVISOR #2

Yes, sir. The petroleum industry data seems to suggest ...

SENATOR STEVENS

(interrupting)

Good.

The Senator reaches into his pocket, removes his mobile phone, and uses it to check his email.

SENATOR STEVENS

Look – I don't understand why everyone is making such a big deal out of this bill. The oil companies aren't evil. They must know what they're doing – right?

CHIEF OF STAFF

Regardless of their motives, sir – your survival in the Senate depends on their funding.

ADVISOR #1

Senator, allow me to remind you that next year is an election year. And you're currently behind in the polls.

SENATOR STEVENS

Thanks for the reminder.

(pointing at his Chief of Staff)

All the more reason to keep the Petroleum Association happy.

Senator Stevens stands up from his chair and deliberately walks over to a window. He glances at a large grove of trees. He then returns his gaze to the television. He misses a tour group from his home state as they walk by the window.

SENATOR STEVENS

Of course, I need to be balanced and fair in my view. What does the data say about the environmental impact of increased oil production?

ADVISOR #2

It depends who you believe. Scientists from the petroleum industry are certainly experts, and they claim the impact will be minimal.

(shuffling papers)

On the other hand, the Environmental Protection Agency says that increased oil production will lead to higher levels of damaging greenhouse gases.

Seemingly deep in thought, Senator Stevens paces the room for a moment and stops next to the sofa where Advisor #2 is sitting. He sits down on the sofa and looks her in the eye.

SENATOR STEVENS

Who is a more credible? The petroleum industry or the Environmental Protection Agency?

ADVISOR #2

In my humble opinion, the Environmental Protection Agency is more credible. They're an objective government organization with no private funding – and no vested interest in the bill.

ADVISOR #2

(fidgeting nervously on the sofa)

If I may share another opinion, Senator, I don't think we should continue to invest in antiquated fossil fuel technology when the climate is already choking on greenhouse gases.

SENATOR STEVENS

That's your opinion. I'm sure there are lots of good arguments on the petroleum side, as well.

The Senator turns his back on Advisor #2 and addresses Advisor #1.

SENATOR STEVENS

What do the voters think?

ADVISOR #1

The population seems to be mostly unaware of the bill. But those who know about it oppose an increase in oil production ... almost unanimously.

SENATOR STEVENS

I see.

Senator Stevens rises from the sofa and slowly walks back to his desk. A newscaster appears on the television. The Senator stops and watches the announcement.

NEWSCASTER

The Senate will vote on the controversial Petroleum Production Bill this afternoon. We will be broadcasting the pre-vote press conference live on this channel.

The Senator sits down and places his head in his hands.

CHIEF OF STAFF

The press conference is scheduled later this afternoon, Sir. What are you going to tell them?

SENATOR STEVENS

(The Senator addresses his Chief of Staff seriously)

I want to do the right thing, but I can't do any good if I lose the re-election. Maybe the ends justify the means in this case.

SENATOR STEVENS

(The Senator nods at Advisor #2)

I'm sure both the Environmental Protection Agency and the petroleum industry's data are rock solid.

(The Senator looks at Advisor #1)

But I need the "oil money" to win next year's campaign.

The Senator rises from his chair and walks over to the window. He closes the drapes.

SENATOR STEVENS

I'm leaning towards "Yes," but I don't have enough data to substantiate my vote. Cancel my appearance at the press conference. I'm going to lay low until the dust settles.

FADE OUT:

Remove your Truth Goggles.

Refer to Figure 5.4 for an illustration of Senator Stevens' quasi-credibility fingerprint.

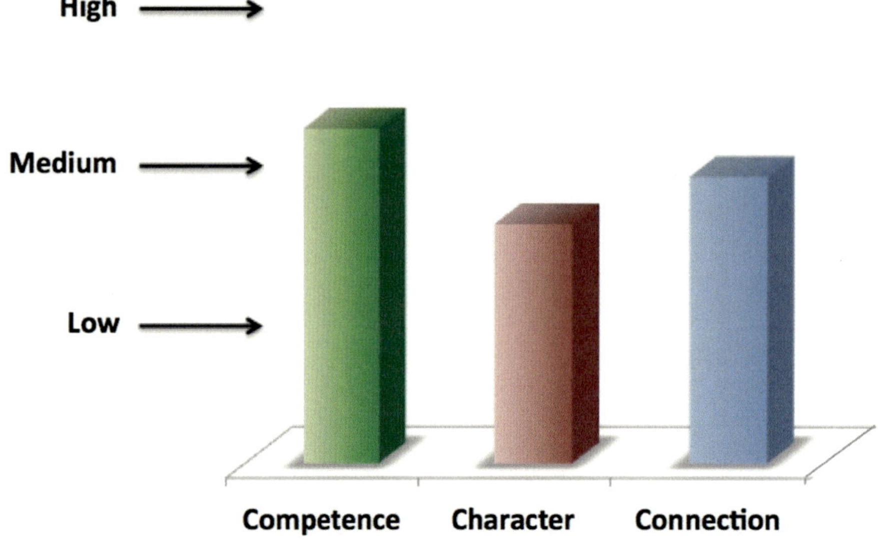

Figure 5.4
Quasi-Credibility Fingerprint

In summary – Senator Stevens exhibited the following characteristics of a quasi-credible messenger:

- **Competence –** the Senator displayed moderate competence in his knowledge of the Petroleum Production Bill. He asked for research and evidence to review – but he didn't seem committed to studying the data from either the petroleum industry or from the Environmental Protection Agency. Statements such as "Maybe the ends justify the means in this case" and "I don't have enough data to substantiate my vote" suggest that he's basing his decision on the "path of least resistance" to getting re-elected, rather than on the merits of the matter.

- **Character –** the Senator exhibited moderate character when considering the impact that voting against the Petroleum Production Bill would have on his prospects for winning re-election for Congress. He was somewhat fair and balanced – or at least tried to be. But his trustworthiness vacillated (moved) based on the situation. Indeed, he made an effort to learn about the opinions of his voters and asked his senior advisors for guidance. However, when their points-of-view interfered with his desire to support the petroleum industry, he rationalized away their evidence and plans to vote for the bill, anyway.

- **Connection –** the Senator demonstrated moderate connection with his staff by alternating between attentiveness and distraction. He was somewhat approachable during some of his interactions (sitting next to Advisor #2), but he disrespected the Chief of Staff when he tried to turn off the television. The Senator's connectedness with each member of his staff seemed linked to their support or opposition of his preferred point-of-view – engaging with Advisor #1 when he supported the petroleum industry, but turning away from Advisor #2 because she opposed the Petroleum Production Bill.

Overall Rating: Senator Stevens is a quasi-credible messenger.

NON-CREDIBLE MESSENGERS

"The American people are tired of liars and people who pretend to be something they're not."

That famous quote was expressed by former First Lady Hillary Clinton – and she's not alone in her thinking. Indeed, her sentiment (point-of-view) is widely shared by a huge segment of the population who also believe that too many people lie and pretend to be someone they're not. For our purposes – I'll refer to that group as "non-credible messengers."

Unlike credible messengers, who only express opinions on topics they have deep knowledge about – non-credible messengers are more than willing to share their unsubstantiated opinions on a host of topics, even those they know precious little about. And these "know-it-alls" do so consistently.

As we did for credible and quasi-credible messengers, let's focus on the three factors that comprise credibility – competence, character, and connection. What follows is a brief description of how each one applies to non-credible messengers:

- **Competence –** non-credible messengers are phony baloney imposters, masquerading around as subject matter experts who "know-it-all." They offer a plethora (multitude) of opinions but exhibit very little expertise in any of their expressed points-of-view (unlike credible messengers who are subject matter experts). Yes – they seem convincing, but they really don't know what they're talking or writing about.

- **Character –** non-credible messengers are unscrupulous and biased. They manipulate people for their own selfish purposes – usually at the expense of other people (unlike credible messengers who are selfless). Non-credible messengers habitually choose greed over integrity, and use any means necessary to achieve their selfish objectives. As a result, they look to game the system whenever they can – no matter how negative the consequences are for other people.

- **Connection –** non-credible messengers are disconnected and off-limits in their dealings with other people. They display a disengaged communication style when interacting with other people (unlike credible messengers who build genuine relationships). In addition, non-credible messengers become distracted quickly when the interaction doesn't benefit them.

Summarizing – non-credible messengers are defined by credibility factors that are woefully low relative to their credible and quasi-credible counterparts. Together these scores define a non-credibility fingerprint that provides evidence that the person is a phony, unscrupulous, disconnected liar.

* * * * *

Once again, activate your Truth Goggles to observe the Senator Stevens scenario from a new perspective.

Put on your goggles now.

INSIDE SENATOR'S OFFICE – WASHINGTON, D.C.

It's Tuesday morning inside Senator Stevens' office. Tuesdays are voting days in the U.S. Senate and today's vote is especially controversial. The Senator is joined by his Chief of Staff and two senior advisors. There's also a television in the room that's broadcasting a news show.

SENATOR STEVENS

Let's go over the pros and cons of the Petroleum Production Bill one more time.

CHIEF OF STAFF

Yes, Senator – did you get a chance to review the detailed briefing our advisors prepared for you?

SENATOR STEVENS

No. I was too busy. From my perspective, the conflicting data from both sides cancel each other out.

The Senator turns away from his staff and fixates on the news coverage coming from the television.

SENATOR STEVENS

I'm going to go with my well-educated gut on this one.

The Chief of Staff walks over to the television to turn it off.

CHIEF OF STAFF

That's not the point, Senator.

SENATOR STEVENS

Good idea – switch it over to the sports show.

The Chief of Staff shakes his head and switches the channel. He returns to his chair.

CHIEF OF STAFF

Your largest campaign contributor, United Petroleum Association, expects a "Yes" vote on this bill to guarantee it passes.

SENATOR STEVENS

Remind me – what's the status of their contribution to my re-election campaign?

CHIEF OF STAFF

Over one million dollars, so far. And likely to get bigger if you vote "Yes" on the bill.

SENATOR STEVENS

Where do I sit in the polls?

ADVISOR #1

You're currently 4 points behind, Sir.

SENATOR STEVENS

(snarling at Advisor #1)

You need to fix that.

Senator Stevens stands up from his chair and deliberately walks over to a window. He mumbles while checking the status of his stock portfolio on his mobile phone. He then returns his gaze to the television – and as a result, completely misses a tour group from his home state as they walked by the window.

SENATOR STEVENS

What does the data say about the environmental impact of increased oil production?

ADVISOR #2

It depends who you believe. Scientists from the petroleum industry are certainly experts, and they claim the impact will be minimal.

(shuffling papers)

On the other hand, the Environmental Protection Agency says that increased oil production will lead to higher levels of damaging greenhouse gases.

Senator Stevens walks over to watch the television again. After a moment, he moves to where Advisor #2 is sitting. He turns his back on her and looks towards Advisor #1 who is sitting in a nearby chair.

SENATOR STEVENS

What's the level of voter awareness for climate change and the role of increased oil production?

ADVISOR #1

Um – let me check.

(typing into a laptop computer)

Here it is. There's a 38% awareness level ...

SENATOR STEVENS

(interrupting)

Good – that's low enough, which means they aren't well versed on the situation.

Senator Stevens turns to walk back to his desk.

ADVISOR #1

... but the majority of them oppose an increase in oil production and support the conclusions reached by scientists at the Environmental Protection Agency.

CHIEF OF STAFF

A "Yes" vote could hurt your bid for re-election.

SENATOR STEVENS

Not if we change their minds.

Senator Stevens sits back at his desk and checks his mobile phone, again.

SENATOR STEVENS

We'll use the extra campaign funding to film a public service announcement and sponsor some supportive research.

CHIEF OF STAFF

It worked before.

Senator Stevens leans back in his chair and places his feet on the desk.

SENATOR STEVENS

(The Senator nods at Advisor #2)

Find an impressionable young scientist to appear in my commercials – and have him deliver a pro-oil message that will resonate with the voters.

SENATOR STEVENS

(The Senator looks at Advisor #1)

The press conference is later this afternoon. I need some research that will convince the press that oil production and global warming have nothing to do with each other.

(The Senator addresses his Chief of Staff seriously)

This is a shrewd political maneuver. If I play my cards right, this could mean six more years in office.

CHIEF OF STAFF

Are you sure about this Senator?

SENATOR STEVENS

The choice is crystal clear. I'm voting "Yes" on the Petroleum Production Bill this afternoon.

FADE OUT:

Remove your Truth Goggles.

Refer to Figure 5.5 for an illustration of Senator Stevens' non-credibility fingerprint.

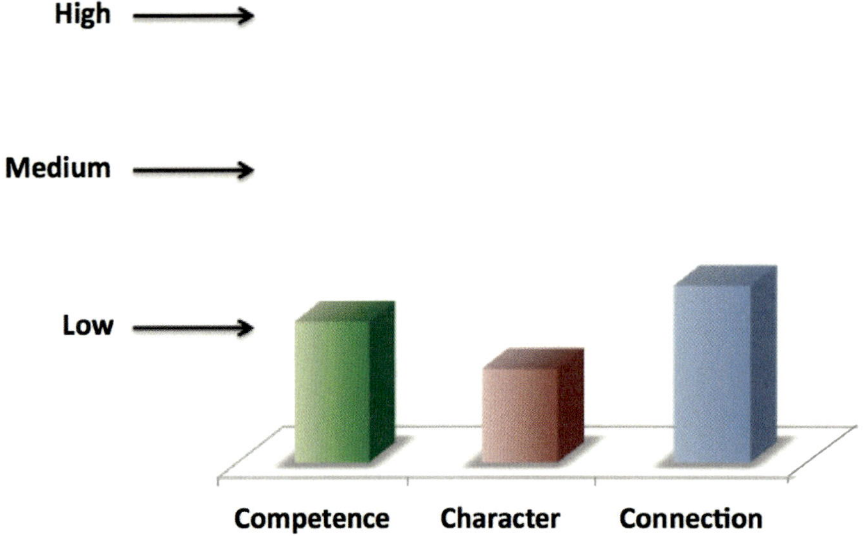

Figure 5.5
Non-Credibility Fingerprint

In summary – Senator Stevens exhibited the following characteristics of a non-credible messenger:

- **Competence –** the Senator exhibited low competence in his understanding of the Petroleum Production Bill – and a complete disregard for studying the facts. He was biased against the Environmental Protection Agency's point-of-view and refused to consider the evidence opposing the bill. Instead, he acted like a "know-it-all" saying, "I'm going to go with my well-educated gut on this one." Beyond that, he attempted to fool the voters and press by funding public service announcements and biased research that support his position.

- **Character –** the Senator displayed low character by completely ignoring the responsibilities of his position as a U.S. Senator. He was unscrupulous and biased in a number of ways – by focusing attention on his re-election campaign and investing extra campaign funding in an attempt to "change the minds" of the voters. He also behaved in an untrustworthy manner by advancing fabricated lies as truth at the press conference.

- **Connection –** the Senator demonstrated low connection with members of his staff. Specifically – he refused to read the report prepared by his senior advisors, disrespected his Chief of Staff when he tried to turn off the television, and snarled at Advisor #1. In addition, the Senator was aloof and off-limits throughout the interaction – watching a sports show, putting his feet on the desk, turning his back on Advisor #2, and checking his mobile phone throughout the meeting.

Overall Rating: Senator Stevens is a non-credible messenger.

* * * * *

I devoted this chapter to discuss how credibility fingerprints (based on competence, character, and connection) categorize various types of messengers – credible, quasi-credible, and non-credible. My goal was to help you to develop the skills necessary to understand who was telling the truth, stretching it, or downright lying.

Before moving onto my Concluding Thought – let's revisit how credibility factors are related to messengers. Refer to Table 5.1 for a brief summary.

Table 5.1
Summary Of Credibility Factors For Messengers

	Competence	Character	Connection
CREDIBLE	**HIGH** ... competence because they're subject matter experts in their fields.	**HIGH** ... character because they rely on their conscience to make good decisions.	**HIGH** ... connection to the people around them because they listen carefully with undivided attention.
QUASI-CREDIBLE	**MODERATE** ... competence because they don't have the depth of knowledge to be experts.	**MODERATE** ... character because their trustworthiness "waffles" based on the defining characteristics of the situation.	**MODERATE** ... connection because they get distracted quickly when better options present themselves.
NON-CREDIBLE	**LOW** ... competence because they masquerade around as "know-it-alls" even though they have little or no expertise on most subjects.	**LOW** ... character because they choose greed and selfish interests over trustworthiness and integrity.	**LOW** ... connection because they're too self-consumed with their own interests and goals.

As stated above – my goal at the beginning of this chapter was to help you learn the skills necessary to classify messengers based on their level of competence, character, and connection. My ultimate objective is for you to apply them when evaluating the messengers you encounter in your everyday life.

The task will be easy enough with credible messengers because they always tell the truth. However, the assignment will be challenging when interacting with quasi-credible messengers because of their proclivity (tendency) to stretch the truth in order to secure benefits, even when doing so penalizes other people. And the exercise will be especially problematic when encountering non-credible messengers because of their uncanny aptitude (ability) to mask the truth behind cleverly disguised lies.

The key will be for you to continue developing your critical thinking skills in order to evaluate the reliability of information and the messengers who deliver it.

Onward – and don't forget to wear your Truth Goggles.

A CONCLUDING THOUGHT

Date: 1980 (yes, I know – that probably seems like ancient history to you)
Time: 2:30pm EDT
Place: Dulles International Airport, Washington, D.C.

What a great day. I remember it like yesterday.

I just finished my Ph.D. – and was getting ready to board an airplane to return to my home campus in California. There I was – with a big smile on my face proudly thinking: "Dr. Ridel – that certainly has a nice ring to it."

After settling into my seat, the person next to me introduced herself in a friendly manner: "Hi, I'm Seiko." I returned the greeting with, "I'm Dr. Ridel – nice to meet you." We chatted for a few minutes and then drifted into our private thoughts as the plane taxied and lifted off into the sky.

Just about the time we reached cruising altitude – Seiko turned to me and asked:

> *"I don't' want to bother you – but given that you're a doctor, do you have any suggestions about how I can treat my aching back?"*

Well – you can imagine my predicament. What should I tell her? Do I "come clean" and admit that my doctorate was in the social sciences – not in medicine? Or should I offer her a treatment plan even though I was clueless about what strategy to propose? Apply heat or cold to the painful area? Take two aspirins? Clueless, indeed.

I spent a few minutes stalling – trying to figure out a way to bluff my way through the awkward dilemma I had unintentionally created for myself. And then I realized that I had no choice and stated the following:

> *"I'm not that kind of doctor."*

Yes – I was honest and told Seiko the truth. Because back then, just like now, I placed a high premium on honesty – even when doing so produced some level of embarrassment.

Seiko appreciated my trustworthiness – and the remainder of the flight was comfortable. We engaged in a wonderful, lengthy (five hour) conversation about all sorts of topics (most of which I knew something about) – and departed company as "friends." And best of all – as she said "goodbye," Seiko referred to me as Dr. Ridel.

I learned an important lesson that day and it was – don't masquerade around as being someone I'm not. Importantly, I've carried that lesson with me ever since. Indeed, I seldom if ever introduce myself as Dr. Ridel, and most definitely not to people on airplanes. ☺

* * * * *

Fast forward to today – 35 years later (almost to the day).

Let's borrow some of the concepts I introduced earlier in this chapter and determine what my credibility fingerprint was at the time of the flight. Refer to Figure 5.6 for an illustration.

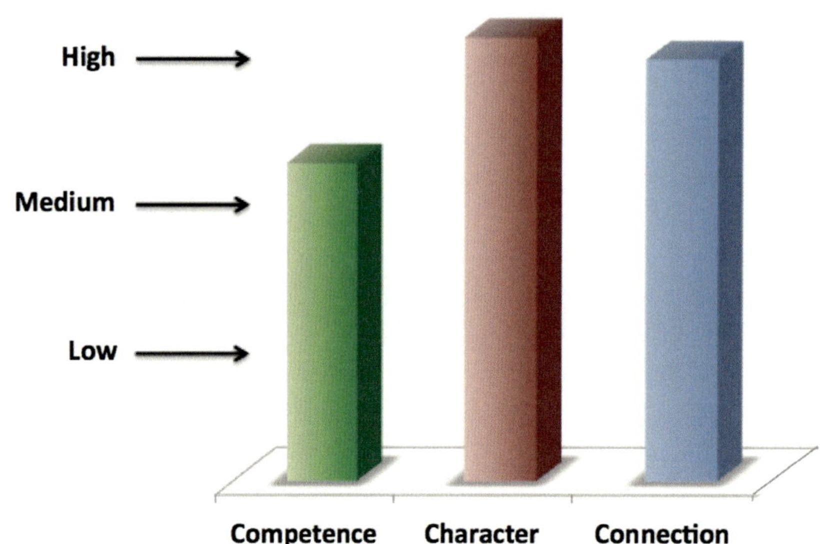

Figure 5.6
My Credibility Fingerprint

In summary – I exhibited the following characteristics of a credible messenger during my flight with Seiko:

- **Competence –** I exhibited moderate competence because, even though I didn't know much about medical (chiropractic) science, I was fairly knowledgeable about the other topics we discussed during the flight.

- **Character –** I displayed high character because I was candid and trustworthy in dealing with Seiko's "back issue," as well as when speaking to her about other topics (sociology and psychology).

- **Connection –** I demonstrated high connection because I offered Seiko considerable attention and was engaged in the conversation (verbally and nonverbally). It was a two-way, fluid, and well-balanced interaction.

Overall Rating: I am a credible messenger.

Interestingly, the credibility fingerprint I possessed 35 years ago (coincidentally when President Reagan discussed nuclear disarmament with Mikhail Gorbachev) remains in evidence today. And I suspect it will continue to be my profile for the rest of my life.

Let me briefly explain why.

Believe it or not, as I type this chapter, I'm competent in "only" six content areas (critical thinking being one of them). Yes, you read that correctly. Me – a Ph.D. for 35 years (since that memorable flight), the author of this textbook, a teacher of tens-of-thousands of students, a person well respected by my family, friends, colleagues, students, and the public at-large on several continents – and I'm competent in **only** six content areas.

How can that be?

One obvious reason is that I set the bar exceedingly high for establishing an "area of expertise." Very high, indeed. While other people acquire content areas like they acquire tee shirts, I believe it takes years (decades?) to really develop an area of expertise. Who knows – I might settle at eight before my career comes to a close. But I won't develop the extra two overnight. The process will take time – and plenty of it.

But there's another reason – a more important one.

From my perspective, one doesn't have to be "smart" to be credible or successful. Not at all.

And I'm a poster child for that statement.

To be frank, I'm not nearly as "smart" as people think I am. While I'm flattered they have that perception of me – it's not entirely true. Mind you, I'm not a fool – but I'm also not an intellectual. What I am is someone who possesses the highest level of character and who easily and thoroughly connects with people. All types of people – ranging from presidents to janitors who clean office buildings and refugees in Third-World countries.

What I want you to understand is that being credible and successful doesn't require you (or anyone) to be "smart." Very few people become intellectuals. I didn't – and you probably won't, either. But I achieved credibility and success because of my high level of character and connection – and I'm confident you can, as well.

Yes you can.

Chapter 6
Understanding Problem Solving In Everyday Life

The fact that people solve problems is hardly noteworthy. What is – is when they proactively prevent them from occurring in the first place.

Robert W. Ridel, Ph.D.

There you are – relaxing on your living room couch, quilt wrapped around your legs, and feet propped up on the ottoman. Of course, a huge bowl of popcorn is easily within arm's reach. You decide to watch television – and begin "surfing" various channels. Venturing here, wandering there – you stumble across a mystery movie and consider whether to view it. Nah – not interested. Synchronized swimming – I don't think so. Dancing with stars and athletes – absolutely not. And then you wander over to a news channel. Eureka. That's it – you decide to learn about what's happening in the country.

The newscast opens with a discussion about health care problems. Before you have a chance to munch on another handful of popcorn – the commentator introduces a panel of "talking heads" who passionately discuss the rising costs of health care and huge numbers of uninsured and underinsured people in the nation, including children. Millions of them. Millions.

You begin to squirm on the couch in disbelief. And I can certainly understand why.

After all – with respect to the health care problem:

- A number of respected think tanks recently ranked the United States dead last when compared to 11 other industrialized nations on several health-related metrics (measurements), such as quality of and access to care. Our dreadfully low position is especially discouraging given that the United States spends more money per capita (per person) on health care than any other country on Earth. For example, the United Kingdom (England, Scotland, Wales, and Northern Ireland) is ranked first even though it spends less than half ($3,405) of what the United States does ($8,508) per year. Hard to believe – but it's true. See Figure 6.1.

	AUS	CAN	FRA	GER	NETH	NZ	NOR	SWE	SWIZ	UK	US
Overall	4	10	9	5	5	7	7	3	2	1	11
Quality	2	9	8	7	5	4	11	10	3	1	5
Access	8	9	11	2	4	7	6	4	2	1	9
Expenses	$3,800	$4,522	$4,118	$4,495	$5,099	$3,182	$5,669	$3,925	$5,643	$3,405	$8,508

Figure 6.1
Health Care Problem

And all of that trickles down to the level of the individual. For example:

- Heart disease, which is the leading cause of death in the United States, accounted for over 600,000 deaths last year alone. The most significant risk factors contributing to heart disease include obesity, smoking, and high cholesterol.
- The second leading cause of death in the country is lung cancer – eclipsing (exceeding) all other forms of cancer combined. Almost 160,000 Americans died of lung cancer last year, and 90% of them smoked cigarettes.

In the next segment of the broadcast, the commentator presents a series of convincing slides that address the staggering economic problems facing the country. One of them nearly knocks you off the couch – showing that the national debt exceeds $18T (as in trillions of dollars denoted by 12 zeroes), which is the equivalent of $56,200 per man, woman, and child.

All-of-a-sudden – the popcorn you were happily devouring doesn't taste so good. And I can certainly understand why.

After all – concerning the financial debt problem:

- Several well-known, respected economists (including recipients of the Nobel Prize) warn that the United States is heading down a dangerous financial path from which there might not be any escape. The amount of debt the nation owes has increased over 200% in the past ten years – and the total paid for interest alone is over $1,100,000,000 per day. Yes – that's more than a billion dollars per 24-hour cycle on just interest (not principal) associated with the national debt. The situation is becoming so dire that many economic experts believe our growing debt, if left unchecked, will eventually bankrupt important social programs, such as Medicare and Social Security. Hard to believe – but it's true. See Figure 6.2.

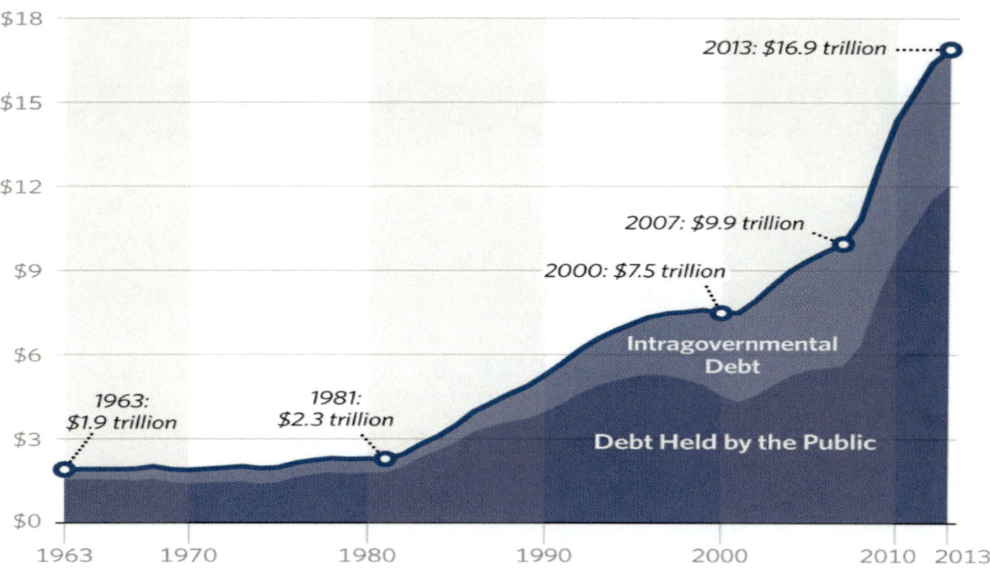

Figure 6.2
National Debt Problem

And just as the effects of health care trickle down to the level of the individual – so do the consequences of national debt. For example:

- On average, every household in the United States owes $15,000 in credit card debt and every student owes $32,000 in student loans. Believe it or not – the personal debt of all Americans is more than half the size of the entire national debt – which, as I mentioned above, is measured in trillions of dollars. That's a lot of personal debt.
- Spending huge amounts of money to make interest payments on the debt negatively impacts people by diverting money away from fixing roads and bridges, building schools, and funding research projects for medicine and technology – all of which lowers people's standards of living.

No wonder your popcorn lost its appeal.

What I hope you haven't lost is your newly developed interest in asking questions – as an aspiring critical thinker. To the extent that you haven't – I suspect you're asking the following:

> *"Why does the nation and its people experience so many problems?"*

That's a good question – just what I would expect from you as an aspiring critical thinker. And, not surprisingly, I have an answer.

I'll develop part of it, the portion that deals with the nation, in Chapter 8. In this chapter – attention will be focused on helping you understand the concepts associated with problem solving and why people experience personal problems. Of course, the social

environment plays a huge role (which I discussed in earlier chapters) – but so do people themselves because of the haphazard, almost random approach they utilize to solve problems in their everyday lives. Ironic, isn't it – that people bring about their own problems, as well as cause them to persist and actually worsen.

Throughout this chapter, I'll make the case that the key to solving personal problems is to understand and implement a structured process that I call the "Five-Step Model for Problem Solving," or abbreviated as the "Five-Step Model." It involves defining problems, identifying causes, and creating, evaluating, and implementing options to solve them – as well as monitoring and modifying them, whenever necessary. Then in Chapter 7, I'll specifically address how the Five-Step Model can be applied to solve several personal problems, including financial problems, health problems, school problems, relationship problems, and work-related problems. I suspect some, most, or all of them apply to your everyday life.

That's a lot of "stuff" – and it's important that you learn this material so you can apply the process to solve problems in your everyday life. Allow me to begin by presenting the Five-Step Model.

Everyday Life with David
"Day 27: Problems"

I've spent most of my life in a state of "oblivious contentment." I was comfortable living in a bubble that didn't expose me to problems like health care and the national debt. They didn't have an impact on me (or so I thought) and, as such, I didn't think about them at all.

Thanks to Dr. Ridel, my bubble has burst – big time.

As an aspiring critical thinker, I now understand that these problems affect me everyday in subtle – and not so subtle – ways. Consider the following examples from my life:

> The nation's struggling health care system has increased my doctor's co-pays and the cost to have my prescriptions filled. Also, my employer recently increased my health insurance contribution because of skyrocketing premiums.
>
> The growing national debt has caused several local and state problems, including bad roads throughout my neighborhood and surrounding areas, larger class sizes for my children, and library closures in my county.

Wow – I never noticed these problems before. My unreflective thinking must have camouflaged these and other situations from my awareness. Well – that's not going to happen anymore. Now that I'm an aspiring critical thinker, I see life's problems much more clearly.

And I also feel a sense of responsibility to get involved. How about you?

THE FIVE-STEP MODEL FOR PROBLEM SOLVING

Imagine how many problems people attempt to solve during the course of a day, week, or month – much less a year. Dozens, hundreds – even thousands. Problems related to finance, health, school, work, children, and so on. To make matters worse, they're woefully unprepared to contend with the avalanche of problems they experience during their everyday lives.

Of course, there are several reasons why people are doomed to being poor problem solvers – but there's one factor that takes precedence (priority) over the rest – and it deals with the fact that they don't employ a structured method to solve them. What's needed is for them to adopt a more systematic, thoughtful approach – such as the one I'm about to describe below. As mentioned a moment ago – I refer to it as the Five-Step Model:

- Step 1: Identify the problem
- Step 2: Discover the causes of the problem
- Step 3: Create options to solve the problem (creative thinking)
- Step 4: Evaluate the best options to solve the problem (critical thinking)
- Step 5: Act, monitor and modify selected options, if necessary

Refer to Figure 6.3 for an illustration of the sequential process of solving problems.

Figure 6.3
Five-Step Model

Let's discuss each step in more detail.

Step 1: Identify the Problem

The beginning of any process to solve problems is to actually define them. It's absolutely futile (useless) to try to solve problems unless you actually know what you're attempting to solve.

Albert Einstein, who arguably possessed one of the greatest minds in the history of humankind – once stated the following about problem solving:

> *"If I had one hour to save the world, I would spend fifty-five minutes defining the problem and the last five minutes finding the solution."*

Absolutely brilliant.

Einstein's quote illustrates the importance of investing time to understand the nature and scope of a problem before attempting to solve it. If you don't take the necessary time to thoroughly define the problem, you may end up reacting to its symptoms rather than identifying the underlying causes of the problem.

For example, imagine if your pants were too tight (which is the symptom). You could "open them up," reposition the attaching button, or simply purchase a larger size. But that wouldn't address the fact that you're consuming too many calories and not exercising enough (which is the problem). Again, if you only react to a problem's symptoms, the underlying causes of the problem would remain – and, as such, the problem would persist.

Here's how Step 1 works:

- **Step 1: Identify the problem**

See Figure 6.4.

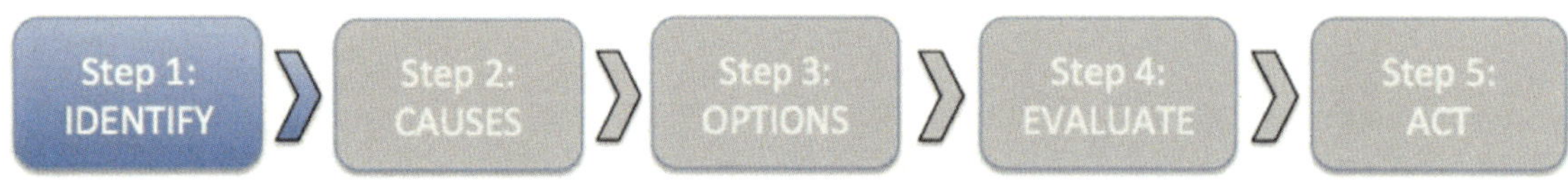

Figure 6.4
Step 1 Of The Five-Step Model

In this step, the key is to spend as much time as possible to identify what the problem actually is – before proceeding with the remaining steps. Once that's accomplished – it's time to figure out what caused it, which is the next step.

Step 2: Discover the Causes of the Problem

In Step 1, you learned the importance of defining a problem you want to solve.

No cause for celebration. That's only one step toward solving it – many more need to take place.

In Step 2, the process shifts from defining the problem to figuring out what factors actually caused it to surface in the first place. This step, which is often referred to as "root cause analysis," involves understanding the "cause and effect" profile of the problem. Stated simply, a problem can't be solved unless you understand the "root" (cause) of its symptoms (effects) – as depicted in the above example of dealing with tight pants. Then, and only then, will you be prepared to solve it.

Here's how Step 2 works:

- Step 1: Identify the problem
- **Step 2: Discover the causes of the problem**

See Figure 6.5.

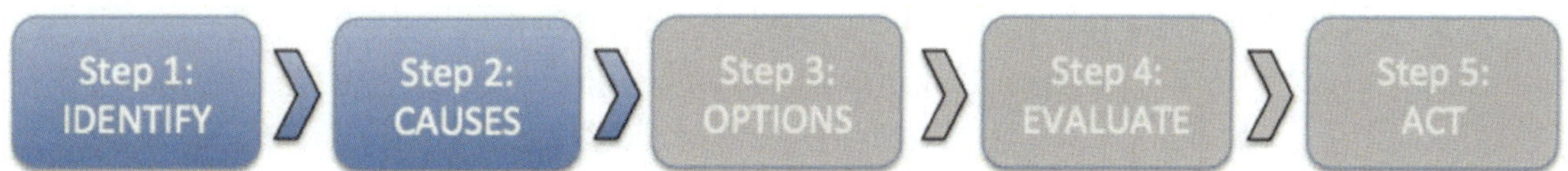

Figure 6.5
Step 2 Of The Five-Step Model

In this step, the key is to spend as much time as possible to evaluate the problem and accurately determine the root cause of it. Once that's accomplished – it's time to figure out what to do about it, which is the next step.

Step 3: Create Options to Solve the Problem (Creative Thinking)

In Step 2, you learned about the importance of discovering what causes problems.

Little cause for celebration. That's just another step toward solving problems – and several more need to take place.

In Step 3, the process shifts from discovering what caused the problem to figuring out what options would actually solve it. This step involves creative thinking – the ability to generate ideas that would solve the targeted (identified) problem. In addition to being creative, this step also requires resourcefulness, patience, some courage, and time for your ideas to develop and mature.

Here's how Step 3 works:

- Step 1: Identify the problem
- Step 2: Discover the causes of the problem
- **Step 3: Create options to solve the problem**

See Figure 6.6.

Figure 6.6
Step 3 Of The Five-Step Model

In this step, the key is to avoid proceeding in a robotic, automatic, jump-to-conclusion fashion. Instead, you should use a free-flowing, imaginative approach to think about options that would solve the problem. Try not to reject an option just because it seems unpopular or impossible to implement. It's also important to set aside enough time to process as many new ideas as possible – realizing that the more you create, the greater your chances are of selecting one that would effectively solve your problems.

In summary, adopt a creative approach to generate options to solve the problem – as depicted below:

- Option 1
- Option 2
- Option 3
- Option 4

Once that's accomplished – it's time to use your critical thinking skills to evaluate which one is best to solve the problem, which is the next step.

<u>Step 4: Evaluate the Best Options to Solve the Problem (Critical Thinking)</u>

In Step 3, you learned the importance of creating several options to solve the problem.

Some cause for celebration. But there are other important steps required in order to solve problems.

In Step 4, the process shifts from creatively figuring out what options can solve problems to critically evaluating which one is the best alternative.

It's important to understand that this step involves a dynamic interplay between creative thinking and critical thinking. The former (creative thinking) provides the options to solve problems, while the latter (critical thinking) serves as the mechanism to evaluate the alternatives. Neither component (creative, critical) is more important than the other – and successfully solving problems requires the involvement of each of them. I mean, how can you critically evaluate options if none exist? And how can you effectively solve problems without making decisions on which option is the best to implement? Not possible in either case. You must have both – or you have "nothing" when it comes to solving problems.

But when the two come together – well, it's an impressive, magical partnership to behold. Reminiscent of a beautiful mental ballet that unfolds in people's minds. Bravo.

With that by way of backdrop – let me re-focus on the critical thinking component and how it determines the best option to solve problems. Importantly, it's during this step that decision making comes into play.

Decision making is the centerpiece of Step 4. See Figure 6.7.

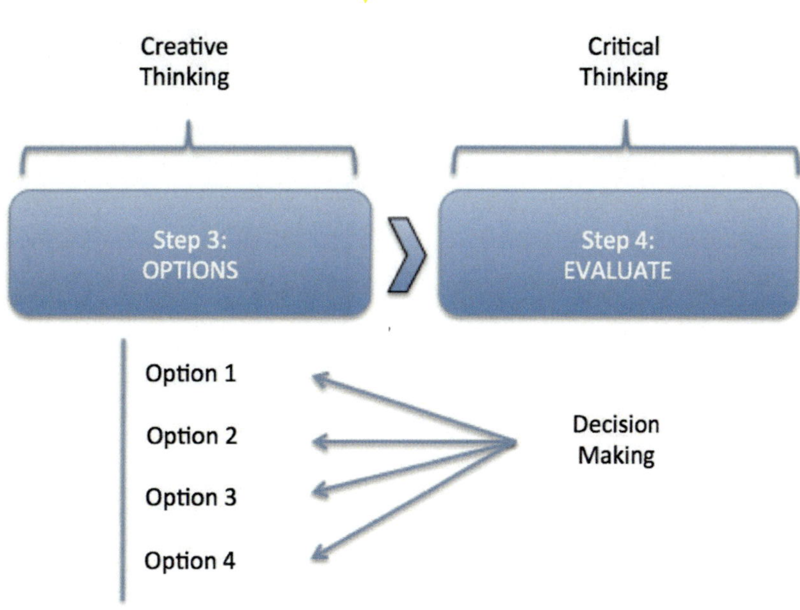

Figure 6.7
Mental Ballet Between Creative Thinking And Critical Thinking

As the figure clearly demonstrates, decision making is connected to problem solving when it comes to evaluating the options generated by creative thinking. More specifically, the process involves "tabulating" the pluses (+) and minuses (–) associated with the alternatives you created in Step 3 (cost benefit analysis), and selecting the best option to solve the targeted problem.

Here's how Step 4 works:

- Step 1: Identify the problem
- Step 2: Discover the causes of the problem
- Step 3: Create options to solve the problem
- **Step 4: Evaluate the best options to solve the problem**

See Figure 6.8.

Figure 6.8
Step 4 Of The Five-Step Model

As you recall from the previous step, you created several options that would potentially solve your problem. But you mustn't stop there – you need to evaluate each of them before deciding which alternative makes the best sense to solve it. Let's evaluate a few of the hypothetical options generated in Step 3 to demonstrate how Step 4 actually takes place.

Option 1:

Refer to Table 6.1 for a list of the pros (+) and cons (-) associated with Option 1.

Table 6.1
Pros (+) And Cons (-) Of Option 1

PROS (+)	Score	CONS (–)	Score
Outcome A	+15	Outcome E	-3
Outcome B	+8	Outcome F	-3
Outcome C	+5	Outcome G	-1
Outcome D	+2	Outcome H	-1
TOTAL SCORE	**+30**	**TOTAL SCORE**	**-8**

Option 1 resulted in a **Net Score of +22**.

After evaluation, you determine that Option 1 would be a very good solution. Of course, it wouldn't come without costs – but the significant pros (+30) would greatly outweigh the minor amount of cons (-8), which makes this option a viable alternative to select in order to solve the problem.

Option 2:

Refer to Table 6.2 for a list of the pros (+) and cons (-) associated with Option 2.

Table 6.2
Pros (+) And Cons (-) Of Option 2

PROS (+)	Score	CONS (–)	Score
Outcome A	+15	Outcome D	-8
Outcome B	+7	Outcome E	-5
Outcome C	+3	Outcome F	-3
TOTAL SCORE	**+25**	**TOTAL SCORE**	**-16**

Option 2 resulted in a **Net Score of +9**

After evaluation, you determine that Option 2 wouldn't be a good solution. True – it would generate considerable benefits (+25), but it would also come with a high level of costs (-16), which makes this alternative less attractive than Option 1.

Option 3:

Refer to Table 6.3 for a list of the pros (+) and cons (-) associated with Option 3.

Table 6.3
Pros (+) And Cons (-) Of Option 3

PROS (+)	Score	CONS (–)	Score
Outcome A	+7	Outcome C	-10
Outcome B	+5	Outcome D	-8
TOTAL SCORE	**+12**	**TOTAL SCORE**	**-18**

Option 3 resulted in a **Net Score of -6**.

After evaluation, you determine that Option 3 would be a bad idea. It would generate some benefits (+12), but it would also come with a considerable amount of costs (-18), which makes this alternative relatively undesirable.

Option 4:

Refer to Table 6.4 for a list of the pros (+) and cons (-) associated with Option 4.

Table 6.4
Pros (+) And Cons (-) Of Option 4

PROS (+)	Score	CONS (–)	Score
Outcome A	+5	Outcome C	-15
Outcome B	+5	Outcome D	-11
TOTAL SCORE	**+10**	**TOTAL SCORE**	**-26**

Option 4 resulted in a **Net Score of -16**.

After evaluation, you determine that Option 4 would definitely be a bad idea – a very bad idea, indeed. It would generate some benefits (+10), but it would also generate an extreme, unacceptable amount of costs (-26), which makes this alternative completely unacceptable.

The final task in Step 4 is to rank the options based on the "Net Scores" calculated for each of them. Here's a summary of findings for each hypothetical illustration that was creatively identified in Step 3.

- Option 1 – Score: **+22**
- Option 2 – Score: **+9**
- Option 3 – Score: **-6**
- Option 4 – Score: **-16**

So – which alternative would you choose?

* * * * *

I know the above illustrations seem robotic and oversimplified. Of course, the actual process of thinking is more fluid and complicated than what I just depicted for purposes of illustration. But that doesn't invalidate the Five-Step Model.

In essence – that's actually how critical thinkers think. Instead of simply acting on inclinations without evaluating possible consequences – they consider the costs and benefits of every option before they choose one. Unfortunately, unreflective thinkers don't think this way and, as a result, miss opportunities to effectively solve personal (and professional) problems in their everyday lives.

What a shame.

If you need further convincing, I'll provide specific illustrations in Chapter 7 that convincingly demonstrate how the Five-Step Model can effectively solve problems in your everyday life.

But for now – let's return to the Five-Step Model.

Step 5: Act, Monitor, and Modify Selected Options

In Step 4, you learned the value of critical thinking when it comes to evaluating options that are creatively developed to solve problems.

Considerable cause for celebration. But you still have one step to go.

In Step 5, the process shifts from evaluating options to completing the Five-Step Model with three key sub-steps:

- Act – this sub-step involves actually implementing the selected option identified as the best approach to solve the targeted problem.
- Monitor – this sub-step involves re-evaluating the selected option to ensure its solving the problem. Nothing is worse than implementing a "solution" that isn't effective.
- Modify – this sub-step involves adjusting the selected option or, if that doesn't improve matters, abandoning it and re-visiting the list of options and selecting a better alternative for implementation.

Here's how Step 5 works:

- Step 1: Identify the problem
- Step 2: Discover the causes of the problem
- Step 3: Create options to solve the problem
- Step 4: Evaluate the best options to solve the problem
- **Step 5: Act, monitor, and modify selected options, if necessary**

See Figure 6.9.

Figure 6.9
Step 5 Of The Five-Step Model

Great – you successfully progressed through each step of the Five-Step Model. Problem solved. Absolute cause for congratulations.

Or is it?

Well – it depends on your point of reference.

PROBLEM CREATORS VS. EXPERIENCERS VS. SOLVERS VS. ELIMINATORS

Don't get me wrong. Solving any problem is noteworthy, whether it deals with financial problems, family problems, school problems, work-related problems, and so on. As I stated earlier, I suspect some, most, or all of these problems are evidenced in your everyday life. And that observation brings us back to the question I posed earlier in the chapter. In abbreviated form, it asks:

"Why do people experience so many problems?"

To answer the question, you must first understand that there are two types of problems:

- **Out of Your Control –** some problems spring on the scene unexpectedly and are beyond control. People can't be held accountable for them, any more than they can be responsible for the high cost of health care or the recent financial crisis and resulting Great Recession it produced. No one could have prevented these problems from occurring – any more than someone could thwart a meteor from crashing into the Earth (despite what Hollywood movies would have us believe).
- **In Your Control –** on the other hand, most problems are predictable and controllable. They are problems-in-waiting – lying dormant (inactive) until the right triggers bring them to life at a moment's notice. Like weeds, needing only proper soil conditions, water, sunlight, and negligent homeowners to grow – problems also spring to life under "ideal" problem-growing conditions.

For purposes of illustration, refer to Figure 6.10 – which suggests that about 1/4 of the problems people experience are beyond their control, while a whopping 3/4 are within their control. Ironically, but most assuredly, people cause the vast majority of problems they experience in everyday life. Not that they invite problems unto themselves; rather, people experience them because they're doing something or not doing something that causes the actual problem.

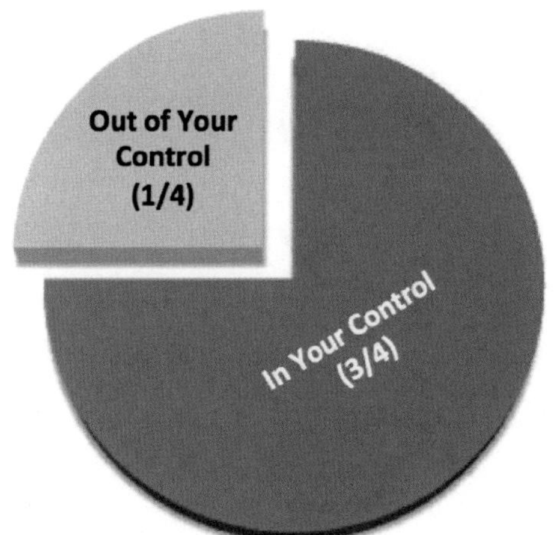

Figure 6.10
Problems In and Out of Your Control

Again – people have control over many of the problems they experience, and the fact they experience them suggests they're to some degree culpable (responsible).

Consider the following:

- Unpreparedness produces problems
- Impatience produces problems
- Shortsightedness produces problems
- Complacency produces problems
- Negligence produces problems
- Pride and ego produce problems

In each of these cases – people experienced problems because of what they did or didn't do. Yes, yes – I know. The social environment plays a huge role – but so do people themselves because of their actions and inactions, as well as their inability to effectively proceed through the Five-Step Model. Ironic, indeed – that people bring about their own problems, as well as cause them to persist and actually worsen.

It's clear that solving problems in-and-of-itself isn't the ultimate objective of critical thinking. The true goal should be to proactively anticipate problems before they actually occur – and take whatever action is necessary so they don't take place. Imagine how valuable it would be if you were able to "see" the future and take preventive actions to avoid problems before they surfaced. In that case, people would be free-and-clear from problems, at least from those under their control. And that would be a lot – 3/4 of the total.

Now – that's what I would call powerful problem solving.

Let me discuss this point more thoroughly, starting with a quick story.

Story from Dr. Ridel

I once delivered a seminar on problem solving to a group of business executives. I started the presentation by inviting a few attendees to briefly share some of their experiences with solving problems. Fortunately – 3 of them agreed to participate. It's beyond the scope of this section to provide details about their individual experiences – except to state that each of their stories clearly depicted them as effective Problem Solvers.

Once the last executive finished – I offered the following comment:

> *"Respectfully, I'm not impressed."*

Well – the conference room was absolutely silent. The audience was undoubtedly surprised by my comment – and the executives who spoke were certainly embarrassed and perhaps even put off by it. Makes sense – I mean, how often are leaders questioned? Not frequently enough would be my guess.

In any event, I proceeded to explain why I wasn't impressed:

> *"Why should I congratulate you for solving a problem that shouldn't have occurred in the first place? The hallmark achievement of leadership is to establish and maintain a problem-free working environment, as much as possible. To the extent that a problem occurred – no congratulations are warranted."*

My point is as important as it is straightforward.

Solving problems is one thing – but preventing them from occurring is something much more notable. Indeed, there's a huge difference between reactively responding to problems once they occur and frantically scrambling to solve them – as opposed to proactively anticipating their occurrence and skillfully acting to make certain they aren't evidenced in the workplace (or elsewhere).

That's a true sign of leadership – and critical thinking.

Now – I want you to read what I'm about to write very, very carefully. No – I mean very, very, very, very carefully.

The moral of the above story, and the core theme of this chapter and Chapter 7, is to be proactive and anticipate problems before they surface. As I mentioned earlier – solving them isn't the ultimate objective. Anticipating problems before they happen, and taking corrective action, is the vital goal for critical thinkers. And that's why I didn't complement the business executives in the above story, because they reacted to problems instead of trying to proactively eliminate them. Let me develop this important point further.

Recall the critical thinking continuum I introduced in Chapter 1, which differentiated beginning, intermediate, and advanced critical thinkers (refer to Figure 6.11). I'd like to build on that representation – adding another layer that predicts how well various categories of people manage problems when (or if) they arise. They are as follows:

- **Problem Creators –** people who create their own problems and don't make an attempt to solve them.
- **Problem Experiencers –** people who experience problems inadvertently and make an attempt to solve them. However, Problem Experiencers are not skilled enough to complete all stages of the Five-Step Model.
- **Problem Solvers –** people who are skilled at solving problems. Problem solvers effectively proceed through all stages of the Five-Step Model.
- **Problem Eliminators –** people who proactively anticipate the occurrence of problems and take whatever "steps" are necessary to prevent them.

Refer again to Figure 6.11:

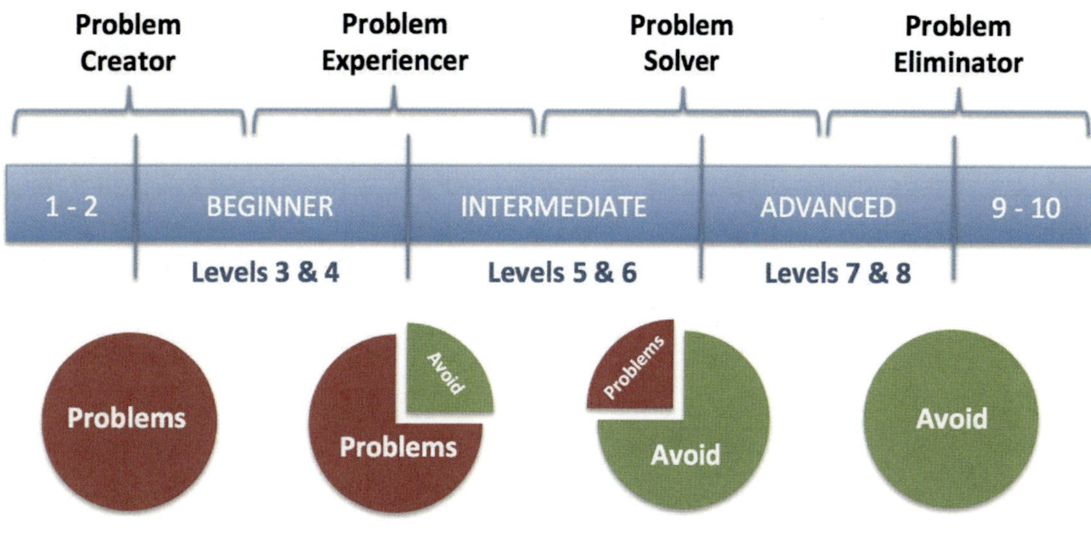

Figure 6.11
Critical Thinking Continuum

Let me briefly describe how people in each of these categories differ when it comes to managing problems. Again, how they respond to problems is influenced by their classification along the critical thinking continuum – as a Problem Creator, Experiencer, Solver, or Eliminator.

Problem Creators

Problem Creators operate on the beginner (left) side of the continuum and experience lots of problems in their everyday lives. What differentiates them from people in the other categories is that they actually create their own problems – intentionally or unintentionally. Three expressions immediately come to mind when I think about Problem Creators:

- "They are their own worst enemies"
- "They shoot themselves in their feet"
- "They can't get out of their own way"

Refer to the pie chart underneath the critical thinking continuum – which depicts Problem Creators as living 100% in the red portion of the circle.

Here's an example: Imagine if a fire recently broke out in your house. That's a serious problem, to be certain. If you were a Problem Creator, you would be the cause of the problem – either inadvertently (accidently) or intentionally (in order to collect an insurance payoff or for other dubious reasons). The important point is – you started the fire on your own. You created the problem.

Problem Experiencers

Problem Experiencers operate on the left-center of the continuum and also experience a multitude of problems in their everyday lives. What differentiates them from Problem Creators is that they don't create problems for themselves. Problem Experiencers try to solve them when encountered, but their critical thinking skills are limited to a significant degree. They can define problems (Step 1) and, to their credit, identify causes (Step 2) – but they don't possess the creative and critical thinking skills necessary to proceed through Steps 3 and 4 of the Five-Step Model. Refer to the pie chart underneath the critical thinking continuum – which depicts Problem Experiencers as living with more red than green.

For example, if you were a Problem Experiencer and encountered a fire – you would try to contend with it (unlike a Problem Creator) – but would be unsuccessful because your skills would breakdown when you reached the creative and critical thinking stages of the Five-Step Model. In that case, the fire would rage until the fire department arrived to extinguish it.

Problem Solvers

Problem Solvers function in the right-center of the continuum and skillfully proceed through each step of the Five-Step Model. Unlike Problem Creators and Experiencers – Problem Solvers are pretty darn good at solving problems because they are skilled at all stages of the Five-Step Model, including identifying them, discovering causes, creating options, choosing the best one, and implementing it.

However, although Problem Solvers manage problems more effectively than Problem Creators and Experiencers – the fact remains they experience problems just like members of the other two categories. They solve them, yes – but they also experience them. Refer to the pie chart underneath the critical thinking continuum – which depicts Problem Solvers as living with more green than red.

Let's return to our fire example for a moment. If you were a Problem Solver, and noticed a fire – you'd immediately identify the problem and try to discover its source (root cause analysis). Not stopping there, as would Problem Experiencers, you would creatively think of several solutions and critically evaluate the pros and cons associated with each of them. Finally, you'd select the best option to put out the flames.

After the shock faded away and you calmed down, you'd think about what just happened. You'd still feel shaken – but you'd also feel a sense of accomplishment. Of being proud that you put the fire out (after all, you always wanted to be a fireperson).

But wait a moment – why should you be proud? Yes – I get it. You extinguished the fire – but why did it occur in the first place? Pausing for a moment – you wonder to yourself:

"What could I have done to prevent the fire from occurring?

Problem Eliminators

Problem Eliminators occupy on the advanced (right) side of the continuum and bypass the Five-Step Model, all together. Imagine what it would be like to enjoy your days, weeks, months, and years without confronting the self-inflicted problems that Problem Creators impose on themselves, problems that Problem Experiencers experience on an ongoing basis, and problems that Problem Solvers solve. (Yes, I know that's a discombobulated sentence.) Refer to the pie chart underneath the critical thinking continuum – which depicts Problem Eliminators as living 100% in the green portion of the circle.

For one final time – let's revisit the fire illustration. **Oh – wait a moment. Silly me. My mistake.** There's no example – the fire didn't take place, because you built preventive mechanisms into your problem solving process. No fire. No problem. You simply bypassed the entire Five-Step Model.

Does that mean that there's something wrong with the Five-Step Model? Not quite correct? Something's missing? I wonder what it would be?

My suggestion would be to build another component into the Five-Step Model – let's call it Step 0. It would represent people who proactively anticipate the occurrence of problems and take whatever "steps" are necessary to prevent them from happening in the first place.

Refer to Figure 6.12.

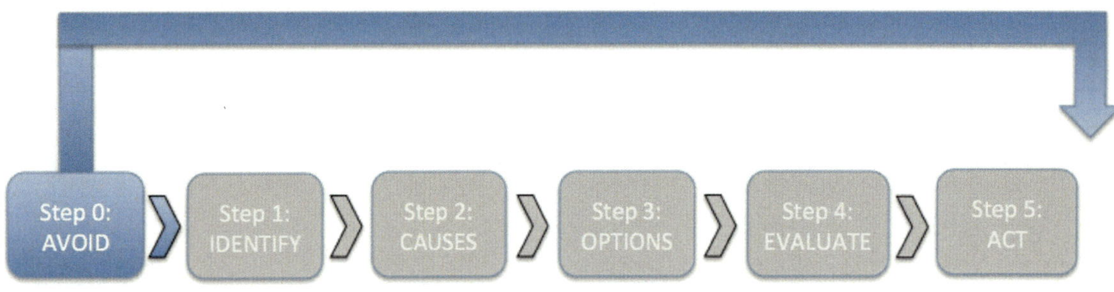

Figure 6.12
Step 0 And The Avoidance Of Problems

As depicted in the above figure, Problem Eliminators (hypothetically) avoid problems, altogether. They "simply" determine what conditions generate problems – and then take action to prevent them from occurring.

Essentially Step 0 makes the Five-Step Model obsolete.

Returning to my earlier weed analogy – Problem Eliminators utilize their ability to anticipate consequences in order to keep their everyday lives relatively free of problems – in the same way homeowners utilize "Round Up" (weedicide) to keep their lawns and gardens weed-free. In both cases – undesirable situations and the adverse consequences they produce never surface because the conditions required for them to develop are eliminated before they can spring into action.

Yes – I know, completely avoiding problems (Step 0) isn't easy to accomplish. But it's certainly achievable for critical thinkers.

* * * * *

As the above scenarios clearly demonstrate – there's a huge difference between people who create and experience problems (Problem Creators and Problem Experiencers, respectively), people who continually solve them (Problem Solvers), and people who prevent them from occurring in the first place (Problem Eliminators).

For people in the first two categories – problems-in-waiting become real problems, necessitating the activation of the Five-Step Model. Unfortunately, Problem Creators and Problem Experiencers aren't motivated or skilled enough to complete it – which explains why problems become real, ever-present features of their everyday lives.

Problem Solvers, on the other hand, are motivated and skilled enough to complete the Five-Step Model. But even they, like Problem Creators and Problem Experiencers, experience problems. Yes, I know – they eventually solve them. And yes I know that solving problems is better than not solving problems. But that outcome isn't as preferred as not experiencing them, at all.

Only people who occupy the last category (Problem Eliminators) are relatively free-and-clear from problems in their everyday lives. For them, problems-in-waiting remain in waiting. There's no need to proceed with the Five-Step Model. None. Step 0 makes certain of that. It's simply bypassed because problems don't surface. They remain unrealized potential. Dormant. Inert. Sleeping.

Take away water, soil, and sunlight – and weeds won't grow. Remove matches and repair faulty electrical circuitry and fires won't take place in your house. Proactively anticipate and eliminate the factors that generate problems in your life, and they won't occur – at least not for the 3/4 of problems that are in your control. Complicated yes – but at the same time, certainly not impossible (at least not for critical thinkers).

Make sense, doesn't it?

So – which category do you call "home?" As an aspiring critical thinker, I'm confident you're moving closer and closer towards the right side of the continuum – toward becoming a Problem Eliminator.

Now – that's cause for a champagne popping, fireworks exploding, and confetti flying celebration.

A CONCLUDING THOUGHT

I have two older brothers – who I got along with decently enough while growing up. We co-existed, but that's about it. You know how older siblings treat their younger counterparts –they're bossed around, teased, and treated with disrespect. And my situation with my older brothers was no different.

Actually – my brothers were and remain good people and trusted friends. Just don't tell them I wrote that.

In any event, I have countless stories about how my older brothers and I co-existed while I was growing up – but one stands out as a good way to conclude this chapter and set up the next one. Here it goes.

One of my brothers once asked me to pick up a pizza he ordered for himself and his girlfriend. I was 16 at the time, a new driver – and happily accepted his request because it would give me a chance to go cruising in his neat car. I mean – how cool would it be to honk the horn and wave to my friends on their bicycles as I drove along. Nothing like "showing off" and making them envious. Again, how could I say "no?" So – with money in hand (given to me by my brother), off I went to the pizza parlor, which was located about 15 minutes from my house.

I picked up the pizza, which really smelled good, and I started to drive home. The journey took me along several streets – with about 6 traffic lights. As luck would have it – I had to stop at practically every one of them. Oh – I forgot to mention, I was really, really hungry. You get the picture – don't you? Hungry driver with a New York-style pizza sitting idly in the passenger seat begging for attention. A prescription for disaster, if ever there was one.

I immediately got caught at the first red light on the drive home – which lasted for about a minute. There I was waiting for the light to turn green, listening to my favorite rocking-roll FM station on a powerful sound system (Jimmy Hendrix, as I recall) – and thinking you know what:

> *"I'm going to nibble on the pizza. What the heck, he (my brother) won't notice some of the cheese and toppings missing. No way."*

So, of course, I placed my hand in the box, carefully placed it on top of the pizza, pronated (twisted) my wrist ever so slightly, and carefully peeled off some of the contents. I didn't take any crust – because doing so would have produced incriminating evidence against me. No cookie (pizza) crumbs on my face or fingerprints to trace. I watched enough detective movies. Off with the cheese and some toppings.

Well – if you're familiar with the art of devouring pizza, you know that pulling off a small portion of a slice is a tricky affair. A larger portion of the contents (cheese along with a lone pepperoni and mushroom) usually ends up being dislodged from the pizza core – which ultimately disappears into your tummy-tum-tum. And that's precisely what happened to me. Multiply that by 3 or 4 more traffic lights – and you'll understand why the pizza was nearly devoid of cheese and toppings by the time I arrived home to my anxiously waiting (and hungry) brother.

The funny thing about it – I had no clue I devoured most of the cheese and toppings. Remember – I was 16 at the time, hungry, and the lid of the pizza box was open just enough for me to skillfully place my hand into it and sample the contents. And I did so at practically every traffic light – not to mention while crushing between them listening to great music and waving to friends as I drove along. And it was "goooood."

Well – you don't want to know what happened when I got home. World War III. I was caught "red-handed" – literally with tomato sauce on my hands, shirt, and pants. Incriminating evidence all over me (I was a messy eater.) I can laugh about the experience now, but it was no funny matter then – for none of us. And my most vivid memory was my brother's girlfriend saying, with surprise in her voice:

"Something is missing."

What a sleuth (detective) she was – there wasn't any cheese or toppings remaining on the pizza.

I'll never forget that experience – and I've used it more than occasionally to demonstrate an important point. I'd like to do so again for you – in this context.

You've learned a great deal about **understanding** the Five-Step Model. Let me briefly summarize:

- Step 1: Identify the problem – the process begins with a targeted definition of a specific problem and its sub-components
- Step 2: Discover the causes of the problem – the process continues from defining the problem to discovering the root causes that allow it to surface and persist
- Step 3: Create options to solve the problem (creative thinking) – next, you employ creative thinking to compile an array (collection) of options to solve the problem
- Step 4: Evaluate the best options to solve the problem (critical thinking) – then, you critically evaluate the identified options, weigh the pluses and minuses associated with each of them, and determine the best solution
- Step 5: Act, monitor and modify selected options, if necessary – finally, you implement the best option, monitor its effectiveness, and make modifications

The Five-Step Model provides you with all the fundamental ingredients you need to solve the problems you would otherwise experience in your everyday life – the equivalent of the water, flour, dough, and delectable red sauce to make a truly excellent "problem solving" pizza. Everything, that is – except the cheese and toppings. To quote my brother's girlfriend, again:

"Something is missing."

The point I'm trying to make is as follows: If you simply learn the Five-Step Model and don't apply it to your everyday life, it's like pizza without cheese and toppings. Frankly, knowledge is inanimate (dead) without application. Recall one of the statements I made in Chapter 1:

> *"... all of your learning about critical thinking will count for naught unless you **apply** lessons learned when making everyday decisions and solving everyday problems. Failing that – you'll never realize your potential to become a critical thinker. Never."*

That statement was true in Chapter 1 – and it applies (pun intended) even more so in this chapter.

Application is the pay-off. It's the required follow-through from all of the concepts you learned in this chapter. Without it, the information provided represents a mere encyclopedia of "dead facts." But with application – the material becomes a living, breathing, pulsating body of knowledge with direct relevance (application) to your everyday life.

It will also provide you with a heck of a slice of pizza.

Everyday Life with David

"Day 30: Problem Solver – Before and After"

Problems. We all have them. Some of us have more than others – personal, professional, financial, health, and so on. To be candid – and I always am while blogging – I have experienced all of these problems, and more. You too? At least I'm in good company.

So, let's be honest with each other – just you and me. Nobody else is listening. Tell me the truth. How do you solve your problems? I can tell you what I used to do before reading this textbook – 1) I would flip a coin, 2) I would throw darts while blindfolded, or 3) I would follow my gut. I'm not particularly proud of these "unreflective" approaches, but I can understand why I was using them. I didn't know any better.

So – how do you think these strategies worked for me? Not well at all. Why? They were based on chance – no process, no scientific method – and worst of all, no critical thinking. Sure, I imagined potential options, sometimes. I might have even evaluated those options from time-to-time. But I never followed a structured, repeatable process for defining my problems and evaluating creative solutions. Never.

Until now.

Learning Dr. Ridel's Five-Step Model really opened my eyes. It certainly makes more sense than my inexperienced, random, unreflective "gut." Don't get me wrong, I like my gut – but it's only right 30% of the time. That's a pretty good batting average in baseball, but it's a complete disaster in everyday life – I was wrong two out of three times. Case in point – buried in debt, overweight, bad grades, and so on.

Okay – I'm going to let you in on another secret. Just you and me. I'm more excited about this lesson than any so far. Sure – the skills I have acquired have been terrific – neutralizing the Puppeteer, detecting unreliable messages, and exposing non-credible messengers. But the prospect of carefully and methodically overcoming debt, health, and school problems has me very fired up!

The only remaining question is which problem to tackle first.

Chapter 7
Applying The Problem Solving Model To Everyday Life

The fact that problems are universal features of everyday life doesn't mean they need to define your existence. "Misery," as the old saying reminds us, "loves company" – but you don't have to be in that company.

Robert W. Ridel, Ph.D.

Barbers do it. Athletes do it. Teachers and doctors do it. So do lawyers, parents, electricians, firefighters, accountants, cooks, postal workers, gas station attendants, engineers, plumbers, gardeners, politicians, and police officers. Indeed, people from all walks of life do it. Including you – on several occasions during your everyday life. And I mean everyday.

So, you ask:

"What are they doing?"

The answer is solving problems:

- How to tackle a "bad hair day"?
- What to do about a season-ending injury?
- How to handle a dispute between students?
- What to prescribe for a particular ailment?
- How to cross-examine a hostile witness?
- Whether to discipline a disruptive child?

The list is practically limitless – covering all areas of life. From the cradle to the coffin – people are confronted with innumerable (numerous) problems that need solving. Some are acute and require immediate attention, while many others are relatively unimportant and hardly matter. But all of them, in their own way, make life more complicated and burdensome than it otherwise needs to be.

Given all the practice people have with problems – you'd think they would be proficient at solving them. But surprise, surprise – that's not the case.

The fact is – solving problems isn't easy. A lot of factors come into play when trying to deal with them, and it's no wonder people are unsuccessful when attempting to do so.

One thing is for certain – and that's the important role played by the Five-Step Model introduced in Chapter 6.

Let's re-consider the process – but this time, instead of simply learning the concepts, I want you to also understand how they can be **applied** to solve problems in your everyday life.

Before continuing – let me re-introduce you to each step in the Five-Step Model and to the sequential representation of them (refer to Figure 7.1):

- Step 1: Identify the problem
- Step 2: Discover the causes of the problem
- Step 3: Create options to solve the problem (creative thinking)
- Step 4: Evaluate the best options to solve the problem (critical thinking)
- Step 5: Act, monitor, and modify selected options, if necessary

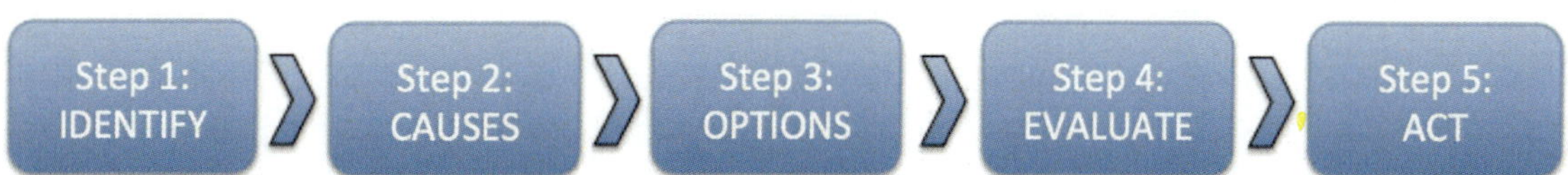

Figure 7.1
Five-Step Model

OK – time to demonstrate how the Five-Step Model can be **applied** to solving problems in your everyday life. I'll begin by addressing two common problems that most people experience – one dealing with financial matters and the other with health. I will present other examples later in the chapter to demonstrate the Five-Step Model's breadth of coverage when it comes to solving a wide variety of personal problems.

SOLVING PERSONAL FINANCIAL PROBLEMS

The economy has been stagnant (unmoving) for several years – and as a result, millions of people have dropped out of the middle class.

Don't be fooled by the all-time highs recently reached by the major stock markets (DOW, S&P) and the spectacular rebound experienced by the NASDAQ. The wealth generated by those achievements don't apply to the vast majority of people who were left behind. The specific numbers tell a sobering tale.

Refer to Figure 7.2 for an illustration of the divergence between the economic classes when it comes to income distribution.

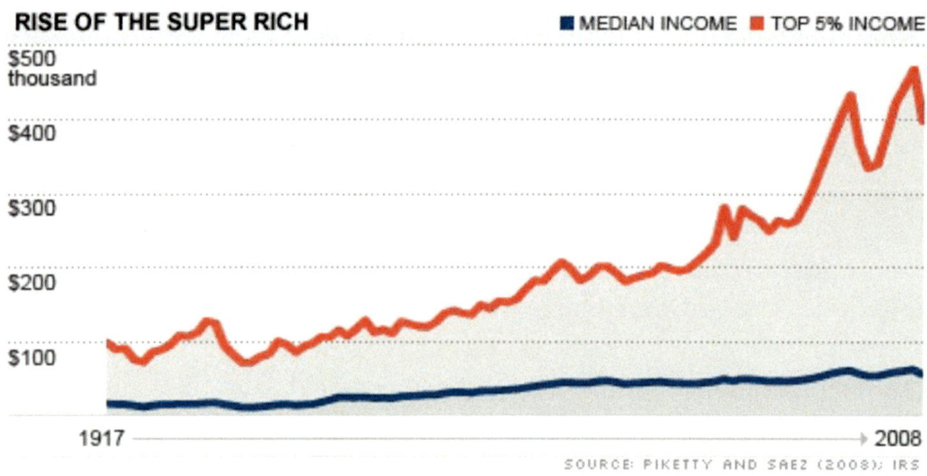

Figure 7.2:
Income Divergence Between The Middle Class And The Super Rich

It's evident from Figure 7.2 that the vast majority of the population has been flat-lined (stagnant) for a long time (and I mean a very long time). No wealth-boom for them – as was the case for the top 5% of earners in the country. And the gap is widening. By 2016, the wealthiest people in the world (1%) will have more money than the rest of the world's population combined – and that's over 7 billion people. This increasing disparity has caused financial problems for a significant portion of the remaining 99% in the form of stagnant income and higher debt.

As mentioned in Chapter 6, personal debt in America is at an all-time high – more than half of the size of the entire national debt. And the situation is getting worse. For example, the current population (Generation X) carries 42% more debt than previous generations, and over 1 million families go bankrupt every year.

Record-high personal debt. Stagnant wages. It's a disastrous financial scenario for the economy and the people impacted by it.

If you have any doubts, let me introduce you to Ming who is using the Five-Step Model to help solve her financial problem.

Step 1: Identify the Problem

Ming's debt keeps rising. She barely earns enough to make the minimum interest payment on what she owes – much less pay down the principal (core amount) on her debt. As a result, her debt keeps getting higher and higher – and the financial hole she's digging for herself keeps getting bigger and bigger. Ming realizes that at some point she needs to pay down her debt, otherwise bankruptcy and foreclosure will be in her future. But how will she respond to that insight?

Fortunately, Ming recently completed a critical thinking course and learned about the Five-Step Model. Importantly – she made the wise decision to **apply** lessons learned in order to solve her debt problem.

Below is Step 1 in Ming's Five-Step Model:

- **Step 1: Identify the problem – Ming determines that her primary financial problem is growing personal debt.**

Now that Ming identified her problem (growing personal debt), it's time for her to figure out what's causing it.

Step 2: Discover the causes of the problem

Ming begins to seriously think about what caused her to accumulate financial debt over time. With the Five Step Model securely in her mind – she decides to compile a list of possible culprits (causes). She identified several, including:

- Spending more money than she makes
- Accumulating credit card debt
- Earning insufficient income at work
- Paying back student loans
- Raising two young children with no child support from their father (her ex-husband)

Below is Step 2 in Ming's Five-Step Model:

- Step 1: Identify the problem – Ming determines that her primary financial problem is growing personal debt.
- **Step 2: Discover the causes of the problem – Ming traces her debt problem back to its root causes – she spends more money than she makes and doesn't receive child support.**

Now that Ming understands what's causing her financial problems (spends more money than she makes and doesn't receive child support), it's time for her to figure out how she can reduce her debt.

Step 3: Create options to solve the problem (creative thinking)

As you learned in Chapter 6, creative thinking is an important part of the Five-Step Model – and this step requires Ming to creatively develop strategies that are designed to solve her debt problem.

Here's a list of the options Ming generated during several creative thinking sessions:

- Option 1: Prepare a weekly budget that's designed to produce a surplus, and apply the extra funds to pay down her credit card debt
- Option 2: Take legal action against her ex-husband to force him to pay child support
- Option 3: Sell her house and use the profits to get out of debt
- Option 4: Cut up her credit cards and pay only with cash
- Option 5: File for bankruptcy

Below is Step 3 in Ming's Five-Step Model:

- Step 1: Identify the problem – Ming determines that her primary financial problem is growing personal debt.
- Step 2: Discover the causes of the problem – Ming traces her debt problem back to its root causes – she spends more money than she makes and doesn't receive child support.
- **Step 3: Create options to solve the problem – Ming thinks creatively about options that will enable her to reduce her high level of personal debt.**

Now that Ming created a list of options to solve her financial problem, it's time for her to use her critical thinking skills and select the best ones to implement.

Step 4: Evaluate the best options to solve the problem (critical thinking)

In Step 4, the process shifts from creatively figuring out what options can solve problems to critically evaluating which alternatives are best suited to solve them.

Before continuing – it's important to reiterate (repeat) that effective problem solving involves the ongoing interplay between creative thinking and critical thinking. The former (creative thinking) identifies options designed to solve problems, while the latter (critical thinking) evaluates which alternatives are best suited to accomplish that important objective. As I stressed in Chapter 6, you can't have one form of thinking without the other and expect to solve problems. Remember what I mentioned about the interplay between the two forms of thinking:

> *"... it's an impressive, magical partnership to behold. Reminiscent of a beautiful mental ballet that unfolds in people's minds. Bravo."*

With that recap in place – let's continue. Below is Step 4 in Ming's Five-Step Model:

- Step 1: Identify the problem – Ming determines that her primary financial problem is growing personal debt.

- Step 2: Discover the causes of the problem – Ming traced her debt problem back to its root causes – she spends more money than she makes and doesn't receive child support.
- Step 3: Create options to solve the problem – Ming thinks creatively about options that will enable her to reduce her high level of personal debt.
- **Step 4: Evaluate the best options to solve the problem – Ming uses her critical thinking skills to evaluate her creative options and select the best alternatives.**

Let's track Ming's decision making process for three of the five identified options.

Option 1: Prepare a weekly budget that's designed to produce a surplus, and apply it to pay down her credit card debt

Refer to Table 7.1 for a list of the pros (+) and cons (-) that Ming produced for Option 1.

Table 7.1
Pros (+) And Cons (-) Of Preparing A Weekly Budget With A Surplus

PROS (+)	Score	CONS (–)	Score
Stop spending more than income	+15	Requires personal sacrifice	-5
Pay less interest expense	+8	Can't afford extra childcare	-2
Pay off credit cards faster	+3	Not dining out	-1
Learn how to save money	+2	Requires math skills	-1
TOTAL SCORE	**+28**	**TOTAL SCORE**	**-9**

Option 1 resulted in a **Net Score of +19**.

After evaluation, Ming determined that preparing a weekly budget and applying the surplus to pay down her credit card debt would be a very good option to deal with her debt problem. The reason she reached that conclusion is straightforward enough – doing so would compel her to curtail (cease) her excessive spending and provide her with additional money necessary to pay down her debt. Of course, honoring her weekly budget would require personal sacrifice on her part – no more dining at restaurants, attending concerts and sporting events, and forget about that trip to Europe she planned on taking next summer. Still – a **Net Score of +19** makes this option worthy of serious consideration.

Option 2: Take legal action against her ex-husband to force him to pay child support

Refer to Table 7.2 for a list of the pros (+) and cons (-) that Ming produced for Option 2.

Table 7.2
Pros (+) And Cons (-) Of Taking Legal Action Against Her Ex-Husband For Child Support

PROS (+)	Score	CONS (–)	Score
Ex-husband pays for childcare	+10	Emotional for her children	-5
Budget surplus helps pay debt	+5	Legal action is stressful	-2
Less personal sacrifice	+2		
TOTAL SCORE	**+17**	**TOTAL SCORE**	**-7**

Option 2 resulted in a **Net Score of +10**.

After evaluation, Ming determined that taking legal action against her ex-husband for unpaid child support would be another very good option to deal with her money woes. The reason she reached that conclusion is straightforward enough – doing so would generate much needed money to raise her children more comfortably and help pay off her credit card debt more quickly. On the other hand, pursuing legal action against her ex-husband would be emotionally difficult for her and her children. All in all, a **Net Score of +10** makes this solution worth considering, as well.

Option 3: Sell her house and completely pay off her credit card debt

Refer to Table 7.3 for a list of the pros (+) and cons (-) that Ming produced for Option 3.

Table 7.3
Pros (+) And Cons (-) Of Selling Her House And Paying Off Her Credit Cards

PROS (+)	Score	CONS (–)	Score
All personal debt is paid off	+8	Forced into small apartment	-15
Homeowner expenses decrease	+3	Downgraded school district	-4
No more credit card interest	+3	No mortgage tax deduction	-2
TOTAL SCORE	**+14**	**TOTAL SCORE**	**-21**

Option 3 resulted in a **Net Score of -7**.

After evaluation, Ming determined that selling her house to pay off her credit card debt would be counter-productive. Doing so would require her and her children to move into a small apartment, and for them to relocate into a less desirable school district. Sure – the solution would help Ming pay off her credit card debt faster, but her personal sacrifices (and that of her children) would be too high from a cost-benefit perspective. Bottom Line – a **Net Score of -7** disqualifies this option as a possible solution for Ming's debt problems.

Once she finished evaluating her options – Ming ranked them based on generated net scores. Here's a summary of her findings for all five options she considered – not just the three summarized above:

- Score: **+19** – Prepare a weekly budget with a surplus, and apply it to credit cards
- Score: **+10** – Force her ex-husband to pay child support (legal action)
- Score: **+5** – Cut up her credit cards
- Score: **-7** – Sell her house and pay off her credit cards
- Score: **-15** – File for bankruptcy

So – which options do you think Ming selected?

Yes – that's correct. Ming decided to prepare a weekly budget that produced a surplus and apply the extra funds to pay down her credit card debt. Importantly, she also decided to take legal action against her ex-husband to provide child support for her children.

Now that Ming selected her two best solutions, it's time for her to implement and monitor them, as well as modify (if necessary).

<u>Step 5: Act, monitor, and modify selected options</u>

The Five-Step Model concludes in Step 5, which introduces three key sub-steps – to act, to monitor, and to modify. Below find a brief summary of how Ming completed each of them to solve her debt problems:

- Act – Ming has done a fabulous job up to this point, but it will count for naught (nothing) unless she **applies** the selected strategies to solve to her debt problem. And Ming accomplishes just that in this sub-step. For example, she adheres to her weekly budget in order to generate the additional money needed to pay down her credit card debt. Ming also engages the services of a pro-bono (free) community lawyer who promptly contacted her ex-husband demanding that he provide child support payments or face damaging legal action.

- Monitor – Ming is on the road to financial recovery, but she still has a long journey ahead. She understands that it'll take years to become debt-free – and that she must continually monitor her strategies to ensure the chosen options do, in fact, solve her financial problems. The process requires that she routinely examine her spending levels, regularly scrutinize her income balances, and carefully watch her pay-down amounts on her credit card debt. And all of this needs to be accomplished on an ongoing basis. Failure on her part to monitor results would spell doom for Ming – and she knows it.

- Modify – In all probability, Ming's journey won't be without twists and turns, bumps and thuds. And when they come about – she'll need to modify her strategies as quickly as possible. For example, she might need to replace one of the selected options with another one, or actually create other alternatives as her situation changes over time. Regardless of what caused the change, Ming will need to make whatever strategy alterations are necessary to achieve her primary objective – which is to become debt-free. If not, recidivism (repeating an undesirable behavior, such as overspending) is a real possibility.

Below is Step 5 in Ming's Five-Step Model:

- Step 1: Identify the problem – Ming determines that her primary financial problem is growing personal debt.
- Step 2: Discover the causes of the problem – Ming traces her debt problem back to its root causes – she spends more money than she makes and doesn't receive child support.
- Step 3: Create options to solve the problem – Ming thinks creatively about options that will enable her to reduce her high level of personal debt.
- Step 4: Evaluate the best options to solve the problem – Ming uses her critical thinking skills to evaluate her creative options and select the best alternatives.
- **Step 5: Act, monitor, and modify selected options, as necessary – Ming prepares a weekly budget, applies surplus funds to pay down her credit card debt, and requests that a legally-sanctioned notice be sent to her ex-husband for child support payments. She's now in the process of monitoring her balances – and is prepared to modify her spending and saving strategies, if necessary.**

* * * * *

So – how did Ming actually do? Is she still spending beyond her means? Or did she successfully reduce or eliminate her financial debt problems? Let's settle into our critical thinking time machine, fast-forward 12 months into the future, and find out.

Lo and behold – Ming's situation has dramatically improved over time:

- Her credit card debt is significantly lower. She's now able to pay the interest on her debt and pay-down some of the principal on what she owes. Fortunately, her spending habits are now under control.
- She just landed a new position that pays her more than what she earned in her last position. To her credit (no pun intended), Ming proudly resists spending the extra money – and instead, deposits it into a savings account she recently opened at a local bank.
- Her ex-husband, no doubt motivated by avoiding legal action, continually sends her monthly child support. Happily, he hasn't missed a payment.

What a pleasant journey in our critical thinking time machine.

All in all, the Five-Step Model seems to be working "miracles" for Ming. Lessons learned – she's brought her debt problem under control.

Care to try?

Everyday Life with David

"Day 33: Money, Trouble, and Motivation"

"Money," as the saying reminds us, "is the root of all evil." Well – that's a little dramatic. I wouldn't say money has to be evil, but excessive consumerism (buying a lot of stuff) can certainly cause a lot of problems. And I've experienced my fair share of battles with spending – especially when I spent "free money" provided by credit cards and home equity loans. What a shock to my system (financial, as well as psychological and emotional) – when I realized that money is only free until you have to pay it back. Don't remind me – painful memories.

Please know – my excessive spending made sense at the time. Life was filled with unbridled optimism – and confidence that the good times would continue. So I continued to spend. My job was secure – so I spent. My family was healthy – so I spent. My house was sound and repair-free – so I spent. Then boom -- unfortunately, the good times abruptly changed. Job loss. Sickness in the family. Water heater goes kaput (breaks) leaving me with an unwanted indoor swimming pool. Unanticipated reality, yes. Unwelcomed reality, yes. Underserved reality, absolutely yes. No matter – it was a financial reality that I wanted to change.

Fortunately, my family and I rebounded quickly.

Yes, I lost a lot – but I also gained a lot in terms of knowledge about when, where, and how much to spend. Beyond that, I also learned the important lesson of saving for the future. I built a budget and watched it closely when it came to spending and saving. As a result, I now feel safe when I lay my head down at night – knowing that I'm living within my means and still enjoying life. Of course, I wish I knew about the Five-Step Model before I experienced the hard-knocks of reality years ago – but I'm certainly glad I integrated its lessons into the very fabric of my everyday life.

I hope you never find yourself buried in financial problems I experienced – but if you do, implement the Five-Step Model immediately and hopefully you'll re-bound like I did.

SOLVING PERSONAL HEALTH PROBLEMS

Akin to suffering from stagnant income levels and financial debt – our nation is also anguishing over the failing health of its citizenry. The evidence is as indisputable (clear) as it is disconcerting (unsettling).

Recall information I presented in Chapter 6 about heart disease and lung cancer – the number one and two causes of death in the United States, respectively. Hundreds-of-thousands of people die on an annual basis – perishing from preventable diseases.

And that's not all.

Adding to the list of the nation's health woes – consider obesity. Amazingly, almost 70% of Americans are obese. Sadly – 18% of children under the age of 11 are also overweight, and this number is steadily growing (having doubled in the last 30 years).

Gee, let me guess where the extra weight comes from – candy bars and cookies at supermarket checkout counters, sugar-laden breakfast cereals, fast foods at countless roadside diners, and high caloric meals delivered at school cafeterias. Refer to Figure 7.3 and review an obesity map of the United States (Centers for Disease Control and Prevention).

Also consider diabetes, high cholesterol, and hypertension – all of which are on the rise with about 50% of the population suffering from one or more of these ailments. Left untreated, each of them can lead to more serious problems, such as heart disease, stroke and, of course, death.

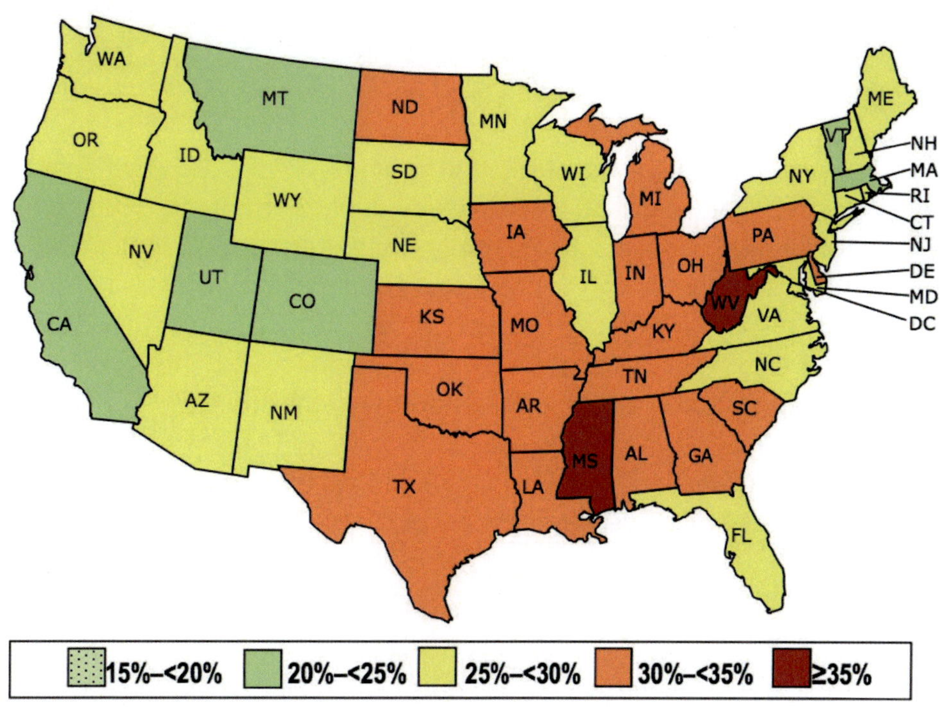

Figure 7.3:
State-By-State Obesity Levels

Still another area of concern, related to obesity – deals with exercise or, more aptly put, lack of exercise. Last year, only 20% of the population met the government's minimum standards for aerobic and muscle-strengthening activity. That's one person in five. What are the other four people doing? And when lack of exercise is combined with obesity – well, it's not a formula for good health and longevity (long life).

Even though people confront many problems during their everyday lives – I can't imagine anything more important than one's physical health. Nothing. It doesn't matter how much wealth people accumulate, how fancy their titles are, and how many awards they earn. As my mother always taught me:

"If you have your health, you have everything."

And I never disagree with my mother, who happens to be 99 years of age.

She's always right. ☺

Seriously, as an aspiring critical thinker, its incumbent (required) of you to evaluate your health continuously and take steps to mitigate (lessen) problems that might otherwise arise. Your life, and the quality of it, depends on you doing so. Yes – health is a matter of serious concern and commitment.

If you have any doubts or need further motivation, let me introduce you to Carlos who is using the Five-Step Model to help solve his weight problem.

Step 1: Identify the Problem

Carlos recently stepped on his scale – and he couldn't believe the digital number that was displayed on the machine. He knew he was overweight, but not by that much. Just then, Carlos began to understand why he's been so tired lately – experiencing difficulty getting up from the couch at home and gasping for breath as he climbed the stairs at work.

Fortunately, Carlos recently completed a critical thinking course and learned about the Five-Step Model for problem solving. Importantly, he decided to **apply** lessons learned in hopes of solving his weight problem.

Below is Step 1 in Carlos's Five-Step Model:

- **Step 1: Identify the problem – Carlos determines that his primary health problem is obesity.**

Now that Carlos understands the specifics of his health problem (obesity), it's time for him to figure out what's causing it.

Step 2: Discover the causes of the problem

The problem now defined, Carlos thinks about how his weight problem developed over time. He decided to use the Five Step Model to identify what caused him to become overweight and out-of-shape. He narrows the list down to the following factors:

- Overeating
- Consuming low-quality junk food
- Exercising infrequently or not at all
- Binging at night – just before going to bed
- Drinking too many soft drinks

Below is Step 2 in Carlos's Five-Step Model:

- Step 1: Identify the problem – Carlos determines that his primary health problem is obesity.
- **Step 2: Discover the causes of the problem – Carlos traces his weight problem back to its root causes – he eats too much low-quality junk food and he doesn't exercise at all.**

Now that Carlos understands what's causing his weight problem (eats too much low-quality junk food and doesn't exercise), it's time for him to figure out how he can lose weight and get in shape.

Step 3: Create options to solve the problem (creative thinking)

As I discussed on repeated occasions, creative thinking is an important part of the Five-Step Model – and this step requires Carlos to develop strategies to solve his weight problem.

Here is a list of the options Carlos generated during several creative thinking sessions:

- Option 1: Start a balanced low-fat diet with 2,000 calories a day
- Option 2: Join a gym and hire a personal fitness trainer
- Option 3: Undergo fat removal surgery (liposuction)
- Option 4: Start an extreme low-carbohydrate diet
- Option 5: Abstain from eating and "body cleanse" every other day

Below is Step 3 in Carlos's Five-Step Model:

- Step 1: Identify the problem – Carlos determines that his primary health problem is obesity.
- Step 2: Discover the causes of the problem – Carlos traces the problem back to its root causes – he eats too much low-quality junk food and he doesn't exercise at all.
- **Step 3: Create options to solve the problem – Carlos thinks creatively about options that will enable him to reduce his obesity and increase his fitness.**

Now that Carlos created a list of options to solve his weight problem, it's time for him to **apply** his critical thinking skills and select the best ones to implement.

Step 4: Evaluate the best options to solve the problem (critical thinking)

In Step 4, the process shifts from creatively figuring out what options can solve problems to critically evaluating which alternatives are best suited to actually solve them.

Below is Step 4 in Carlos's Five-Step Model:

- Step 1: Identify the problem – Carlos determines that his primary health problem is obesity.
- Step 2: Discover the causes of the problem – Carlos traces the problem back to its root causes – he eats too much low-quality junk food and he doesn't exercise at all.
- Step 3: Create options to solve the problem – Carlos thinks creatively about options that will enable him to reduce his obesity and increase his fitness.

- **Step 4: Evaluate the best options to solve the problem – Carlos uses his critical thinking skills to evaluate his creative options and select the best alternatives.**

Let's track Carlos's decision making process for three of the five identified options.

Option 1: Start a balanced low-fat diet with 2,000 calories a day

Refer to Table 7.4 for a list of the pros (+) and cons (-) that Carlos produced for Option 1.

Table 7.4
Pros (+) And Cons (-) Of Starting A Balanced Low-Fat Diet

PROS (+)	Score	CONS (–)	Score
Lose weight safely (over time)	+20	Requires personal discipline	-7
Control food quality & quantity	+8	Time consuming to cook	-2
Save money on food	+4	Takes time to track food	-2
Gain energy	+2	Have to buy different clothes	-1
TOTAL SCORE	**+34**	**TOTAL SCORE**	**-12**

Option 1 resulted in a **Net Score of +22**.

After evaluation, Carlos determined that a balanced low-fat diet with a daily 2,000-calorie limit would be a very good solution. The reason he reached that conclusion makes sense – after all, dieting would enable him to lose weight by controlling the quality and quantity of food he consumed. Nothing more complicated than that. Of course, the new diet would require discipline and time management on his part. Unfortunately, Carlos doesn't possess those two attributes in abundance. That stated – a **Net Score of +22** makes this a worthy solution.

Option 2: Join a gym and hire a personal fitness trainer

Refer to Table 7.5 for a list of the pros (+) and cons (-) that Carlos produced for Option 2.

Table 7.5
Pros (+) And Cons (-) Of Joining A Gym And Hiring A Personal Fitness Trainer

PROS (+)	Score	CONS (–)	Score
Live longer	+15	Hard to schedule in work day	-5
Get fit and lose weight	+5	Expensive	-3
More energy	+2	Painful and tiring	-2
Look better	+2		
TOTAL SCORE	**+24**	**TOTAL SCORE**	**-10**

Option 2 resulted in a **Net Score of +14**.

After evaluation, Carlos determined that the idea of joining a gym and hiring a personal fitness trainer would be an effective strategy to solve his obesity problem. It would help him lose weight, get fit and, as a fringe benefit, potentially live longer. How can you argue with that? On the downside, daily workouts will take a lot of time away from his family and cause some physical pain. Ouch! Nevertheless – a **Net Score of +14** makes this solution worth pursuing.

Option 3: Undergo fat removal surgery (liposuction)

Refer to Table 7.6 for a list of the pros (+) and cons (-) that Carlos produced for Option 3.

Table 7.6
Pros (+) And Cons (-) Of Getting Fat Removal Surgery

PROS (+)	Score	CONS (–)	Score
Immediate weight loss	+15	Dangerous surgery	-15
No diet or exercise required	+10	Painful recovery	-5
		Very expensive	-3
		Obesity may return	-2
TOTAL SCORE	**+25**	**TOTAL SCORE**	**-25**

Option 3 resulted in a **Net Score of 0**.

Carlos was initially interested in this option because it would bring about immediate weight loss without having to exercise. However, upon further evaluation, he determined that fat removal surgery wouldn't be the panacea (cure-all) he thought it would be. For example, the research stated that the surgery might be dangerous. Besides – the procedure wouldn't address the underlying root cause of the problem; namely, overeating and lack of exercise. What would happen if Carlos eventually returned to his old eating habits? To his sedentary (inactive) lifestyle? He'd probably become obese, again. Bottom Line – a **Net Score of 0** disqualifies this option as a solution for Carlos's weight problem.

Once he finished evaluating his options – Carlos ranked them based on the generated net scores. Here's a summary of his findings for all five options he considered – not just the three summarized above:

- Score: **+22** – Start a balanced low-fat diet with 2,000 calories a day
- Score: **+14** – Join a gym and hire a personal fitness trainer
- Score: **0** – Get fat removal surgery
- Score: **-3** – Start an extreme low-carbohydrate diet
- Score: **-25** – Don't eat for a week each month

So – which options do you think Carlos chose?

Yes – that's correct. Carlos decided to start a balanced low-fat diet restricted to 2,000 calories a day. Importantly, he also decided to join a gym and hire a personal fitness trainer.

Now that Carlos selected his two best solutions, it's time for him to implement and monitor them, as well as modify (if necessary).

<u>Step 5: Act, monitor, and modify selected options</u>

The Five-Step Model concludes in Step 5, which introduces three key sub-steps – to act, to monitor, and to modify. Below find a brief summary of how Carlos completed each of them to solve his health problems:

- Act – Carlos has performed admirably up to this point. He researched several popular low-fat diets and implemented his own balanced program with a daily threshold of 2,000 calories. For example, he removed all of the junk food from his house and even mapped a different route between his home and workplace – in order to avoid fast food restaurants along the way. Ice cream and pizza became things of the past, as did candy bars and potato chips. And no more late evening snacks. Carlos also joined a local gym and engaged the services of a fitness trainer to help him remain on track and accomplish his goal of losing weight – and keeping it off.

- Monitor – Carlos is doing exceptionally well, but he knows it's too premature to celebrate. As an aspiring critical thinker, he understands that losing weight is one thing – but keeping it off will be another matter, altogether. With that caution squarely in his mind, Carlos monitors his weight everyday – and charts it religiously (consistently). He even asked members of his family to participate in monitoring his eating habits. Carlos also exercises every other day at the gym – again, devotedly. He's not a fanatic about his routine – just dedicated to the process. Failure at monitoring isn't an option for him. Not going to happen.

- Modify – Carlos, like other people trying to lose weight – isn't going to lose pounds continuously. His weight will probably fluctuate somewhat, which is actually quite normal. Whenever he gains some weight – he'll need to make adjustments in his eating and exercise regime (routine). Maybe dine on half a sandwich instead of a full tuna-melt (hold the cheese) or bacon-lettuce-tomato (hold the bacon). Perhaps run an extra half-a-mile – or take a sauna after working out at the gym. Regardless of the strategy change selected – Carlos will need to make whatever adjustments are necessary to achieve his primary objective – which is to lose weight and keep it off indefinitely. If not, recidivism (repeating an undesirable behavior such as overeating) is a real possibility.

Below is Step 5 in Carlos's Five-Step Model:

- Step 1: Identify the problem – Carlos determines that his primary health problem is obesity.
- Step 2: Discover the causes of the problem – Carlos traces the problem back to its root causes – he eats too much low-quality junk food and he doesn't exercise at all.
- Step 3: Create options to solve the problem – Carlos thinks creatively about options that will enable him to reduce his obesity and increase his fitness.
- Step 4: Evaluate the best option(s) to solve the problem – Carlos uses his critical thinking skills to evaluate his creative options and select the best ones.
- **Step 5: Act, monitor, and modify selected options, as necessary – Carlos starts a balanced low-fat diet, removes junk food from his house, joins a gym, and hires a personal fitness trainer. He's now in the process of monitoring his weight on a daily basis – and is prepared to modify his diet and exercise strategies, as necessary.**

* * * * *

So – as we did with Ming, let's settle into our critical thinking time machine and fast-forward 12 months into the future to discover how Carlos is doing with his weight and overall health.

Consistent with Ming – his situation has dramatically improved over time:

- He lost a considerable amount of weight – largely because of his improved eating habits. Remarkably, Carlos hasn't consumed any junk food in over 6 months (well, there was that candy bar on his birthday).
- His commitment to exercise continues to be strong. Carlos hasn't missed any time at the gym since he started almost a year ago. Amazingly, his stamina has improved to the point that he's able to run up the stairs at his office building without losing his breath (or calling the paramedics).
- Unexpectedly, Carlos' success motivated his wife and two children to start their own diets and exercise programs, as well. Every week they compare weight totals – and the resulting competitive atmosphere has encouraged them to remain focused on their collective objective of becoming healthier.

What another wonderful journey in our critical thinking time machine.

As is the case with Ming – the Five-Step Model seems to be working wonders for Carlos. It just goes to show the value of **applying** lessons learned. He's brought his weight under control and is healthier than he's ever been.

Care to try?

If so – I'll gladly settle into my critical thinking time machine and travel 12 months into the future to evaluate how you're faring. I'm confident you'll be fine – as long as you honor the critical thinking principles you're now learning.

Onward.

SOLVING OTHER PERSONAL PROBLEMS

Many people can relate to the personal problems faced by Ming (too much debt) and Carlos (overweight). However, life's challenges don't end with those two. Indeed – there are several other personal problems that negatively impact people during their everyday lives. The good news is the Five-Step Model can help overcome them – just like it assisted Ming tackle her debt problem and helped Carlos manage his health problems.

Here's a brief preview of three additional personal problems:

- **School problems –** Hannah is pursuing her college degree, but challenges at home and work are negatively impacting her ability to study and pass her courses.
- **Relationship problems –** Isaac's marriage is on the brink of collapsing and he desperately wants to avoid becoming a divorce statistic.
- **Work problems –** Aisha is stuck in a "dead end job" and wants to land a position that offers opportunities for her to develop her professional skills.

Do any of these challenges sound familiar? If not, you're either a very, very lucky person – or someone who's prone to being overly optimistic in your self-assessments. Seriously, I'm guessing at least some of them sound familiar to you. If so – there's no need to fret (worry). You're in exceptionally good company. School, relationship, and work problems apply to many, many other people, as well.

Fortunately, the Five-Step Model provides you with a proven method to lessen the negative impact they exert on your life. Let me briefly discuss each in turn.

Solving School Problems

Hannah decided to go back to school after learning that holders of college-degrees earn more money than their non-degreed counterparts (according to the Department of Labor). The problem is Hannah hasn't attended school in almost 15 years and she's experiencing difficulty adjusting to the discipline and rigor of college. Try as she might – she's struggling in school, especially when it comes to keeping up with her course assignments (readings and papers).

After reading a book entitled "Critical Thinking in Everyday Life," Hannah vowed to **apply** the Five-Step Model to overcome the difficulties she was experiencing in school. She identified poor grades as her problem (Step 1) and used root cause analysis to trace her difficulties back to the following factors (Step 2):

- Struggling to understand textbooks that are lengthy and complicated
- Declining assistance offered by her teachers and academic advisor
- Procrastinating on her assignments
- Straining to find the time needed to complete her assignments (20+ hours per week)

In Step 3, Hannah shifted gears from considering what's causing her school problems to creatively imagining potential solutions. Here's a list of the options she came up with:

- Option 1: Take advantage of the assistance offered by her teachers and academic advisor
- Option 2: Set aside 20 hours a week to read her textbooks and complete her assignments
- Option 3: Use an online scheduling program to manage her time
- Option 4: Set attainable goals to improve her grades
- Option 5: Create a support group that consists of family members and friends to help her study and pass her classes

Next in Step 4, Hannah tapped into her critical thinking skills to evaluate the pluses (+) and minuses (-) associated with each of these options and select which ones would help her perform better in school. After careful consideration, she decided that she needed

to accept the assistance offered by her teachers and academic advisor, as well as purchase (and use) an online scheduling program that would help her manage her time more effectively.

Ah – but Hannah didn't stop there.

After implementing her selected strategies (Step 5), Hannah continually monitored her progress to make certain she stayed on track with her studies (also Step 5). Importantly, she made adjustments to her chosen strategies whenever it became apparent she was falling behind in school (Step 5, again).

Bottom Line: Hannah's grades will improve because she's **applying** the Five-Step Model.

Solving Relationship Problems

Isaac met a lovely lady in college and they dated for two years. He proposed to her at graduation (ah, romance) and they married 6 months later in a cozy, fantasy-themed wedding on the beach. Unfortunately, the pixie dust began to fade from their "happily ever after" marriage about a year ago. No dates or movies – and romance has become a "thing" of the past. And worst of all, Isaac and his wife seldom speak with each other – and when they do, the exchange is uncomfortable and usually laden (burdened) with arguments and disagreements.

After reading a book entitled "Critical Thinking in Everyday Life," Isaac endeavored to **apply** the Five-Step Model to his marriage. He identified his collapsing marriage as the problem (Step 1) and used root cause analysis to uncover the following possible causes (Step 2):

- Avoiding contact with each other
- Suspecting that the other was having an affair
- Distrusting one another
- Arguing incessantly (continually)

In Step 3, Isaac thought deeply about his marriage and compiled the following list of options to solve his relationship problem:

- Option 1: Schedule "dates nights" together once a week
- Option 2: Embark on a second honeymoon to an exotic locale
- Option 3: Seek assistance from a marriage counselor
- Option 4: Arrange opportunities to join social networking groups
- Option 5: Communicate more frequently and honestly

Next in Step 4, Isaac evaluated the pros (+) and cons (-) associated with each of his creative options and, after careful consideration, decided to schedule a series of "date

nights" with his wife – complete with flowers, chocolate, and tickets to the movies. He also collaborated with her to develop a list of priorities for them to grow closer together – such as communicating more frequently and being transparent (honest) whenever problems surfaced between them.

That's a good start for Isaac, but now it's time for him to implement his strategies (Step 5). So off they went – to baseball and football games, rock climbing, wine tasting, and antiquing (nah, he has to draw the line somewhere). Smartly, Isaac continually monitored the health of their marriage to make certain that he and his wife didn't slip back into old habits (also Step 5). And if that occurred – Isaac figured out ways to modify his chosen options or replace them with better alternatives (Step 5, again).

Bottom Line: Isaac will avoid divorce and improve the quality of his marriage because he's **applying** the Five-Step Model.

Solving Work Problems

Aisha loathes (hates) her job – absolutely detests it. She lays her head down in bed every night with a gnawing feeling in her abdomen region – dreading what's in store for her at work the next day. The best word to describe her situation is "drudgery." She sits for endless hours in a sea of cubicles, endures mind-numbing paperwork, and struggles to bite her tongue in response to the demeaning words uttered by her obnoxious boss. Aisha can't shake the feeling that she's in a dead-end situation and has no alternative but to remain. She's stuck.

After reading a book entitled "Critical Thinking in Everyday Life," Aisha promised herself to **apply** the Five-Step Model and fix her work-related problems. She identified unhappiness as the problem (Step 1) and used root cause analysis to uncover the following probable causes (Step 2):

- Avoiding opportunities to spend time with co-workers
- Settling for low-level positions with her company – and not applying for opportunities that would develop her skills
- Consenting to her boss's unreasonable demands without push-back or complaint
- Procrastinating about returning to school to acquire the skills necessary for career advancement
- Burning out by spending too much time at work

In Step 3, Aisha creatively thought about options to alleviate the problem. Here's a list of alternatives she generated during several creative thinking sessions:

- Option 1: Collaborate with her co-workers to create a more positive working environment
- Option 2: Speak with human resources about her boss's abusive behavior

- Option 3: Quit her job and return to college to finish her degree
- Option 4: Develop more efficient time management skills in order to spend less time at work
- Option 5: Start applying for a different job at her company or somewhere else

Next in Step 4, Aisha evaluated the positives (+) and negatives (-) associated with each of her options and decided to collaborate with her co-workers to create a more positive working environment. In addition, she recently applied to an online college to complete her degree.

Aisha demonstrated great insight in addressing how to improve her miserable working conditions and implementing what she determined was the best strategies (Step 5). Similar to my previous illustrations, Aisha carefully monitors her progress so she doesn't slip back into old habits (also Step 5). If she does, she is prepared to modify her chosen strategies and, if necessary, implement new options in order to improve her work situation (Step 5, again).

Bottom Line: The quality of Aisha's work life will be significantly improved because she's **applying** the Five-Step Model.

* * * * *

I trust the above material demonstrates the importance of **applying** the Five-Step Model when dealing with problems in your everyday life. Here's a quick review of the aspiring critical thinkers who solved their personal problems by utilizing it:

- Ming designed and implemented a budget to control her spending habits and reduce her personal debt
- Carlos created and maintained a balanced, low-fat diet to overcome his obesity
- Hannah applied study techniques and a time management plan to improve her grades at school
- Isaac improved the quality of his interactions with his wife to save their marriage
- Aisha collaborated more with her co-workers and enrolled in college to improve her situation at work

That's five people who significantly improved their lives by applying the general concepts associated with the Five-Step Model – as well as honoring the specific defining characteristics of critical thinking as outlined in Chapter 1. Let me refresh your memory:

> *"Critical thinking is a continuous process of evaluating information, formulating opinions based on facts, and applying learning to effectively solve problems and make sound decisions."*

Let's break down the above definition into its component parts and determine if our five subjects implemented the Five-Step Model correctly and, as a result, behaved as critical thinkers:

- **Critical thinking is a continuous process –** in each example, the individual consistently integrated the Five-Step Model into their everyday life – 24x7x365.
    - ✓ **CHECK**
- **... evaluating information and formulating opinions based on facts –** in each example, the individual creatively evaluated his or her options in the Five-Step Model and critically selected the best solution based on factual evidence.
    - ✓ **CHECK**
- **... applying learning to effectively solve problems and make sound decisions –** in each example, the individual applied his or her understanding of the Five-Step Model to effectively solve his or her personal problem.
    - ✓ **CHECK**

Confirmation.

It looks like all five of our aspiring critical thinkers passed the test. By proceeding through each step of the Five-Step Model, all of them effectively solved their personal problems and established a system to continually monitor their progress and make modifications, if necessary. As I've stated in Chapter 6 – that's the power of the Five-Step Model.

A CONCLUDING THOUGHT

Ming's debt and Carlos's obesity. Hannah's failing grades, Isaac's struggling marriage, and Aisha's drudgery at work. That's quite a laundry list of personal problems.

The obvious question that comes to mind (at least my mind) is the following:

> *"Life is difficult enough under 'normal' circumstances – why do you make it more arduous (demanding) than it needs to be by permitting problems to occur, persist, and worsen?"*

The plain and simple truth is this – *you don't.*

Oh – I can just imagine some people responding:

> *"What a silly question to ask. Foolish, actually. Reality is reality. You're dreaming if you think you can make life*

any less difficult than it is for everyone else. Stop dreaming. Wake and grow up. Live the life everyone else does."

Again, the answer is – *you don't.*

Let me explain.

The French have a great saying – *fait accompli,* which literally means "accomplished fact." A done deal. Something that's irreversible. Beyond alteration. Not to be outdone by the French (shudder the thought) – Americans have their own phrase that captures the same sense of inevitability; namely, "It is what it is."

Yes – it's true:

- You breathe
- You eat and drink
- You eliminate wastes (pee and poop)
- You ... well, you get the idea

Each of those functions is a *fait accompli*, an "it is what it is." Literally. You have to breathe, eat, drink, eliminate wastes, and so on – in order to survive.

But not so when it comes to living with problems.

As I stated in the tagline to this chapter:

> *"The fact that problems are universal features of everyday life doesn't mean they need to define your existence. 'Misery,' as the old saying reminds us, 'loves company' – but you don't have to be in that company."*

Just because problems are common and widespread doesn't mean you have to be encumbered (burdened) with them during your everyday life.

Critical thinkers often refer to the phrase "myth of given" – in an attempt to counter (oppose) a *fait accompli* and an "it is what it is" orientation. To argue against the position that certain things in life, such as problems, are prearranged, set, and certain.

Responding to that position – critical thinkers would boldly and confidently state:

> *"Nonsense. Absolute rubbish."*

For critical thinkers – what seems to be "given" isn't automatic. Isn't a certainty. It might appear to be "true" or "reality" on the surface – but if you think about the matter critically, you'll find that most problems are not a *fait accompli* or an "it is what it is."

Critical thinkers know better.

They understand that "myths of given" are simply conceptual hallucinations that convince people that prevailing, undesirable situations are permanent – and as such, people display little commitment or motivation to change it.

Consider the following "myths of given" about so-called everlasting problems:

- "The poor will always be with us."
- "Cancer will never be cured"
- "The United States will never balance the budget"

Yes, each of these problems is commonly evidenced – but must they be that way? Always? For everyone? No. No. And no.

Let me explain.

- The poor are with us not because they must be poor – rather, the poor struggle financially because of various circumstances related to education, geography, health, and the economy.
- Cancer is a widespread killer not because it can't be cured – rather, cancer prevails because of unhealthy lifestyles, toxic environments, a lack of preventive care, and limited funding for research.
- The budget deficit in the United States persists not because it has to – rather, the national debt grows because the government has an insatiable appetite for spending and doesn't collect enough tax revenue to cover the expenses.

Here are some other "myths of given" that history actually demystified (exposed) to be untrue. It was once considered that:

- Small Pox would never be eradicated (eliminated) – but it was
- The New York Mets would never win the World Series – but they did
- People would never walk on the Moon – but they did
- The human genome code would never be broken – but it was

Need further "convincing?"

Everyday Life with David

"Day 35: Five Steps To A Better Future"

"I'm as mad as h_% and I'm not going to take this anymore!"*

That's a famous quote from the movie, "Network" in the 1970s – and it applies even more today than it did over four decades ago. It certainly applies to me when I think about what's happening with health care and the national debt – and several other important problems.

As I said in one of my recent blogs, I didn't even realize how problematic the situation was until I started reading Dr. Ridel's textbook. Wake up, David! Now I'm really mad as h_%* and I want to do something about it.

Hey – I have a crazy idea.

Let's use the Five-Step Model to solve some of our national problems. Crazy? Maybe – but worth a try. Imagine what would happen if we confronted each of our national problems with the same structured, clearly effective process that we use to solve our personal problems?

First we could identify the problems – done, easily enough. Then – we could identify some potential causes, such as high-cost, low-quality health care and government overspending.

Next we could think about creative options for each of the national problems. Improved access to health care. Balanced budget. Then we could evaluate the options and choose the best solutions. How cool would that be? I know I'm just an inspiring critical thinker like you, but the Five-Step Model makes complete sense to me.

Ah – but what do I know? I'm sure there are smarter people than I am who don't share my optimism about the effectiveness of the Five-Step Model. But wait a moment – what are their reasons? Is their information reliable? Are they credible messengers?

Actually, upon further reflection, I don't really care what they think. Let's give it a try anyway. I mean – if I learned anything from this chapter it's that no problem is insurmountable (insolvable) – especially if you apply a structured process to solving them. No *fait accompli* or an "it is what it is" for me. And no "myths of given." You know – I'm really beginning to feel my critical thinking skills developing. This is really exciting.

Chapter 8
Eureka:
Your Journey To Become A Critical Thinker

When I close my eyes for the last time – I want my final thought to be that I did something, even in a minuscule way, to improve the human condition.

Robert W. Ridel, Ph.D.

Ah – the final chapter. I hope you've enjoyed reading the textbook as much as I've enjoyed writing it. I'm sincerely honored to participate in the process of you becoming a critical thinker. Serving you in the capacity of a writer and teacher is an important role in **my** everyday life. I take that responsibility very, very seriously – just as you should the task of becoming a critical thinker in **your** everyday life.

And it seems like you have.

Let me offer a partial listing of what you've learned up to this point. You've discovered that becoming a critical thinker requires that you:

- Admit you don't yet possess the skills needed to become a critical thinker
- Identify external and internal barriers that impede your development as a critical thinker
- Replace external barriers with shaping agents that encourage you to seek evidence and ask questions, as well as modify internal barriers that are self-generated
- Determine the reliability of messages by distinguishing fact from fiction, fiction from fact, and postponing judgment until enough evidence is gathered and evaluated
- Recognize the credibility and non-credibility of messengers, and continually evaluate their competence, character, connection, and charisma
- Understand the problem solving process by defining problems, identifying causes, and creating, evaluating, and implementing options to solve them
- Apply a structured problem-solving approach (Five-Step Model) in order to overcome problems in your everyday life

That's an impressive list – and the lessons contained in it collectively laid the foundation for you to become an aspiring thinker.

No longer do you believe you're someone you're not (a critical thinker) – at least not yet. No longer are you thwarted by barriers, either external or internal. No longer are you duped into believing that every piece of information (messages) you read or hear is reliable, or every person (messenger) who delivers it is credible. No longer are you helplessly impacted by problems without methods to effectively solve them.

Again, you've successfully transitioned from being an unreflective thinker into becoming an aspiring thinker – and have earned my sincerest respect and congratulations.

Let's take a look at a visual representation of your accomplishment. Refer to Figure 8.1:

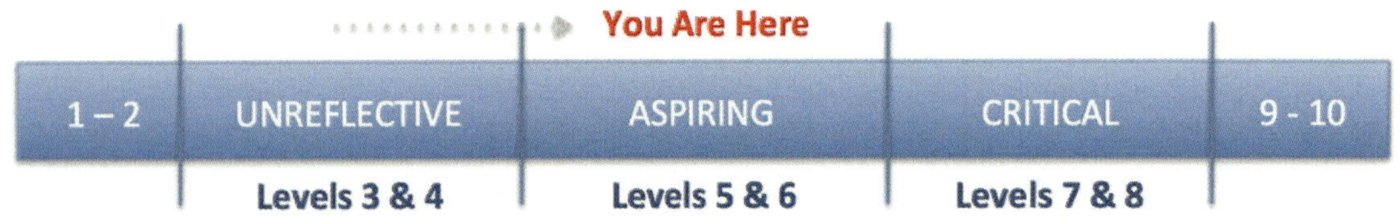

Figure 8.1
Your Journey To Become A Critical Thinker

As Figure 8.1 clearly demonstrates – you've certainly come a long way from the beginning of your journey. It might not have been easy – but it certainly was worth it.

Any doubts?

If so, refer to Table 8.1 for a list of the benefits (+) and costs (-) associated with transitioning from being an unreflective thinker into becoming an aspiring thinker.

Table 8.1
Benefits (+) And Costs (-) Associated With Becoming An Aspiring Thinker

BENEFITS (+)	Score	COSTS (–)	Score
Identify barriers	+158	Invest time and effort	-37
Replace and modify barriers	+177	Abandon substantiated opinions	-27
Determine reliability of messages	+180		
Ascertain credibility of messengers	+174		

Table 8.1 (Cont.)
Benefits (+) And Costs (-) Associated With Becoming An Aspiring Thinker

BENEFITS (+)	Score	COSTS (–)	Score
Develop a structured approach to address problems	+191		
Implement strategies to solve problems	+194		
TOTAL SCORE	**+1,074**	**TOTAL SCORE**	**-64**

As is evident from the above table, the benefits of your transition greatly outweigh the costs. In this hypothetical illustration, becoming a critical thinker results in an amazing **Net Score of +1,010**. (Ok, so I exaggerated the numbers used to compute the final total – prerogative of the writer. ☺)

But before you get carried away with heightened enthusiasm – let's revisit Figure 8.1. It also illustrates that more learning needs to take place in order for you to continue your journey from being an aspiring thinker into becoming a critical thinker.

And that will take time and effort.

The journey won't happen quickly. It will take time – well beyond the amount necessary to complete a class and read a textbook (no matter how good it might or might not be). It will represent a lifelong endeavor that won't come without challenges. What goal in life ever comes easy? I know of none. And transitioning from being an aspiring thinker into becoming a critical thinker will be no exception. It will require a high-level of dedicated effort and commitment on your part.

The obvious question is – how will you complete your journey from being an aspiring thinker into becoming a critical thinker? The less than obvious answer is that you'll need to develop a deeper base of knowledge about the problems that interest you and develop a more expansive mindset about their existence around the world.

Figure 8.2
Deepen Your Knowledge

Let me explain.

Up to this point, I've focused attention on the application of critical thinking to your everyday life. By my calculations, I've used the phrase "everyday life" upwards of a hundred times. That's good.

However, to become a critical thinker – you must deepen your base of knowledge about the problems that interest you (refer to Figure 8.2). What's more, you must also venture beyond the boundaries of your everyday life – you must expand your thinking beyond yourself and immediate surroundings to encompass a world at-large perspective (refer to Figure 8.3).

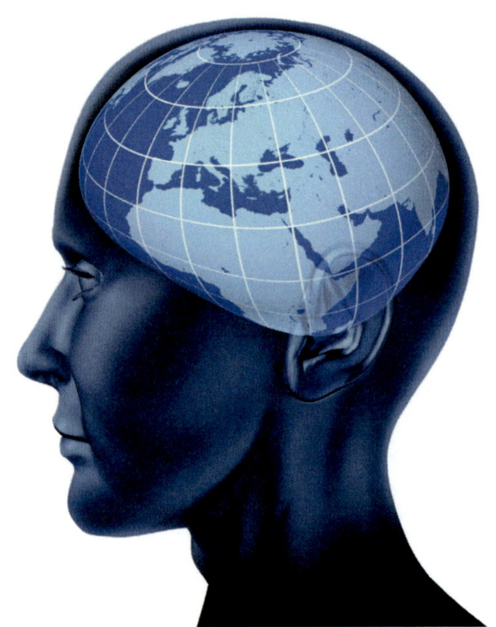

Figure 8.3
Expand Your Thinking

And you're not quite there, yet – on both counts.

In the past, as an unreflective thinker – you didn't possess a deep understanding of the causes and conditions that maintain problems, nor did you pay much attention to how they impacted the national and global scene.

Presently, as an aspiring thinker – you're beginning to develop your own research-based opinions on problems that interest you. In addition, you're also trying to broaden your view beyond local problems.

All of that is good – but there's still more learning that needs to take place. To become a critical thinker – you'll need to deepen your knowledge about problems. A surface understanding of them won't be sufficient.

And beyond that, you'll need to expand your understanding about how they impact different parts of the world. Restricting your attention to local settings won't be enough to qualify you as a critical thinker.

The differences between how unreflective, aspiring, and critical thinkers consider national and global problems is depicted in Table 8.2.

Table 8.2
Different Perspectives On National And Global Problems

PROBLEM	Unreflective Thinker	Aspiring Thinker	Critical Thinker
Health Care	"I don't get Obama Care. What's the big deal with health insurance? I don't need it."	"I just started to think about the Affordable Care Act (Obama Care). I'll study the particulars in the weeks to come."	"I reviewed the research on the Affordable Care Act and am beginning to understand both sides of the debate. I will reserve judgment until I collect and evaluate more information."
Climate Change	"Yea – it's hot. So what. It's hot everywhere. I don't think scientists know what they're talking about."	"I'm not certain what caused the climate to change. Perhaps it happened naturally – or maybe it took place because of pollution. I'm going to take a science class to find out."	"I've looked at the evidence – and there's considerable disagreement over whether humans or nature are responsible for climate change. I need to conduct considerable research and assessment on both sides before I make my decision."
National Debt	"The government can print money, right? If we run out of it, it can simply print more."	"I need to research why the national debt is increasing so much. It's time for me to become better informed about the economy."	"Our allies in Europe use austerity measures to battle recession – while we in the U.S. attempt to spend our way out of recession. I need to research which approach is more effective."

As Table 8.2 demonstrates – levels of thought become deeper and more expansive as people progress from being unreflective thinkers to aspiring thinkers – and especially as they transition to becoming critical thinkers.

Unreflective thinkers don't satisfy any of those requirements. Not even close. Aspiring thinkers come closer – but they also lack depth and range when it comes to speaking

and writing about problems. Beyond that, aspiring thinkers are "zip code centric" – meaning that their base of knowledge is restricted to their own "backyard" or local area. The profiles of unreflective and aspiring thinkers are in marked contrast to that of critical thinkers. For them, thinking isn't curtailed by lack of knowledge or restricted to any geography. Quite the contrary, everything and everyone, no matter the location, is subject to evaluation. To question. All the time.

But let's not get ahead of ourselves. As I stated earlier:

"... you're not quite there, yet."

In an attempt to help you get "there" – I'll try to deepen your base of knowledge about three national and global problems (health care, climate change, and the national debt). I'll also try to provide you with a "world at-large" perspective for each of them.

Of course, I trust the following exercise will propel you along your journey to become a critical thinker.

Evidence – Starting Your Journey
As you proceed through the following sections – *I will provide evidence, in the form of questions,* *that demonstrate you're making progress* *toward reaching your goal of becoming a critical thinker.*

Let's revisit our visual representation of your journey to become a critical thinker. Refer to Figure 8.4 – which identifies your current location on the critical thinking continuum. At this point, you're just starting your journey from being an aspiring thinker to becoming a critical thinker. Upcoming figures will track how far you've progressed toward that goal.

Figure 8.4
Starting Your Journey To Become A Critical Thinker

So – without further adieu, it's time for you to push ahead to get "there."

STARTING YOUR JOURNEY

The selected national and global problems are all catastrophic. Health care costs are skyrocketing, climate-related disasters are at an all-time high, and the national debt is suffocating the middle class and nation as a whole. You need to understand these problems in more depth and scope in order to successfully make the transition from being an aspiring thinker to becoming a critical thinker. Otherwise your journey will peter-out and stall.

Consider the following evidence:

- The health care system in the United States ranks 38th globally by the World Health Organization (WHO), behind such countries as Morocco, Cyprus, and even Costa Rica. Specifically, we rank 46th in infant mortality, 192nd in affordability of care, and 24th in life expectancy. And still, for some reason, many Americans believe the nation's health care system is the best in the world.
- Extreme climate conditions now affect almost 50% of the country and cause a staggering $450 billion dollars in damage every year (National Oceanic and Atmospheric Administration). Carbon dioxide gases are rising to dangerous levels, and global temperatures are breaking records on an annual basis. And still, for some reason, many Americans believe climate change is nothing to worry about.
- Foreign countries (such as China, Japan, and Belgium) fund a third of what we as a nation borrow – which is roughly equivalent to our annual Gross Domestic Product, or GDP (Treasury Department of the United States, Bureau of Public Debt). That means that we owe as much money as we produce in a year. Imagine what would happen if those countries "called in" their loans (required us to pay them back). Catastrophic. Disastrous. Cataclysmic. And still, for some reason, many Americans believe the nation's financial system is stable.

The evidence clearly demonstrates that the fiasco associated with health care, the debacle associated with climate change, and the disaster associated with the national debt are pressing problems, even if they aren't perceived that way by many Americans.

Review Table 8.3 for a summary of the dangerous state of these national and global problems.

Table 8.3
Evidence For National And Global Problems

Problem	Evidence
Health Care (World Health Organization)	U.S. ranks #1 in the world in health care expenses per person
	U.S. health care ranks 38th in overall quality
	U.S. ranks 46th in infant mortality
Climate Change (National Aeronautics and Space Administration)	CO_2 gas has risen to over 380 parts per million – highest level in 400,000 years
	61% increase in global temperatures since 1980
	50% of U.S. is currently experiencing extreme climate conditions
National Debt (Congressional Budget Office of the United States)	National debt has increased 228% in past 10 years – now totaling almost $18 trillion
	U.S. owes as much as it earns
	Interest payments amount to $1,100,000,000 (billion) per day

Yes, I know – that's a lot of information to digest. And you no doubt have several questions, such as:

Evidence – Starting Your Journey
"What the heck is going on?"
"Why do these problems (health care, climate change, and national debt) remain unsolved?"
"How did they come about?"
"Who is responsible?"
"How come our leaders aren't solving them?"

Good – these are the questions a critical thinker would ask. Well done.

Your last question especially intrigues me. Indeed, given the dangers associated with the previously highlighted problems – you'd think our leaders (government, business, media) would be consumed with the task of solving them, regardless of what political party they are aligned with or where they fall on the socio-economic scale. So yes – I

certainly understand why you'd question the inability of our leaders to solve the health care fiasco, the climate change debacle, and the national debt disaster.

By way of contrast – consider the following example of a problem that, if it were to occur, would generate immediate action by our leaders to solve it.

Imagine if a meteor was hurtling (racing) toward the Earth, and the demise (death) of hundreds of millions of people was an absolute certainty once it struck. That would be a problem of epic proportions. Everyone in his or her right mind would consider the situation deeply troubling. Panic would be rampant (widespread) – with massive numbers of people trampling over each other trying to escape. I imagine the situation would be like a scene from a "Godzilla" movie – with the beast running amuck (out of control) throughout the streets of Tokyo trampling buildings, cars, trains, and anything or anyone in its path.

So – what do you think our leaders would be doing under that threatening scenario? Sitting around playing board games? Taking a nap on the couch? Drinking lattes at the local coffee shop? Absolutely not. Quite the contrary, they would be intensely focused on how to solve the problem – in this case, on how to divert or destroy the rapidly approaching meteor.

You betcha – no question about it.

Our leaders in government, business, and media would be galvanized (fired up) in a single-minded (determined) way to take collective action. The government (Federal and State) would be in emergency session to craft and pass laws designed to protect the country – its people, infrastructure, and its overall way of life. Business would marshal (organize) its resources to provide financial support and humanitarian aid. And the media, operating through its affiliates and the emergency broadcast system, would keep the country informed of breaking developments.

Certainly.

So obvious, in fact, that you're compelled to ask the following "why" questions:

Evidence – Starting Your Journey
"Why isn't anything being done about these problems?"
"Why aren't people upset about them? Demanding that action be taken? I mean – they're not life-threatening meteors, but in some ways they're just as serious."

Once again, these are the questions of a critical thinker. Excellent.

But you don't stop there – oh no. You continue your "inquisition" by confronting me with a request to offer my opinion:

Evidence – Starting Your Journey
"Why, Dr. Ridel, aren't the problems associated with health care, climate change, and the national debt being solved?"

This is the question of a seasoned critical thinker – you're clearly learning your lessons. Well done, again.

However, while I respect your question and understand why you'd ask it – it's not my place to provide an answer, at least not in this context. That's for you to figure out after you assess your information about the highlighted problems – and evaluate your sources (refer to Chapters 4 and 5, respectively).

What I believe isn't important – again, at least not in this context. My role isn't to influence you to think one way or another about the targeted problems; rather, my responsibility is to help you develop your ability to think critically about them. And that's a huge difference.

Again – my responsibility is to help you develop your critical thinking skills. To help you make the transition from being an aspiring thinker to becoming a critical thinker. Nothing more. Alas, the question you skillfully asked is **your** question to answer.

I can only imagine what you're thinking after reading my response to your question:

Evidence – Starting Your Journey
"That's an unacceptable copout, Dr. Ridel. A convenient excuse, plain and simple. I'm surprised and disappointed. That's not like you to be vague. Tell me it ain't so. Come on – please answer my question about why these problems aren't being solved?"

Wow – that's what I would call an insightful question, with a tinge of spice and directness. Give me a moment to organize my thoughts and think about how best to answer it.

Before I do – let me state that your questions provide ample evidence that you've progressed from being an unreflective thinker into becoming an aspiring thinker. Well done – congratulations. Refer to Figure 8.5 which depicts your journey.

Figure 8.5
Continuing Your Journey To Become A Critical Thinker

Congratulations, again.

CONTINUING YOUR JOURNEY

Ok, ok – I've had my moment to reflect on your challenging question – and I'm now ready to answer it. Again, I usually wouldn't offer my point-of-view. But since you asked (☺) – I always answer "why" questions about problems with this follow-up question:

"Who benefits?"

From my perspective, questions about problems are best answered by asking **who benefits** from their origin and continuation. Yes, I know – answering questions with a question seems odd – but in my experience, the answer to the question "who benefits" yields important insight into questions about the origin of problems and why they continue.

Let me apply my reasoning to two of the previously discussed national and global problems – health care (national) and climate change (global).

Pharmaceutical Companies Benefit from the Health Care Problem

As you learned earlier in this and other chapters – the evidence strongly suggests that health care is a serious national problem. And yet, for some reason, it remains unsolved.

So, you ask inquisitively:

"Why?"

To which I answer straightforwardly:

"Who benefits?"

While supporters and opponents spend valuable time debating the success or failure of our health care system, pharmaceutical companies continue to benefit from skyrocketing health care costs – to the tune of $300 billion per year.

Refer to Table 8.4 for a revenue and cost breakdown for the most profitable pharmaceutical companies in the world (Source: GlobalData).

Table 8.4
Profitability Of Global Pharmaceutical Companies

Pharmaceutical Company	Revenue	R&D	Sales & Marketing	Profit Margin
Pfizer	$52B	$7B	$12B	43%
Hoffmann-La Roche	$50B	$9B	$9B	24%
AbbVie	$19B	$3B	$4B	22%
GSK	$41B	$5B	$10B	21%
Eli Lilly	$23B	$6B	$6B	20%

Not surprisingly, pharmaceutical companies have received tremendous criticism for generating huge profits, especially when so many people are unhealthy and suffer from assorted medical conditions. Disapproval has also been expressed about the amount of money they spend on marketing drugs – in some cases twice as much – versus the amount they invest in researching and developing medicines designed to treat illnesses and cure diseases (again, refer to Table 8.4). One can only wonder how many medical breakthroughs would take place if that ratio were reversed.

Adding insult to injury (no pun intended) – the health care system isn't designed to cure patients as much as it's structured to treat them. Such an emphasis provides pharmaceutical companies with a never-ending stream of revenue from the medicines they research, produce, market, and sell. The fact is – they benefit from the ongoing existence of sick people, not from patients who recover or die. Healthy people don't buy medicine. And pardon the morbid imagery – but neither do the deceased.

And if that wasn't troubling enough, pharmaceutical companies operate on profit motives – meaning that research funding is targeted only for illnesses and diseases that yield substantial earning potential. For those that don't – well, they persist because not enough profit is associated with treating and curing them.

Below find a straightforward path that depicts how profit motives drive the decisions pharmaceutical companies make about so-called non-profitable diseases:

- No profit leads to no research
- No research leads to no production of medicine
- No medicine leads to no treatment or cure
- No treatment or cure leads to continued illness and death

There's even a term for this phenomenon – and it's called "Neglected Tropical Diseases" (NTD). The World Health Organization (WHO) identified at least 17 NTDs that affect more than 1.4 billion people in 149 countries around the globe. Again, NTDs can be treated and cured – but the needed medications aren't produced because they aren't profitable.

Refer to Figure 8.6 for a disturbing illustration of the far-reaching impact of a "neglected disease." According to Thomson Reuters Web of Knowledge and WHO, research investments (from 1992 through 2011) to treat and cure HIV/AIDS were 15 times higher than investments earmarked (allocated) to treat and cure Intestinal Worms – even though the latter afflicts many, many more people (1 billion versus 34 million).

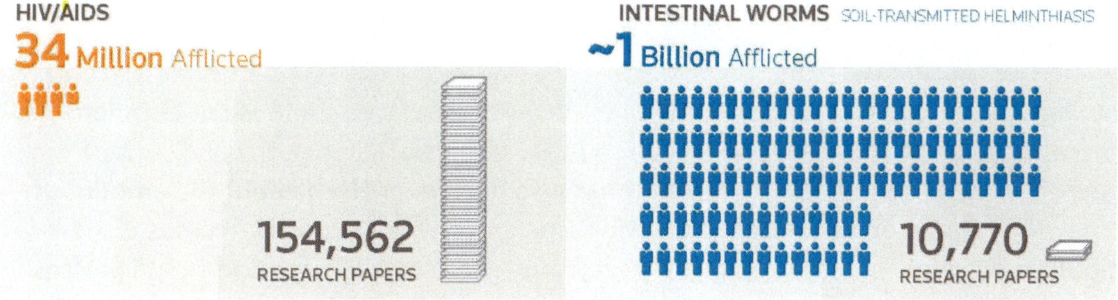

Figure 8.6
NTDs: An Illustration

And that's just one example – several additional types of NTDs exist, such as River Blindness, Soil-transmitted Helminthes, and Snail Fever. In each of these cases, funding is insufficient because there isn't enough projected profit for pharmaceutical companies to justify researching and developing the medicines needed to treat and cure them.

The point is that the allocation of funding for research and development is driven by profit motives. The more financial gain – the more pharmaceutical companies invest to treat and cure patients. Pity those who are afflicted with unprofitable diseases.

* * * * *

So – what's a critical thinker to think?

As persuasive as these finding are – it's important to remember that, as a critical thinker, you mustn't jump to conclusions based on only one side of the story. You need to evaluate unbiased, reliable information from a multitude of credible sources in order to establish a more balanced perspective concerning this (and other) problem(s).

Refer to Table 8.5 which counters the negative information previously presented in Table 8.4. It offers a glimpse into the positive side; specifically, how pharmaceutical companies attempt to solve health care problems.

Table 8.5
Pharmaceutical Companies: The Other Side Of The Story

Source	Evidence
U.S. Bureau of Labor Statistics	Pharmaceutical companies develop and produce products that treat a variety of health problems and save millions of lives every year. They distribute drugs that treat and cure various types of illnesses across the entire human lifespan, including influenza, cardiovascular disease, diabetes, arthritis, and cancer, as well as other ailments and diseases.
Pharmaceutical Research and Manufacturers of America	Pharmaceutical companies invest over $50 billion each year researching new medicines to solve health care problems. Not only do they improve health outcomes, but they also help reduce the need for costly healthcare services, such as emergency room admissions, hospital stays, surgeries, and long-term care.
U.S. Food and Drug Administration	80% of prescriptions filled in the United States are for generic drugs – representing an 85% cost savings over brand name drugs. This equates to over $150 billion in annual savings. The development of generic drugs is made possible because pharmaceutical companies invest billions of dollars every year to research and develop medicines to treat illnesses and cure diseases.

The above table presents quite a different story than the negative information offered earlier – doesn't it? Indeed, pharmaceutical companies would argue that they're providing a fundamental and important service; namely – saving lives. And in many ways, they are correct. Think about it – what would the world be like without vaccines and medicines?

Critical thinkers know there are (at least) two sides to every problem, and the health care problem is certainly no exception.

Yes – there are negatives associated with the huge amount of revenue pharmaceutical companies earn, and the fact that their profit motives conflict with treating and curing people who are afflicted with certain types of illnesses and diseases (such as NTDs). However – there's another side to the story, as well. As noted above, pharmaceutical companies invest billions of dollars developing health care solutions that significantly improve and save the lives of people across the nation and globe – including people we know and who are dear to us. And even ourselves.

Again, as a critical thinker – it's absolutely required that you examine this and other problems from a multitude of perspectives. Only then will you be able to answer the probing question:

"So – what's a critical thinker to think?"

Let me give you a hint to help initiate your thinking process – a lesson I learned a long time ago while I was a student studying social problems. It's captured in the following quote:

"The truth falls somewhere in between."

Ponder that as a critical thinker.

Fossil Fuel Companies Benefit from the Climate Change Problem

Evidence has been presented throughout this textbook that climate change is a serious global problem. And yet, for some reason, it remains unsolved.

Once again you ask:

"Why is that the case?"

To which I would reiterate my answer:

"Who benefits?"

While supporters and opponents of the climate change debate remain preoccupied with the causes of global warming, fossil fuel companies continue to benefit from the world's reliance on oil, coal, and natural gas to fuel our automobiles, operate our factories, and heat and cool our homes and offices.

Refer to Table 8.6 for a revenue and profit breakdown for the most profitable fossil fuel companies in the world (Source: Reuters).

Table 8.6
Profitability Of Global Fossil Fuel Companies

Fossil Fuel Company	Revenue	Profit	World Ranking of Profitability	Country
Gazprom OAO	$157B	$36B	#3	Russia
Exxon Mobil	$394B	$33B	#5	United States
BP plc	$380B	$24B	#9	United Kingdom
Chevron	$211B	$21B	#12	United States
PetroChina Co Ltd	$373B	$21B	#13	China

Not surprisingly, many credible organizations (World Resources Institute, Intergovernmental Panel on Climate Change at the United Nations) question the incredible profits earned by fossil fuel companies. As you can see from Table 8.6, five of the most profitable companies in the world earn billions of dollars every year by burning fossil fuels – and releasing damaging gases into the atmosphere.

But profit is only a secondary focus for those critical of fossil fuel companies.

No matter the huge profits, detractors rightly remind us that our primary attention must to be focused on the dangerous levels of "greenhouse gas" (also known as carbon dioxide or CO_2) that fossil fuel companies release into the atmosphere by burning oil, natural gas, and coal. As a result, the planet has become saturated with a blanket of gas that creates a warming condition known as the "greenhouse effect." Stated forcefully, opponents of the fossil fuel industry insist that greenhouse gas is literally "chocking" the planet.

And NASA (National Aeronautics and Space Administration) agrees.

The agency recently reported that atmospheric carbon dioxide reached its highest level in the past 400,000 years – almost twice as high as the previous record (refer to Figure 8.7). NASA also reports that the rate of sea level change has doubled since 1950, and the index for global land-ocean temperatures has increased more than 60% since 1980.

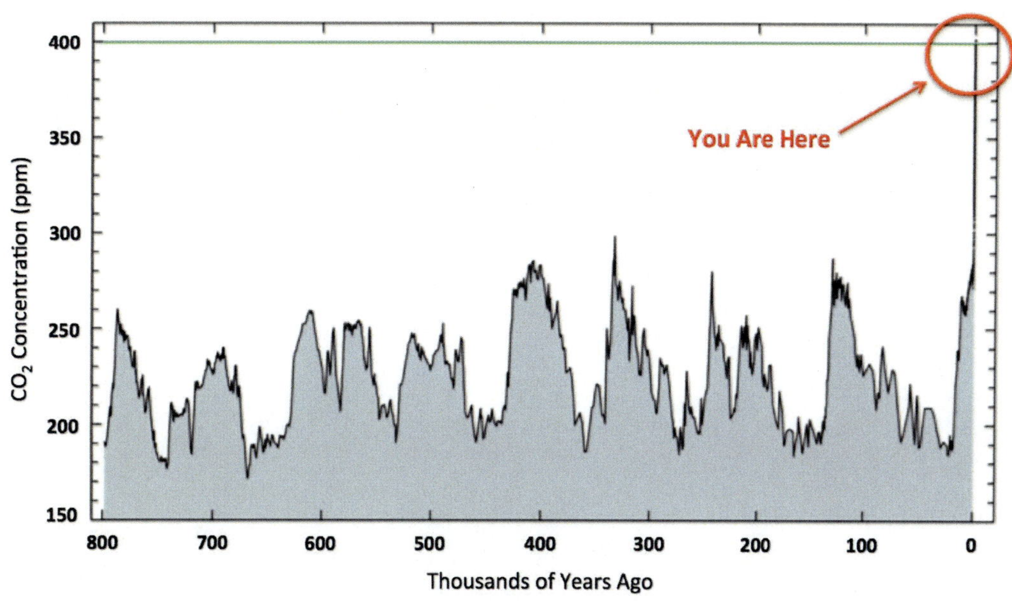

Figure 8.7
Dramatic Increase In Carbon Dioxide On The Planet

Such a trend is unprecedented in the history of the planet – and there's no end in sight. Unfortunately, the numbers are almost certain to worsen – and that wouldn't be good for the Earth and all life forms that inhabit it, including us.

Below find a straightforward illustration that depicts the profit-driven causes and environmental consequences associated with releasing greenhouse gas into the atmosphere, and the humankind results that might ensue if current trends continue.

Profit-Driven Causes:

- Burning of fossil fuels leads to atmospheric carbon dioxide gas
- Building up of carbon dioxide gas leads to the greenhouse effect
- Warming impact of the greenhouse effect leads to increased global temperatures
- Increasing global temperatures cause catastrophic environmental consequences

Next, consider the following environmental evidence that demonstrates the catastrophic consequences of burning fossil fuels.

Environmental Consequences:
(National Aeronautics and Space Administration)

- Tropical Storms (Hurricanes) and Tornadoes – the percentage of people in the United States who are exposed to extreme weather events has doubled since 1950
- Coastal Floods – the rate of rising sea levels in the past decade has doubled compared to the last century
- Melting Ice Caps – the thickness of sea ice in the Arctic has declined 13% per decade since 1980
- Extreme Heat – 10 of the warmest years in recorded history have occurred in the past 12 years
- Ocean Acidification – the acidity of surface ocean waters has increased 30% since the beginning of the Industrial Revolution

Finally, consider the following disastrous fallout that might befall humankind as a result of the continued burning of fossil fuels.

Humankind Results:
(Environmental Protection Agency)

- Coastal City Floods – 216 million people around the globe will experience regular flooding (70% increase), if current trends continue
- Global Drought – 38% increase in the number of people who will be exposed to drought conditions, if current trends continue
- Starvation – 4-degree rise in temperature across the Earth will bring about decreased agricultural production, loss of critical ecosystem functions, and the extinction of many animal and plant species, if current trends continue
- Economic Impact – wealthy countries (United States and China) will lose billions of dollars in Gross Domestic Product (GDP) caused by decreased agricultural output and property loss from tropical storms and flooding, if current trends continue

Please note that the above information isn't "pie-in-the-sky predictions" or "wild guesses." Quite the contrary – it's based on scientific evidence and sophisticated predictive models published by the Environmental Protection Agency. In fact, some of these disastrous scenarios have already begun to occur.

Case in point – scientists at the National Center for Atmospheric Research (NCAR) have confirmed that the planet is beginning to reach the "point of no return" which will occur when fossil fuel companies pour roughly 565 additional gigatons (billion tons) of carbon

dioxide into the atmosphere. At the current rate, NCAR predicts that will happen in the next 15 years.

* * * * *

So – what's a critical thinker to think?

No matter how overwhelming the evidence seems to be, you mustn't – as a critical thinker – jump to conclusions based on only one side of the debate. Quite the contrary, you must develop a balanced evaluation of this and other problems before taking a position.

Refer to Table 8.7 which provides a glimpse of the positive side; specifically, the important role that fossil fuel companies play is providing energy to the world.

Table 8.7
Fossil Fuel Companies: The Other Side Of The Story

Source	Evidence
Nongovernmental International Panel on Climate Change (NIPCC)	The evidence cited to support "unprecedented" warming trends in the 20th Century has been discredited and contradicted by many independent scholars. According to the NIPCC, temperatures around the world were warmer during the Medieval Warm Period of approximately 1,000 years ago, and have on average been 2-3 degrees higher than today's temperatures over the past 10,000 years.
British Broadcasting Corporation (BBC)	A steady increase in the number of sunspots has occurred over the past few hundred years. The data suggest that solar activity might be causing the Earth's temperature to rise – not human actions.
Climate Warming Petition Project	There is no convincing evidence that the human release of carbon dioxide will, in the foreseeable future, cause catastrophic heating of the Earth's atmosphere and disruption of its climate. Moreover, there's evidence that increased levels of atmospheric carbon dioxide might actually be beneficial for plant and animal life.

The above table clearly offers a more positive viewpoint than the negative evidence presented earlier – doesn't it? Indeed, fossil fuel companies would forcefully ask the following question: "What would happen to the infrastructure of our society, and the huge number of people served by it, if fossil fuel companies stopped producing energy?"

As is the case with the debate about pharmaceutical companies and health care – critical thinkers know they must research all points-of-view before they assume a position on the controversy about fossil fuel companies and climate change.

Yes – there is considerable evidence that fossil fuel companies profit from the destruction of the environment, primarily through causing increased levels of carbon dioxide (greenhouse effect) and the resulting consequences associated with a dramatically changing climate. However, they also provide a fundamental and important product to people around the globe – energy. In fact, oil is the only energy source currently available that can support the needs of a huge proportion of the world's population (which currently totals 7+ billion people). Again, from their perspective, what would happen to the world as we know it without energy driven by fossil fuel?

Let me repeat what I wrote in the previous section – about pharmaceutical companies. As a critical thinker – it's absolutely imperative that you examine this and other problems from a multitude of perspectives. Only then will you be able to answer the probing question:

"So – what's a critical thinker to think?"

Again, let me give you a hint to help initiate your thinking process – a lesson I learned a long time ago while I was a student studying social problems. It's captured in the following quote:

"The truth falls somewhere in between."

Ponder that as a critical thinker.

COMPLETING YOUR JOURNEY

I know I've placed huge requirements along your path to transition from being an unreflective thinker to becoming an aspiring thinker. Well – guess what? You've already made substantial progress in several important areas, including:

- Admitting you didn't possess the skills required to be a critical thinker
- Identifying external and internal barriers that impeded your development as a critical thinker
- Replacing external barriers with shaping agents who encouraged you to seek evidence and ask questions, as well as modifying self-generated internal barriers to critical thinking

- Determining the reliability of messages by distinguishing fact from fiction, fiction from fact, and postponing judgment until you gathered and evaluated enough evidence
- Recognizing the credibility and non-credibility of messengers, and evaluating characteristics associated with their competence, character, connection, and charisma
- Understanding the problem solving process by defining problems, identifying causes, and creating, evaluating, and implementing options to solve them
- Applying a structured problem-solving approach (Five-Step Model) in order to overcome problems in your everyday life

As a result of those accomplishments – you successfully made the transition from being an unreflective thinker to becoming an aspiring thinker.

If the above requirements weren't challenging enough, I also introduced stringent criteria that you needed to satisfy in order to take the next step on your journey – from being an aspiring thinker to becoming a critical thinker. Consider the following:

- **Deepen your base of knowledge –** you learned that possessing a surface understanding of problems doesn't qualify you as a critical thinker. In order to make the transition from being an aspiring thinker, you must develop a deeper understanding about the origin of problems, what conditions maintain them, and how they can be solved. Which you've accomplished.
- **Expand your reach –** you learned that remaining within the boundaries of your own everyday life doesn't qualify you as a critical thinker. Making the transition from being an aspiring thinker requires you to develop a more expansive mindset about problems not only in your own "backyard," but also in the world around you. Which you've accomplished.

But you're not done yet.

As you can see in Figure 8.8, the "wall" that separates an aspiring thinker from becoming a critical thinker is much higher, thicker, and insurmountable than any of the barriers you encountered up to this point in your journey. To scale it, you must accomplish more than deepening your knowledge about problems and developing a world-perspective. One more hurdle remains – which must be successfully navigated otherwise you'll remain trapped behind the wall and thwarted from becoming a critical thinker.

So – are you ready to take the next and final step on your journey?

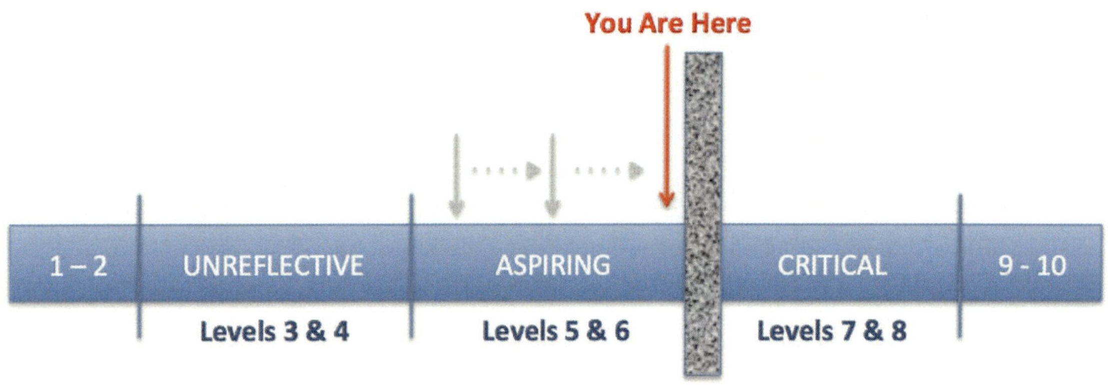

Figure 8.8
Completing Your Journey To Become A Critical Thinker

And that step, required to climb the wall that separates aspiring thinkers from critical thinkers, involves **speaking your mind** about the problems you've learned – specifically, sharing your fact-generated insights with other people to improve their everyday lives and the well-being of their families, friends, communities, and nation. No monopolizing or hoarding information. No camouflaging insights. Doing so would most assuredly deny you entrance to the "other side" of the wall.

Again – speaking your mind is required to continue your transition from being an aspiring thinker to becoming a critical thinker. It's the capstone piece and "crown jewel" of your journey. It's that important.

Yes, I know. Such a requirement seems downright impossible for mere mortals to accomplish. Downright unimaginable. Utter fantasy.

But as a critical thinker – you aren't a "mere mortal," any longer. You're different from aspiring thinkers, and you're a completely different species from unreflective thinkers. Unlike them, you can speak your mind – powered by your deepened base of knowledge about problems and your expanded mindset on how they impact people around the world.

Yes you can.

- You may not be Nelson Mandela who spoke his mind against apartheid in South Africa, but you can be Barry Jones who speaks his mind against prejudice and racial discrimination in neighborhood housing and employment.

- You may not be Eleanor Roosevelt who spoke her mind for the rights of women and minorities in the United States, but you can be Clarita Rodriquez who speaks her mind about equal pay for comparable work at a recent town hall meeting.

- You may not be Mahatma Gandhi who spoke his mind for the rights of the poor in India, but you can be Ashwin Patel who speaks his mind against unfair treatment of the homeless at a recent municipal board meeting.

- You may not be Saint Joan of Arc who spoke her mind against English rule in France, but you can be Li Chen who speaks her mind against political corruption with family members and friends at a weekend barbeque.

- You may not be Martin Luther King, Jr. who spoke his mind against racism in the United States, but you can be Jayden Lewis who speaks his mind against racial profiling at a recent homeowner's meeting.

As critical thinkers, each of these historical heroes and heroines were compelled to speak out – even if doing so resulted in political suicide, imprisonment, or even death. They had no choice because as critical thinkers – they were obligated to speak their minds, just like they were compelled to breathe. And that's what makes each of these famous men and women notable – because they spoke their minds when most other people remained silent.

And you can do the same.

Granted you're not going to become the hero of a country (Mandela), or the namesake of a national holiday (King). But by speaking your mind – you can make a difference in the lives of the people you care about (and who care about you), as well as improve the state of your community and nation.

Again, yes you can – because you are a critical thinker.

A CONCLUDING THOUGHT

Well not so fast – I have to "come clean" with you. I haven't been completely candid by stating that the previously identified criteria will take you to the "Promised Land" of becoming a critical thinker. The truth be told – becoming a critical thinker doesn't end with deepening your base of knowledge, expanding your reach, and speaking your mind. Ah – I wish the process ended there. As it turns out, there's one more requirement that must be accomplished if you're to become a critical thinker **– and that is for you to remain a critical thinker.**

Seems odd, doesn't it?

But if you think about it – the statement makes perfect sense. After all, becoming a critical thinker doesn't guarantee you lifelong membership in the "club." The possibility always exists that you might "slip back" into becoming an aspiring thinker or, worse still, into becoming an unreflective thinker.

Sociologists (and other social scientists) refer to the process of relapsing into a previously undesirable state or type of behavior as "recidivism" – and the people who do so as "recidivists."

Consider the following:

- Have you ever tried to lose weight?
- How about quit smoking?
- Or stop drinking alcohol?

If so, you possess first-hand knowledge about how difficult it is to accomplish those objectives – to lose weight, stay away from cigarettes, and refrain from drinking alcoholic beverages. Recidivism (relapsing) is, as you know, very common.

But even if you accomplish your immediate goal – you also know that the real challenge is not to revert back into old habits. It's hard enough to lose weight, but the real struggle is to keep the weight off. It's hard enough to quit smoking, but the real struggle is to refrain from smoking cigarettes. It's hard enough to stop drinking, but the real struggle is to remain sober. Yes – the real challenge is not to become a recidivist.

And the same applies to critical thinking. It's hard enough to become a critical thinker, but the real struggle is to remain a critical thinker.

Refer to Figure 8.9 for an illustration of a critical thinker who experiences recidivism and returns to being an aspiring thinker or even an unreflective thinker.

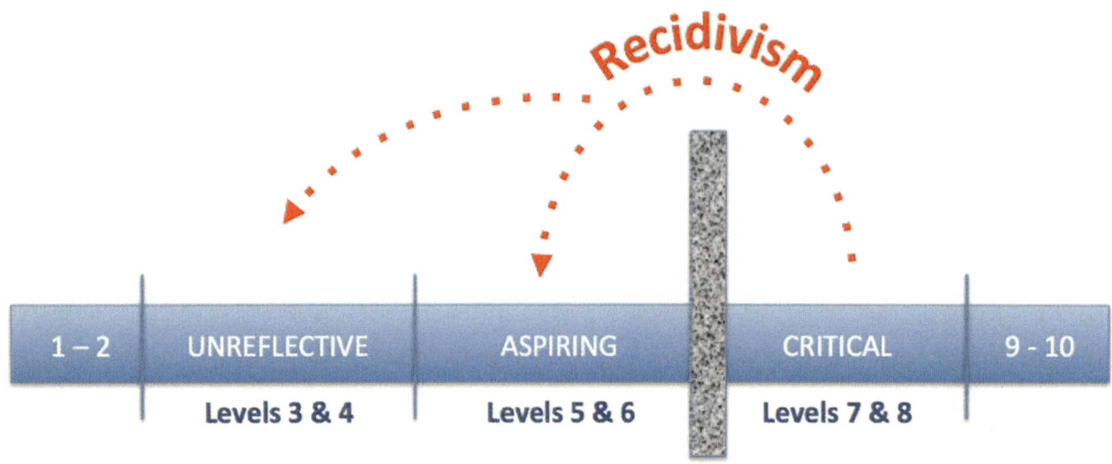

Figure 8.9
Recidivism: Back Over The Critical Thinker Wall

At this point, you're surely wondering:

A Concluding Thought
"OK, Dr. Ridel – how do I avoid becoming a recidivist when it comes to critical thinking?"

Once again – another great question.

Not surprisingly, the answer is derived from the lessons you've learned in this and the preceding chapters.

Let me summarize:

- To avoid recidivism – you need to recognize that your position as a critical thinker will never be completely secured or guaranteed. Never. Everyday life contains innumerable forces that can slowly but surely pull you back over the wall that separates critical thinkers from aspiring and unreflective thinkers. Refer to Chapter 1.

- To avoid recidivism – you need to remain vigilant about external agents who thwart the development of your critical thinking skills (i.e. family, friends, teachers, and media). You also need to combat self-generated internal factors that bring about recidivism (i.e. rationalizing, being emotional, stubbornness, and biases). Refer to Chapter 2.

  Not becoming a recidivist also requires that you replace your external barriers with shaping agents who promote critical thinking, whenever possible, and modify internal tendencies that would otherwise shutdown your development as a critical thinker. Refer to Chapter 3.

- To avoid recidivism – you need to scrutinize the reliability of the information you hear and read (fact versus fiction) – and resist temptation to prematurely adopt an opinion or point-of-view until you evaluate enough data and evidence. Refer to Chapter 4.

  Not becoming a recidivist also requires that you evaluate the credibility of informational sources. Stated bluntly – you need to determine who's telling the truth, who's stretching it, and who's downright lying. Refer to Chapter 5.

- To avoid recidivism – you need to identify problems that define your everyday life, and discover what caused them to surface and persist. You also need to create options to solve the problems (creative thinking) and evaluate each of them to determine the best solution (critical thinking). Refer to Chapter 6.

Not becoming a recidivist also requires that you apply what you learned about the problems that define your everyday life. You need to act – to implement strategies designed to solve them, monitor their effectiveness, and make modifications, whenever necessary. Refer to Chapter 7.

- To avoid recidivism – you need to deepen your knowledge about problems and expand your mindset about how they impact people around the globe. You also need to speak your mind to other people – share the research-based insights you've developed to help them improve their everyday lives.

I trust the above information answers your question about how to avoid becoming a recidivist when it comes to critical thinking.

Of course, I can't promise that satisfying all the highlighted requirements will guarantee you immunity to recidivism. Assure you that you will forever remain a critical thinker. I wish I can – but I can't.

What I can state with confidence is that honoring the concepts presented throughout this textbook will dramatically increase the likelihood you'll remain on the "critical side" of the wall. I can also state with conviction that your life (professional, personal) will be hugely benefited by residing there instead of on the "aspiring side" and, most definitely, compared to occupying the "unreflective side" of the wall.

You've earned my sincerest respect and congratulations for achieving your status as a critical thinker. Enjoy it. Keep it. Relish its benefits. And importantly, share your knowledge and insights about critical thinking with other people – so that they, too, will experience a life they richly deserve.

* * * * *

Let me conclude this chapter with the same words I opened it with:

> *"When I close my eyes for the last time – several decades*
> *in the future, I want my final thought to be that I did something,*
> *even in a minuscule way, to improve the human condition."*

By way of full disclosure – I'm a pessimist by "nature." My friends characterize me as someone who makes a pessimist seem like an optimist. As someone who views the proverbial glass as being broken. Shattered. Not half-empty as other pessimists believe, and certainly not half-full as most people do.

Refer to me as you wish – as a cynic, doubter, skeptic. Oh yes – I'm most definitely a pessimist.

If you knew something about my history – you'd certainly understand why I view life through shadowy, less than sanguine (hopeful) spectacles. It's a deep-seated perception – reinforced by decades of observing and working with people penalized by their financial situation, race and ethnic heritage, and by their gender and age.

Nothing would please me more than helping them live better, more fulfilled lives. Each and every one of them. Of course, I know that's not possible. Unfortunately, there's precious little I can do about poverty and the "isms" that define the lives of billions of people around the world (racism, sexism, and ageism).

What I can do is this – I can assist people to become and remain critical thinkers. I can help them:

- Understand the origin and conditions that maintain problems in their everyday lives
- Recognize that problems impact other people who reside in distant, faraway lands – just as they do family members and friends who live around the corner
- Speak their minds about the consequential nature of problems; specifically, how they negatively impact people's "life chances" (how they live their lives) and "chances for life" (whether they actually live)
- Vanquish the forces of recidivism which, if activated, would pull them over to the "other side" of the wall

Yes – this I can and must do.

Writing a textbook on critical thinking is part of that commitment – as is teaching the subject. Both roles provide me with a platform to "honor the cause" of serving people. Without those opportunities – I would be akin to a "rebel without a cause." An empty shell. Listless. Absent of purpose. In limbo. Lost.

For that reason – you have my deepest appreciation for reading this textbook. Doing so provides meaning to my life – but only if you apply lessons learned to improve your life and the lives of other people. It's the application of content that produces meaning, not the mere learning of it.

You must do something with it.

Let me close by offering you one of my favorite expressions, which I coined long ago:

"Realize potential – the ultimate objective."

I don't know what "potential" means – it's immeasurable. And I don't know what "ultimate" means – it's too subjective. What I do know is that I can "feel" what the expression means. For me it means serving other people by helping them realize **their**

potential, whatever that happens to be. And for you it means becoming a critical thinker. Interesting that our ultimate objectives are in sync.

If tonight turns out to be the last night I close my eyes – I will rest comfortably knowing that I've achieved my ultimate objective – improving my life, the lives of people I care about, and the human condition.

How about you?

Robert

Made in the USA
Coppell, TX
06 April 2022

SUPERPOWER
STEM CHALLENGES

LEARN TO PROBLEM-SOLVE WITH
THE ENGINEERING DESIGN PROCESS
AT HOME OR AT SCHOOL

WRITTEN
BY
DELANDA
COLEMAN
&
TERRENCE
COLEMAN

THIS BOOK IS PART
OF THE SERIES:

WHAT'S MY

978-1-7344158-8-9

Published 2021

Published by Sydney and Coleman, LLC
www.sydneyandcoleman.com
Boston, Massachusetts
Instagram and Facebook @sydneyandcoleman

THIS BOOK BELONGS TO:

TABLE OF CONTENTS

WELCOME

to the 10-day Superpower STEM Challenge!

Have you ever wondered how astronauts land safely on the ground after traveling from the sky? Or have you ever wondered how tall towers are able to stand up without falling over?

Over the next 10 days, we are going to build 10 unique objects that will teach you exactly how to use the engineering design process to learn how!

WHAT IS THE ENGINEERING DESIGN PROCESS?

The engineering design process is a series of 6 steps that engineers use in **creating** products and processes.

GET READY!

Before we begin here are some rules for the challenge:

1. **Create a team!** You can work with others to solve each day's challenge. Join a small team or work with your parents on your activities.
2. **Plan ahead!** Leveraging the calendar below, plan the days you will work on the challenge. You can do one activity a day or more than one.
3. **Gather supplies!** Before you start an activity, gather all the necessary materials listed for the activity. Ask an adult to help you find anything you don't have.
4. **Get a pencil!** Don't forget to get a pencil and eraser to draw out your plans BEFORE you build - it's best to sketch out an idea before you create it.
5. **Document Everything!** Use the Engineering Design Process Worksheets to plan and document your learnings.

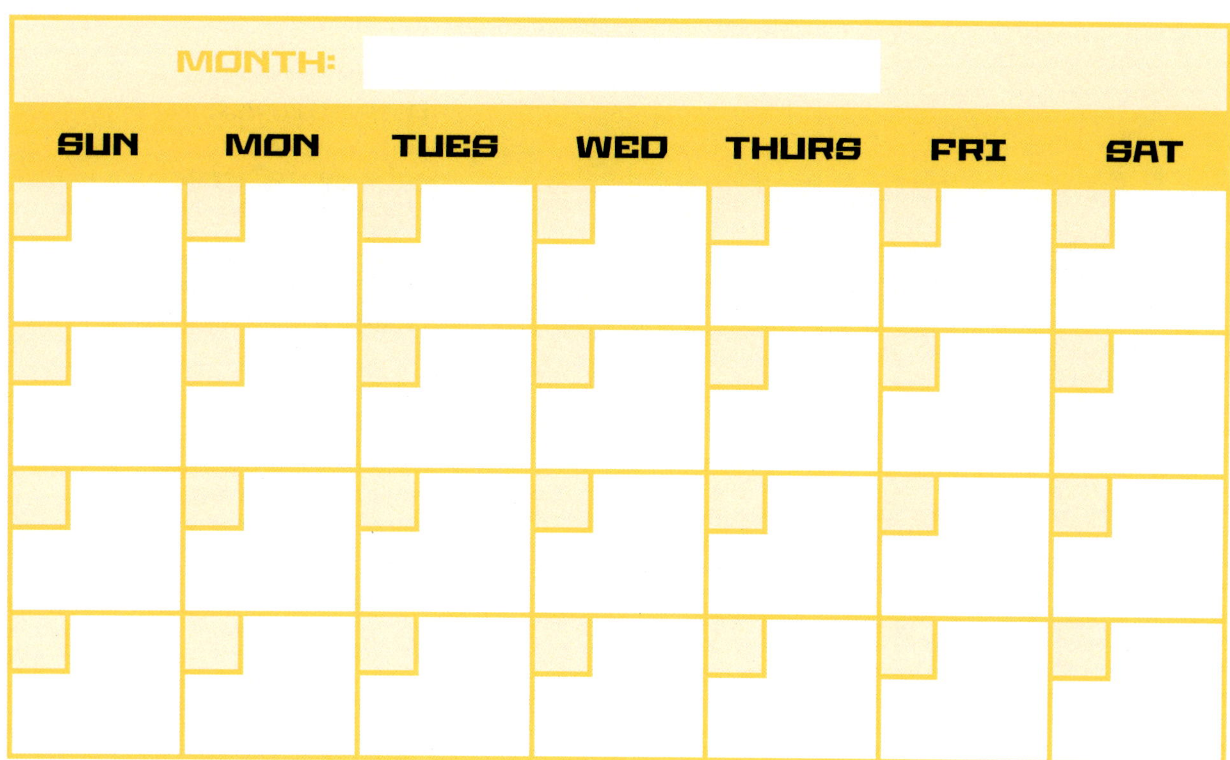

CHALLENGE CHECKLIST

- [ ] LUNAR LANDER
- [ ] STRAW ROCKET
- [ ] STOP THE SPACE CRAFT
- [ ] DNA MODEL
- [ ] GUMDROP TOWER
- [ ] TALLEST TOWER
- [ ] EGG DROP
- [ ] WIND POWERED CAR
- [ ] CREATE A NEW TOY OR GAME
- [ ] MARSHMALLOW CATAPULT

THE ENGINEERING DESIGN PROCESS

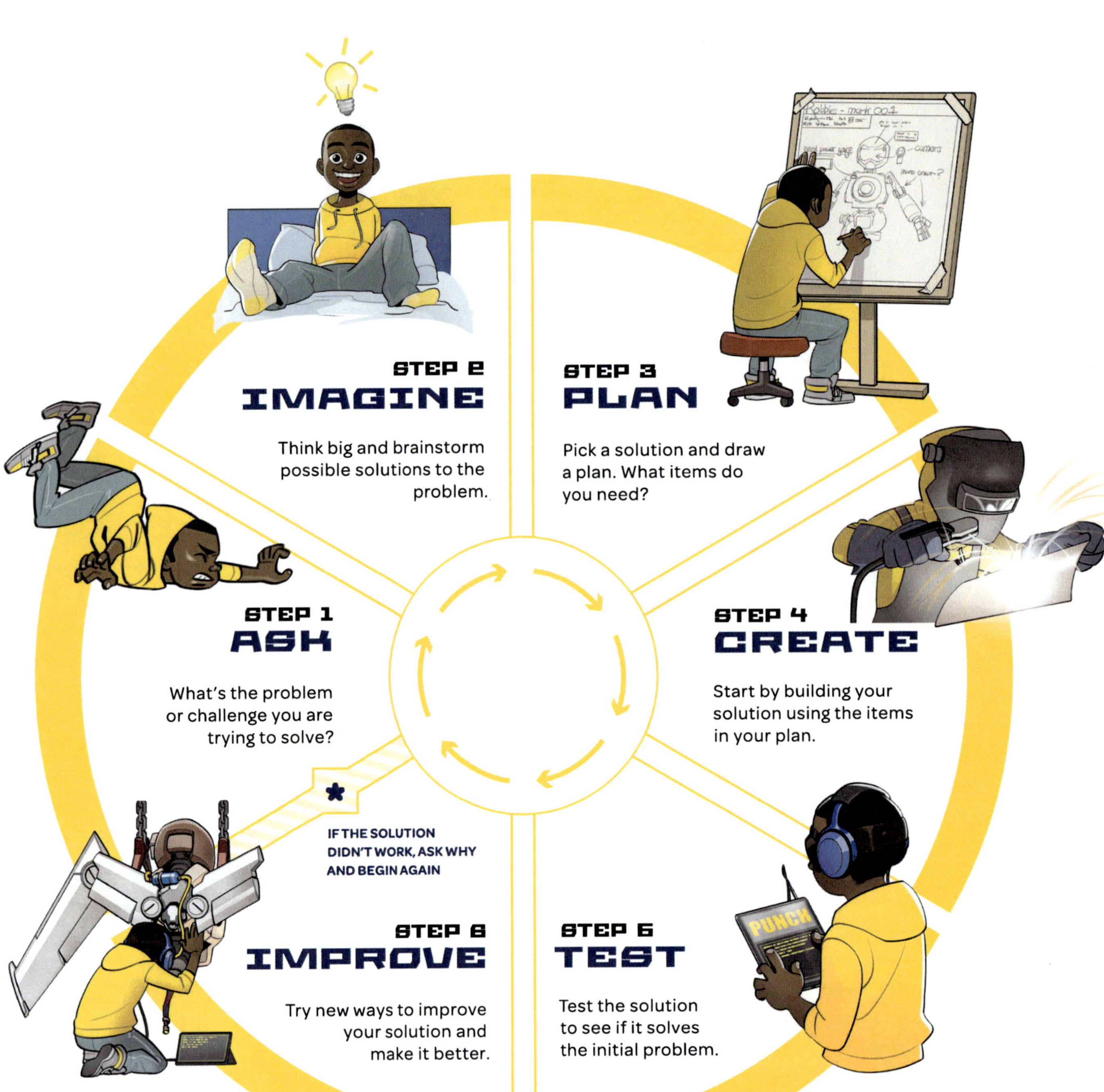

DAY 1 LUNAR LANDER

"Astronauts" (two regular marshmallows) need a spacecraft that can land safely on the moon, so they are not injured, and the spacecraft is not damaged upon landing. It is your job to create a spacecraft that absorbs the shock of landing on the moon using the materials listed. You will drop your spacecraft from a height of 3 feet* to test its ability to withstand the force of the fall.

The "astronauts" should not fall out of the spacecraft or be damaged (smashed etc.) in any way. The spacecraft should remain in one piece and parts should not break apart or fall off the device when testing. If this happens you should adjust by following the engineering design process. Most importantly, HAVE FUN!

*All testing should be conducted by a parent or guardian.

VOCABULARY

- **SHOCK ABSORBERS:** slow down and reduce the magnitude or severity of an impact
- **FORCE:** is a push or pull
- **GRAVITY:** force that all things with mass are brought towards one another
- **AIR RESISTANCE:** the force air exerts on an object as it moves through it; the force acts in the opposite direction from which the object is moving

★ When you jump off a high step, you bend your back and knees to absorb some of the energy and break your fall. That's what a shock absorber does—absorbs the energy of an impact.

MATERIALS

- 1 PIECE OF CARDSTOCK
- 1 PIECE OF COPY PAPER
- 1 INDEX CARD
- SMALL PAPER CUP
- 2 REGULAR SIZED MARSHMALLOWS
- 10 MINIATURE MARSHMALLOWS
- MASKING TAPE
- 10 PLASTIC STRAWS
- 6 RUBBER BANDS

NEXT STEPS:

1. FOLLOW THE ENGINEERING DESIGN WORKSHEET TO BEGIN THINKING OF IDEAS FOR YOUR SPACECRAFT.
2. THEN FOLLOW THE ENGINEERING DESIGN PROCESS TO BUILD, TEST, EVALUATE, AND IMPROVE YOUR DEVICE.

ENGINEERING DESIGN PROCESS WORKSHEET

1. ASK

WHAT IS THE PROBLEM?

2. IMAGINE

WHAT ARE YOUR IDEAS FOR POSSIBLE SOLUTIONS?

4. & 5. CREATE AND TEST

DOCUMENT WHAT HAPPENS:

6. IMPROVE

HOW CAN YOUR CURRENT DESIGN BE IMPROVED?

3. PLAN

DRAW AND LABEL YOUR DESIGN:

DAY 2 STRAW ROCKET

3...2...1...Launch! How far can you get a rocket made from a straw and other household items to travel, using the force from a rubber band launcher you design and create?

Create a straw rocket using clay, card stock, tape, a paper clip, and glue, as well as a slingshot type launcher made from a rubber band and popsicle stick. Most importantly, HAVE FUN!

- Have you ever taken a rubber band, pulled one side, and then let go? What does the rubber band do? It launches forward in the opposite direction that you pulled it. This type of energy will be used to make a launcher or slingshot device for a rocket you make from a straw. Be sure your rocket has a nose cone and fins. Ask your parent or guardian to help you research the parts of a rocket.

VOCABULARY

- **ROCKET:** spacecraft, aircraft or another vehicle that obtains thrust from a rocket engine
- **NOSE CONE:** top part of a rocket that is cone shaped
- **FINS:** flat part which sticks out on bottom of rocket and helps control movement, adding stability
- **THRUST:** sudden push in a specific direction
- **PROPEL:** force that pushes object in a given direction, usually forward
- **KINETIC ENERGY:** energy of motion – a ball rolling down a hill
- **POTENTIAL ENERGY:** energy of position – a ball sitting on top of the hill
- **ELASTIC POTENTIAL ENERGY:** type of energy of position related to an object that can return to its original shape after being moved or changed- think of a trampoline
- **AIR RESISTANCE:** the force air exerts on an object as it moves through it; the force acts in the opposite direction from which the object is moving

MATERIALS

- 1 STRAW
- 1 PIECE OF CARDSTOCK
- CLAY OR PENCIL ERASER CAP FOR NOSE CONE
- TAPE
- GLUE
- PAPER CLIPS
- RUBBER BANDS
- POPSICLE STICKS

NEXT STEPS:

1. FOLLOW THE ENGINEERING DESIGN WORKSHEET TO BEGIN THINKING OF IDEAS FOR YOUR SPACECRAFT.
2. THEN FOLLOW THE ENGINEERING DESIGN PROCESS TO BUILD, TEST, EVALUATE, AND IMPROVE YOUR DEVICE.

ENGINEERING DESIGN PROCESS WORKSHEET

1. ASK

WHAT IS THE PROBLEM?

2. IMAGINE

WHAT ARE YOUR IDEAS FOR POSSIBLE SOLUTIONS?

4. & 5. CREATE AND TEST

DOCUMENT WHAT HAPPENS:

6. IMPROVE

HOW CAN YOUR CURRENT DESIGN BE IMPROVED?

3. PLAN

DRAW AND LABEL YOUR DESIGN:

DAY 3

STOP THE SPACECRAFT

Space travel can be dangerous. Astronauts and spacecrafts are traveling at high speeds and need to be able to slow down before reaching the ground. A spacecraft must be able to slow down as it approaches land so the craft, the passengers, and equipment remain in one piece. You will need to create a device that can attach to a spacecraft to slow it down as it enters the atmosphere from space. Most importantly, HAVE FUN!

The cup will be your spacecraft. Drop the cup from about 6-7 feet (parents should always conduct tests and drops at this height) and time how long it takes to hit the ground. You will add your device to slow down the craft to reduce this time.

VOCABULARY

- **DRAG:** a force caused by friction as a solid object moves through a fluid
- **FRICTION:** resistance one object exerts on another; there are many types of friction
- **FLUID:** anything that flows easily, this can be a liquid or a gas like air
- **AIR RESISTANCE:** the force air exerts on an object as it moves through it; the force acts in the opposite direction from which the object is moving

★ Have you ever seen a skydiver use a parachute on television or in a movie? What happens to the person using a parachute? They are falling through the air rapidly, and once they open the parachute they begin to slow down. Why? Well, parachutes utilize the friction caused by air resistance as their fabric travels through the air to slow down the skydiver.

MATERIALS

- 1 PLASTIC CUP, 8-12 OZ
- 2-3 FEET OF STRING YARN
- 10 RUBBER BANDS
- 2 PIECES OF COPY PAPER
- 2 PIECES OF CARDSTOCK
- 1 PIECE OF PLASTIC WRAP
- 3-4 LARGE COFFEE FILTERS OPTIONAL
- TAPE
- GLUE

NEXT STEPS:

1. FOLLOW THE ENGINEERING DESIGN WORKSHEET TO BEGIN THINKING OF IDEAS FOR YOUR SPACECRAFT.
2. THEN FOLLOW THE ENGINEERING DESIGN PROCESS TO BUILD, TEST, EVALUATE, AND IMPROVE YOUR DEVICE.

ENGINEERING DESIGN PROCESS WORKSHEET

1. ASK

WHAT IS THE PROBLEM?

2. IMAGINE

WHAT ARE YOUR IDEAS FOR POSSIBLE SOLUTIONS?

4. & 5. CREATE AND TEST

DOCUMENT WHAT HAPPENS:

6. IMPROVE

HOW CAN YOUR CURRENT DESIGN BE IMPROVED?

3. PLAN

DRAW AND LABEL YOUR DESIGN:

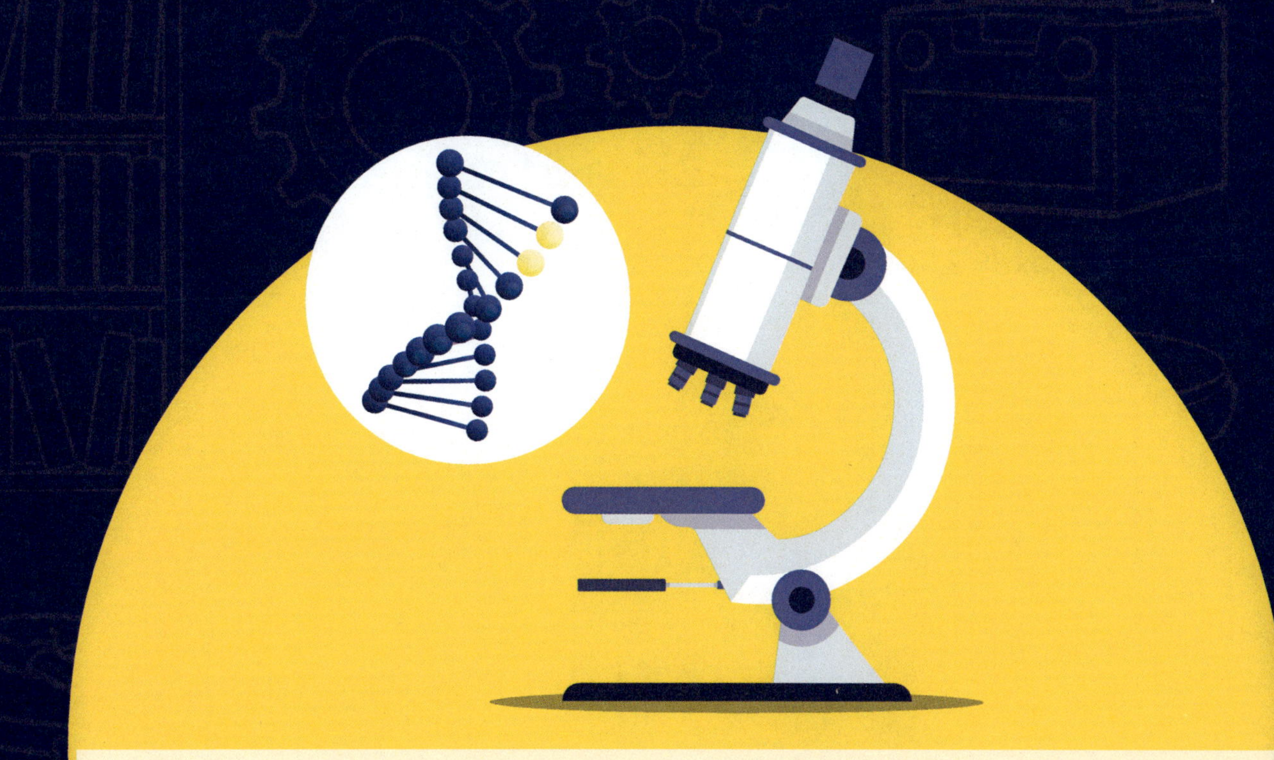

DAY 4 MODEL DNA

Every living thing is made up of a chemical compound known as DNA or deoxyribonucleic acid. DNA is in the shape of a double helix which is just a fancy way of saying it looks sort of like a spiral staircase. DNA has nitrogen bases that fit together like a puzzle. Now, we cannot see DNA without the help of special devices called microscopes. So, you will design a model of DNA using multicolored marshmallows, licorice, and toothpicks to hold it all together.

Ask your parent or guardian to help you find an image of DNA.

Decide which color is which base pair and remember only G can pair with C and only A with T. Use the toothpicks to attach the base pairs (marshmallows) to the licorice as the phosphate backbone or sides.

VOCABULARY

- **DNA:** deoxyribonucleic acid, in each individual organism
- **MODEL:** detailed representation can be either bigger or smaller depending on what is being modeled
- **NITROGEN:** an element found in nature and necessary for life
- **DOUBLE HELIX:** shape of DNA, similar to a twisted ladder

★ Why are models important in science? Have you ever seen a globe? A globe is simply a model of the earth used to help us find locations and structures.

MATERIALS

- **10-12 MULTICOLORED MARSHMALLOWS**
- **5-6 TOOTHPICKS**
- **2 LARGE PIECES OF LICORICE**

NEXT STEPS:

1. FOLLOW THE ENGINEERING DESIGN WORKSHEET TO BEGIN THINKING OF IDEAS FOR YOUR DNA.
2. THEN FOLLOW THE ENGINEERING DESIGN PROCESS TO BUILD, TEST, EVALUATE, AND IMPROVE YOUR DEVICE.

ENGINEERING DESIGN PROCESS WORKSHEET

1. ASK

WHAT IS THE PROBLEM?

2. IMAGINE

WHAT ARE YOUR IDEAS FOR POSSIBLE SOLUTIONS?

4. & 5. CREATE AND TEST

DOCUMENT WHAT HAPPENS:

6. IMPROVE

HOW CAN YOUR CURRENT DESIGN BE IMPROVED?

3. PLAN

DRAW AND LABEL YOUR DESIGN:

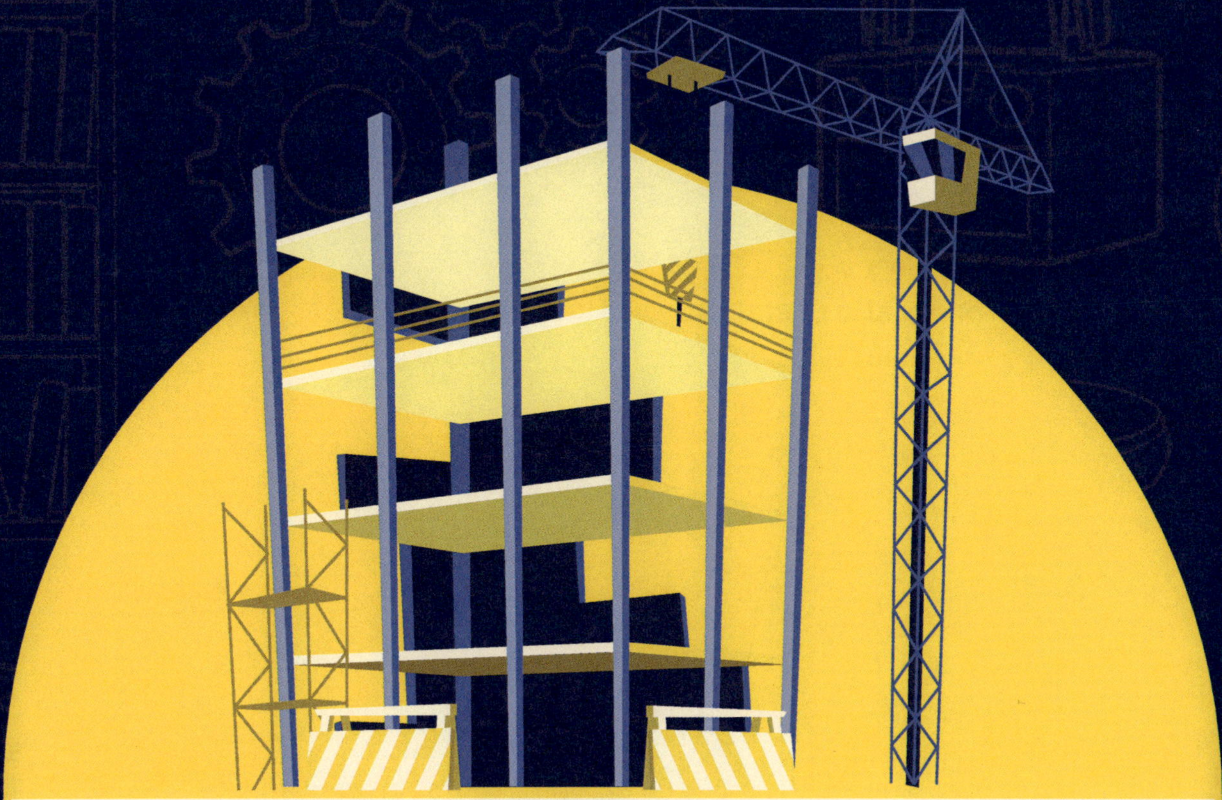

Building structures takes work and an in-depth understanding of all the STEM content areas. Your task is to design, create, and test a structure made from only toothpicks and gumdrops that can hold the weight of a textbook without breaking or falling.

Triangles are the strongest shape and used in structures for their strength. Engineers use trusses or supportive beams in triangular arrangements to make strong buildings. You will use the gumdrops as attachment points and create a structure that can hold up the weight of a textbook.

VOCABULARY

- **TRUSS:** a truss is an assembly of beams or other elements that creates a rigid structure

MATERIALS

- 10 GUMDROPS
- 20 TOOTHPICKS
- TEXTBOOK FOR TESTING

NEXT STEPS:

1. FOLLOW THE ENGINEERING DESIGN WORKSHEET TO BEGIN THINKING OF IDEAS FOR YOUR STRUCTURE.
2. THEN FOLLOW THE ENGINEERING DESIGN PROCESS TO BUILD, TEST, EVALUATE, AND IMPROVE YOUR DEVICE.

ENGINEERING DESIGN PROCESS WORKSHEET

1. ASK

WHAT IS THE PROBLEM?

2. IMAGINE

WHAT ARE YOUR IDEAS FOR POSSIBLE SOLUTIONS?

4. & 5. CREATE AND TEST

DOCUMENT WHAT HAPPENS:

6. IMPROVE

HOW CAN YOUR CURRENT DESIGN BE IMPROVED?

3. PLAN

DRAW AND LABEL YOUR DESIGN:

DAY 6

TALLEST TOWER

In this challenge, you will use only 12 crafting pipe cleaners to build the tallest tower possible in under 15 minutes.

*The tower should be at least 18 inches and must be freestanding, meaning it cannot be taped to the table or floor.

VOCABULARY

- **FOUNDATION:** base of a building, often needs to be wide in nature to support greater height

- What do a house, a skyscraper, and a hotel all have in common? Yes, they are all buildings, and all include a foundation. The base at which you begin a structure is important to its stability and support. How will you construct your tower's foundation to support the tallest possible height?

MATERIALS

- **12 CRAFTING PIPE CLEANERS**

NEXT STEPS:

1. FOLLOW THE ENGINEERING DESIGN WORKSHEET TO BEGIN THINKING OF IDEAS FOR YOUR TOWER.
2. THEN FOLLOW THE ENGINEERING DESIGN PROCESS TO BUILD, TEST, EVALUATE, AND IMPROVE YOUR DEVICE.

ENGINEERING DESIGN PROCESS WORKSHEET

1. ASK

WHAT IS THE PROBLEM?

2. IMAGINE

WHAT ARE YOUR IDEAS FOR POSSIBLE SOLUTIONS?

4. & 5. CREATE AND TEST

DOCUMENT WHAT HAPPENS:

6. IMPROVE

HOW CAN YOUR CURRENT DESIGN BE IMPROVED?

3. PLAN

DRAW AND LABEL YOUR DESIGN:

DAY 7 EGG DROP

Eggs are fragile. One mistake and a carton of eggs can turn into a huge mess as they crash to the ground and crack, spilling egg yolk all over the floor. So, how can we protect an egg, even if the container it is in gets dropped?

You will create a container to protect an egg that will be dropped from at least 10 feet.

*All testing should be conducted by a parent or guardian

VOCABULARY

- **INSULATION:** cushioning or protective layer of material
- **GRAVITY:** force in which all things with mass are brought towards one another
- **AIR RESISTANCE:** the force air exerts on an object as it moves through it; the force acts in the opposite direction from which the object is moving

★ What would happen if you were to drop an egg onto several very soft pillows? Would it break? Most likely not, because the pillows offered a cushion to the falling egg. Your goal is to create a container that utilizes various aspects of air resistance and insulation so the egg does not break.

MATERIALS

- 1 PLASTIC CUP NO LARGER THAN 16 OZ
- 2-3 FEET OF STRING YARN
- 10 RUBBER BANDS
- 2 PIECES OF COPY PAPER
- 2 PIECES OF CARDSTOCK
- 2 PIECES OF NEWSPAPER
- 1 STYROFOAM CUP NO LARGER THAN 8 OZ
- 1 PAPER PLATE
- TAPE

NEXT STEPS:

1. FOLLOW THE ENGINEERING DESIGN WORKSHEET TO BEGIN THINKING OF IDEAS FOR YOUR CONTAINER.
2. THEN FOLLOW THE ENGINEERING DESIGN PROCESS TO BUILD, TEST, EVALUATE, AND IMPROVE YOUR DEVICE.

ENGINEERING DESIGN PROCESS WORKSHEET

1. ASK

WHAT IS THE PROBLEM?

2. IMAGINE

WHAT ARE YOUR IDEAS FOR POSSIBLE SOLUTIONS?

4. & 5. CREATE AND TEST

DOCUMENT WHAT HAPPENS:

6. IMPROVE

HOW CAN YOUR CURRENT DESIGN BE IMPROVED?

3. PLAN

DRAW AND LABEL YOUR DESIGN:

DAY 8 WIND POWERED CAR

Wind is a powerful source of energy. Your challenge is to create a car that can travel at least 2 feet using only wind power (a small fan).

VOCABULARY	MATERIALS
RENEWABLE ENERGY: energy from sources that do not run out; there are many types, including wind ★ For years, the only way people could travel across the water was with ships that utilized sails. These large ships would move by harnessing the power of the wind in large, fabric sails. No wind meant little to no movement. You will use the same sail idea to harness the wind (air from a small fan) to move a model car you build from household items.	- 2-3 PAPER TOWEL ROLLS - 2 PIECES OF CARDSTOCK - 3-4 PIECES OF TISSUE PAPER - 1 PIECE OF COPY PAPER - HARD LIFE SAVERS CANDIES - 6 STRAWS - WOODEN DOWELS OR KABOB STICKS OPTIONAL - 1 FOOT OF STRING YARN - 5 PIPE CLEANERS - TAPE

NEXT STEPS:

1. FOLLOW THE ENGINEERING DESIGN WORKSHEET TO BEGIN THINKING OF IDEAS FOR YOUR CAR.
2. THEN FOLLOW THE ENGINEERING DESIGN PROCESS TO BUILD, TEST, EVALUATE, AND IMPROVE YOUR DEVICE.

ENGINEERING DESIGN PROCESS WORKSHEET

1. ASK

WHAT IS THE PROBLEM?

2. IMAGINE

WHAT ARE YOUR IDEAS FOR POSSIBLE SOLUTIONS?

4. & 5. CREATE AND TEST

DOCUMENT WHAT HAPPENS:

6. IMPROVE

HOW CAN YOUR CURRENT DESIGN BE IMPROVED?

3. PLAN

DRAW AND LABEL YOUR DESIGN:

DAY 9 MARSHMALLOW CATAPULT

Catapults are devices used to launch objects through the air. They have been used for centuries, and your challenge is to create one using the materials listed below to launch marshmallows at least 2 feet.

The catapult must be freestanding, meaning it should be taped to the table or floor when launching. Therefore, it needs a base.

VOCABULARY

- **CATAPULT:** used to launch an object through the air without the help of a chemical propellant
- **KINETIC ENERGY:** energy of motion – a ball rolling down a hill
- **POTENTIAL ENERGY:** energy of position – a ball sitting on top of the hill
- **ELASTIC POTENTIAL ENERGY:** type of energy of position related to an object that can return to its original shape after being moved or changed- think of a trampoline

MATERIALS

- **10 LARGE POPSICLE STICKS**
- **6 RUBBER BANDS**
- **1 PLASTIC SPOON**
- **MARSHMALLOWS FOR LAUNCHING**

NEXT STEPS:

1. FOLLOW THE ENGINEERING DESIGN WORKSHEET TO BEGIN THINKING OF IDEAS FOR YOUR CATAPULT.
2. THEN FOLLOW THE ENGINEERING DESIGN PROCESS TO BUILD, TEST, EVALUATE, AND IMPROVE YOUR DEVICE.

ENGINEERING DESIGN PROCESS WORKSHEET

1. ASK

WHAT IS THE PROBLEM?

2. IMAGINE

WHAT ARE YOUR IDEAS FOR POSSIBLE SOLUTIONS?

4. & 5. CREATE AND TEST

DOCUMENT WHAT HAPPENS:

6. IMPROVE

HOW CAN YOUR CURRENT DESIGN BE IMPROVED?

3. PLAN

DRAW AND LABEL YOUR DESIGN:

DAY 10 CREATE A NEW TOY OR GAME

What is your favorite toy? Toys can be as simple as a ball or as complex as a robot you program to walk around. Toys are a great way to occupy your time and have fun.

Your challenge is to design and create a new toy/game using the supplies listed. Be creative, and most importantly, have fun!

VOCABULARY

- **ENGINEER:** a person who designs, builds or maintains engines, machines, or public works
- **INVENTOR:** a person who invented a particular process or device or who invents things as an occupation
- **DESIGNER:** a person who plans the form, look, or workings of something before it's being made or built, typically by drawing it in detail

NEXT STEPS:

1. FOLLOW THE ENGINEERING DESIGN WORKSHEET TO BEGIN THINKING OF IDEAS FOR YOUR TOY OR GAME.
2. THEN FOLLOW THE ENGINEERING DESIGN PROCESS TO BUILD, TEST, EVALUATE, AND IMPROVE YOUR DEVICE.

MATERIALS

- 6 PAPER TOWEL ROLLS
- 2 PIECES OF CARDSTOCK
- 3-4 PIECES OF TISSUE PAPER
- 1 PIECE OF COPY PAPER
- HARD CANDY LIFE SAVERS
- 6 STRAWS
- 2 FEET OF STRING YARN
- 10 RUBBER BANDS
- 10 PIPE CLEANERS
- GLUE
- TAPE
- LARGE CRAFTING POM POMS
- BEADS
- 10 LARGE POPSICLE STICKS
- 10 SMALL POPSICLE STICKS
- 6 PAPER CLIPS

ENGINEERING DESIGN PROCESS WORKSHEET

1. ASK

WHAT IS THE PROBLEM?

2. IMAGINE

WHAT ARE YOUR IDEAS FOR POSSIBLE SOLUTIONS?

4. & 5. CREATE AND TEST

DOCUMENT WHAT HAPPENS:

6. IMPROVE

HOW CAN YOUR CURRENT DESIGN BE IMPROVED?

3. PLAN

DRAW AND LABEL YOUR DESIGN:

JOIN OUR DIGITAL BOOK CLUB!

Congratulations! You've completed 10 challenges! We'd like to give you a place to start more adventures with the characters in the Sydney and Coleman collection!

WE HAVE CREATED A FREE DIGITAL BOOK CLUB THAT YOU CAN ACCESS WHEN YOU VISIT: CLUB.SYDNEYANDCOLEMAN.COM

INSIDE THE CLUB, YOU'LL FIND:

- **FREE** activity and coloring pages
- **PREVIEW** of future books and products
- **EXCLUSIVE** author readings of all our books
- **DISCOUNT** codes for products offered at SydneyandColeman.com
- **ADDITIONAL** printable worksheets
- **MEMBERS** only offers!

JOIN THE DIGITAL BOOK CLUB FOR YOUR SPECIAL CONTENT!

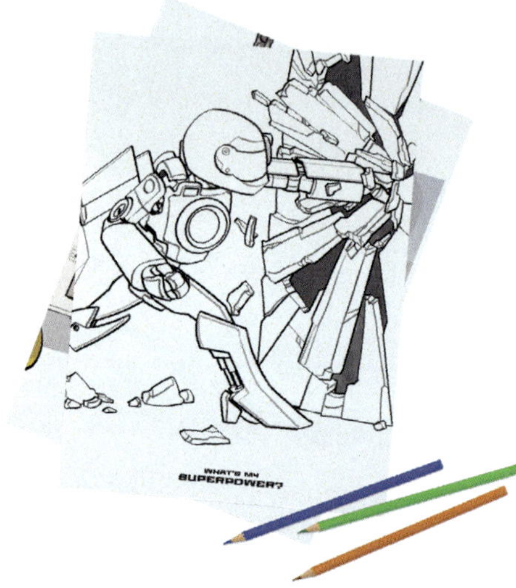

CLUB.SYDNEYANDCOLEMAN.COM

Made in the USA
Middletown, DE
29 April 2022